Reading Hebrews Missiologically

The Missionary Motive, Message, and Methods of Hebrews

Abeneazer G. Urga,
Edward L. Smither,
Linda P. Saunders,
editors

visit us at missionbooks.org

Reading Hebrews Missiologically: The Missionary Motive, Message, and Methods of Hebrews

© 2023 by Abeneazer G. Urga, Edward L. Smither, and Linda P. Saunders.
All Rights Reserved.

No part of this book may be reproduced, stored in a retrieval system, or transmitted in any form or by any means—electronic, mechanical, photocopy, recording, or otherwise—without prior written permission from the publisher, except brief quotations used in connection with reviews in magazines or newspapers. For permission, email permissions@wclbooks.com. For corrections, email editor@wclbooks.com.

Scripture quotations marked CSB are taken from the Christian Standard Bible®, Copyright © 2017 by Holman Bible Publishers. Used by permission. Christian Standard Bible® and CSB® are federally registered trademarks of Holman Bible Publishers.

Scripture quotations marked NIV are taken from the Holy Bible, New International Version®, NIV®. Copyright © 1973, 1978, 1984, 2011 by Biblica, Inc.™ Used by permission of Zondervan. All rights reserved worldwide. www.zondervan.com. The "NIV" and "New International Version" are trademarks registered in the United States Patent and Trademark Office by Biblica, Inc.™

Scripture quotations marked ESV are taken from the ESV® Bible (The Holy Bible, English Standard Version®), Copyright © 2001 by Crossway, a publishing ministry of Good News Publishers. Used by permission. All rights reserved.

Scripture quotations marked AMPCE are taken from the Amplified Bible, Copyright © 1954, 1958, 1962, 1964, 1965, 1987 by The Lockman Foundation. Used by permission.

Published by William Carey Publishing
10 W. Dry Creek Cir
Littleton, CO 80120 | www.missionbooks.org

William Carey Publishing is a ministry of Frontier Ventures
Pasadena, CA | www.frontierventures.org

Cover and Interior Designer: Mike Riester

ISBN: 978-0-87808-455-6 (paperback)
    978-0-87808-457-0 (epub)

Printed Worldwide

27 26 25 24 23   1 2 3 4 5   IN

Library of Congress Control Number: 2023930269

Reading Hebrews Missiologically offers a collection of essays that model for us a new way of reading the Bible with our missional lenses on that is both communal and collaborative. Not only do the authors make a convincing argument that the book of Hebrews has to be understood as a missiological text, but they also uncover for us the beautiful fruit of engaging the Scriptures in community, with different hermeneutic perspectives speaking together and to one another. This book will help you appreciate both mission and Hebrews more. I could not recommend it more.

Harvey Kwiyani, PhD
CEO, Global Connections, UK

Rich in intellectual engagement and scholarly diversity, *Reading Hebrews Missiologically* provides a needed resource to studies of the Epistle and a necessary and vital resource to equip further mission work in the church. Readers will encounter essays that draw from the best of Hebrews scholarship for a fresh missiological end. The volume even includes an essay offering critique and avenues for further development, beginning the "where do we go from here" conversation in the volume itself. I'm eager to use this in my own work on Hebrews and pass it on to my students.

Rev. Amy Peeler, PhD
Associate Professor of New Testament, Wheaton College and Graduate School
Author, *"You Are My Son": The Family of God in the Epistle to the Hebrews*

Reading Hebrews Missiologically is a brilliant integration of missiology, theology, and biblical exegesis. Its contributors don't settle for superficial proof texts or slogans. This book demonstrates a fruitful approach to missiological hermeneutics. Rather than give readers spiritual "milk," they offer theological meat. Chew on each chapter slowly to savor its goodness.

Brad Vaughn, PhD
Author, *Reading Romans with Eastern Eyes, The Cross in Context,*
and *One Gospel for All Nations*

Contents

Preface ... ix

Part 1: The Missionary Motive of Hebrews

Chapter 1 ... 3
Hebrews and Missions: Renarrating the World in Christ
By Matthew Aaron Bennett

Story & Worldview: The Purpose and the Problem	4
Cult & Christ: The Shadow and the Substance	9
Continuity and Contrast: Islam as a Case Study	14
Conclusion: A More Compelling Story	19

Chapter 2 ... 23
***Missio Dei* as the Grand Narrative in the Epistle to the Hebrews**
By Linda P. Saunders

God's Supreme Sacrifice in the Context of the *Missio Dei*	24
Conclusion	34

Chapter 3 ... 37
Christ Outside the Gate: How Hebrews 13 and Galilee Locate Mission for Jesus and Relocate Mission for Us
By Allen Yeh

A Tripartite Salvation History	38
The Tension between Jewish and Gentile Missiology	40
Latin America: Liberation Theology	47
Conclusion	51

Chapter 4 ... 55
The Incarnation and the Mission of God
By Michael P. Naylor

Jesus as Davidic Heir	55
Jesus, Priest according to the Order of Melchizedek	59
Jesus and the People of God	61
Conclusion: The Incarnation and the Mission of God	65

Part 2: The Missionary Message of Hebrews

Chapter 5 ... 71
Missional Hospitality in Hebrews: Welcoming God and Welcoming the Stranger
By Edward L. Smither

Mission and Hospitality	71
Abraham, Israel, and Jesus	72
Imitating Israel in Hospitable Mission	77
Imitating the Patriarchs in Hospitable Mission	78
Welcoming Strangers, God, and Christ	80
Hospitality to Believers and Non-Believers	81
Conclusion	82

Chapter 6   87
Hope as an Anchor: The Missional Message of the Pilgrim People of God
By Jessica A. Udall

Pilgrimage Identity in the Bible	87
Conclusion	98

Chapter 7   101
Mission Hope in a Storm-Tossed World
By Irwyn Ince

The Storm-Tossed World	101
The Glorious Prophet	103
The Glorious Priest	105
The Glorious King	107
Chaos	108
Jesus Is in Control	110
The Calm	111
Conclusion	112

Part 3: The Missionary Methods of Hebrews

Chapter 8   117
Evangelism in the Epistle to the Hebrews
By Abeneazer G. Urga

What Have Others Said about Hebrews and Mission?	117
Hebrews' Missionary Theology	121
Conclusion	130

Chapter 9   135
Superior Communication Skills: Modes of Divine Communication in Hebrews and the Implications for Christian Mission
By Sigurd Grindheim

The Superiority of the New Covenant	135
Mission and Power	143
Conclusion	146

Chapter 10   149
African American Missiological Use of Hebrews: From the Antebellum Period to the Twentieth Century
By Jessica N. Janvier

The Epistle, Jewish Christians, and African American Christianity	149
The African American Matrix of Scripture Interpretation	152
The Missiological Use of the Epistle in African American Christianity	159
Outward and Inward	160

Chapter 11   167
From Milk to Meat: Implications in Hebrews for Missiological Developments in Discipleship Methods
By Sarah Lunsford

Overview of Missiological Developments in Discipleship Methods	167
Analysis of Discipleship Making	170
Implications for Missiological Developments in Discipleship Methods	176

Part 4: Review and Response

Chapter 12   185
    Looking through Three Hermeneutical Lenses:
    A Review of *Reading Hebrews Missiologically*
    By Robert L. Gallagher

    Diversity of Authorship   185
    Scholarly Observations   186
    Missionary Tapestries in Three Parts   186
    Looking through the Lens of Interpreting the Metanarrative   188
    Looking through the Lens of Understanding Hebrews   188
    Looking through the Lens of Exploring "Mission"   189
    Summary of Observations   190
    Bosch Shines a Light on "Mission"   190
    Conclusion   191

About the Contributors   194

Scripture Index   198

Preface

What is the missionary theology of the Epistle to the Hebrews? Is there even a missionary theology in the letter? Several scholars have argued that the epistle is primarily about internal church matters that attempt to convince the believers to remain in the faith rather than engaging in world mission. In this compendium, a few biblical scholars and missiologists argue that the epistle *does contain a theology of mission. To this end,* Reading Hebrews Missiologically *aims to tease out the theology of mission in the book of Hebrews.*

The discussion on the theology of mission in the New Testament usually focuses on Jesus and Paul, with minimal attention given to the General Epistles. This volume will fill this gap by exploring the theme of mission in the Epistle to the Hebrews. Our book will consider Hebrews' missionary theology in three parts: the missionary motive of Hebrews, the missionary message of Hebrews, and the missionary methods of Hebrews.

Part 1 overviews the missionary motive of Hebrews. Matthew Aaron Bennett argues that Hebrews provides a sketch of biblical metanarrative that connects Israel's story, cultus, and worldview as an extension and a fulfillment in the death, resurrection, ascension, and session of Jesus. In doing so, Hebrews not only narrates the story of Israel but also renarrates the world in Christ. Linda P. Saunders contends that *missio Dei* is the grand narrative of Hebrews. The divine plan is to redeem and rescue the descendants of Abraham through the Seed of Abraham from the bondage of sin and death. Allen Yeh discusses that the Epistle to the Hebrews—particularly Hebrews 13:12–14—mandates that Christian mission should emulate the examples of Christ: doing mission from the margin with dishonor and disgrace. In this chapter, Yeh places Hebrews 13:12–14 in the context of *Heilsgeschichte* (salvation history) and echoes the two prominent works of Puerto Rican theologian Orlando E. Costas (*Christ Outside the Gate* [1982] and *Liberating News* [1989]). Michael P. Naylor explicates the significance of the incarnation to carry out God's mission and fulfill the task of the messianic/Davidic heir and the great high priest.

Part 2 discusses the missionary message of Hebrews. Edward L. Smither unearths the motif of missional hospitality in Hebrews. He connects the command to practice hospitality in Hebrews to the paradigms of Abraham, Israel, and Christ in order to delineate the theological and missiological significance of hospitality in mission—both to the original audience and to the contemporary church. Jessica A. Udall denotes that Hebrews presents hope as an anchoring message to the pilgrim people of God. She centers her discussion on Hebrews 6:13–20 to highlight the life of Abraham as a pilgrim who hoped in God in uncertain and desperate times. Similarly, Irwyn Ince highlights the motif of hope in the Epistle to the Hebrews. He posits that Hebrews provides hope as a solution to our storm-tossed and broken world. Christian hope is grounded on Jesus—the glorious Prophet, Priest, and King—who is able to calm the storm and fix the brokenness.

Part 3 probes the missionary methods of Hebrews. Abeneazer G. Urga demonstrates that Hebrews contains verbal proclamation/evangelism as a missionary method. His explication of evangelism pays attention to Hebrews 2:1–4, 4:1–3, and 11:13–16. Sigurd Grindheim explores divine communication and its implications for Christian mission today. He argues that God communicated through the suffering Son, and the contemporary church should emulate the divine communication modes (cf. Heb 13:12–13). Hebrews, Grindheim posits, offers superior communication skills to Christians involved in mission: "a witness that is borne out through suffering and identification with the poor and marginalized." Jessica N. Janvier details how the African American church utilized the Epistle to the Hebrews in mission. She goes as far back as the antebellum period to showcase how the African American Christians used Hebrews to call people to the genuine Christian faith (against enslaving "Christians"), convert those who do not know the gospel, and encourage those who suffer to persevere (enslaved African Americans). Sarah Lunsford challenges the contemporary discipleship methods utilized in Christian mission. Despite the numerical growth seen in the mission field, Lunsford laments that there is a lack of deep theological reflection in contemporary discipleship methods. Therefore, she directs our attention to Hebrews 5:11–6:3 to address the ineffective discipleship methods that have stunted the growth of Christians.

Part 4 concludes the compendium with a review and a response to the essays presented in this volume. Robert L. Gallagher provides a brief synopsis of the essays and assesses the contribution of the compendium to a biblical theology of mission. He denotes that the missionary theology of Hebrews should be interpreted in light of Scripture as a whole. He also insists that the term *mission* should be clearly defined.

In short, this study invites further missiological reflection upon a portion of Scripture that has received little attention regarding questions of mission. This work aims to contribute to a growing body of literature in which all of Scripture is read with a hermeneutic of mission. Finally, we pray that through these reflections God's people will be inspired to fresh approaches to practical mission in the world today.

February 2023
Abeneazer G. Urga, Addis Ababa, Ethiopia
Edward L. Smither, Columbia, South Carolina
Linda P. Saunders, Concord, Virginia

Part 1
The Missionary Motive of Hebrews

Chapter 1

Hebrews and Missions
Renarrating the World in Christ

Matthew Aaron Bennett

The burden of this book is to explore the contribution of the book of Hebrews to Christian missions. The purpose of this chapter, then, will be to investigate how Hebrews contributes to the communication of the gospel among people and in places where the gospel is unfamiliar. In using the word *gospel*, we encounter a term that is broadly used in Christian writings but which is also variously defined. As one who is convinced of the authority and sufficiency of Scripture, it is my preference to defer to biblical texts whenever possible in setting the parameters for the biblical use of terms.

While there are multiple instances of apostolic *kerygma* to which one might appeal, the words of Paul commend themselves as a succinct and helpful biblical definition of the Christian gospel, as he writes to the Corinthians:

> Now I want to make clear for you, brothers and sisters, the gospel I preached to you, which you received, on which you have taken your stand and by which you are being saved, if you hold to the message I preached to you—unless you believed in vain. For I passed on to you as most important what I also received: that Christ died for our sins according to the Scriptures, that he was buried, that he was raised on the third day according to the Scriptures, and that he appeared to Cephas, then to the Twelve. (1 Cor 15:1–5 CSB)

What Paul provides here for his readers serves as one of the most concise biblical definitions of the essential elements of the gospel message.

Among other things that could be highlighted, Paul here includes a recognition that the Christ—the anticipated Messiah of the Hebrew Bible—was crucified for human sins, was raised again, and appeared to multiple witnesses. He notes that this is a message to be received and also to be passed on. And he twice reminds his readers that these events happened in accordance with the Scriptures. For those familiar with the contours of the biblical story, this gospel summary provides clarity regarding the essentials of the gospel.

But in a context where one cannot count on familiarity with the preceding Scriptures that Paul references, the clarity of the message is quickly obscured by the brevity of the destoried summary. Without a knowledge of the story and worldview that the Scriptures—the Torah, the Writings, and the Prophets—provide, an account of a man who is crucified and who comes back to life is interesting and unexpected, yet it has no apparent connection to the forgiveness of sins. Likewise, while those tutored by the elder testament recognize the importance of the title *Christ*, those oblivious to it might simply mistake it for Jesus's family name.

If one of the essential tasks in missions is to communicate the biblical gospel of Jesus Christ, then we must both consider the barriers to such communication as well as the Scriptures that are of most help in explaining the meaning of the gospel in a new place and for a new people. I want to argue in this chapter that Hebrews is ideally suited to renarrating the world according to a biblical story, worldview, and cultus so as to make sense of the gospel for those unfamiliar with the Scriptures.

In order to substantiate this claim, we will need to consider how Hebrews provides a biblical framework for understanding the biblical God who intends to dwell among his creation. In light of this divine intention to dwell with humanity, we will need to explain the problem of sin and its biblically prescribed remedy to show how a sin-stained people could abide a holy and righteous God dwelling in their midst. Using Hebrews, we will be able to demonstrate for non-Christians why Jesus's crucifixion, resurrection, and ascension is good news, as the author extends and retells the biblical story of the world in and through Christ.

Story & Worldview: The Purpose and the Problem

The first aspect of this task is to demonstrate how Hebrews provides a sketch of the biblical metanarrative—and subsequently provides a worldview framework—for the reader. The importance of story for doctrine and worldview is reinforced by missiologist Theodore Curry, who argues,

> If one is to properly comprehend the Bible's teaching on the triune nature of God, the incarnation, the atonement, the church, eschatology, or ethics, these must be understood in the context of their organic relationship to the story narrated in the Bible and its redemptive theme.[1]

---

[1] Many have argued for the centrality of story in biblical communication, not the least of which is Curry, "Mission to Muslims," 222. Leading into the quote cited above, Curry writes, "The Bible's redemptive narrative provides the clue to understanding its overarching message. It communicates its depiction of reality in the one form that is commonly understood across all cultures regardless of time or place—story. Story is so fundamental to the Bible that most of its major teachings, both doctrinally and ethically, are developed within the context of stories."

The biblical story is often simplified by considering the basic plot moves: Creator and Creation, Sin and the Fall of Humanity, Redemption through Covenant, and New Creation.[2] If Hebrews is able to present the basic outline of the biblical story, perhaps it can be useful in both demonstrating Christ to be the climax of the story and also challenging the counter-stories of non-Christian faiths.

As noted above, Paul connects Jesus's death and resurrection with the removal of human sin. Yet such a claim only makes sense within the parameters of the biblical story wherein one finds the logical precursors of substitutionary atonement embedded in ancient Israel's divinely commanded sacrificial system. Likewise, such a sacrificial system only makes sense within the worldview framework in which sin separates image-bearing humans from the one whose image they bear.[3] In other words, the story told about the world, its history, and human roles therein produces a set of basic assumptions about how the world works and how to ascertain value and purpose.

One of the most important elements of the biblical worldview as it relates to producing a system of value and purpose is through the tension created by the desire of a holy and righteous God to dwell among his sin-stained creatures. As we seek to communicate the gospel story and its relationship to atonement to non-Christians, we must engage the context of the biblical story from which these doctrines and values arise and in which they make sense.[4] We turn, then, to an analysis of the metanarrative provided by Hebrews to provide a glimpse of some of the influences that form a biblical worldview and which are necessary for non-Christians to apprehend.

Author and Authority: "God has spoken through the prophets and by his Son."

From the very first verses of Hebrews, the author addresses the fact that there is a God, and he has spoken. Not only has this God spoken through prophets during previous ages, but in recent times he has communicated in and through his Son. For the author of Hebrews, God is the one who is singularly responsible for the creation of the world. This God accomplishes

---

[2] Various scholars conceive of this metanarrative by this basic paradigm with slight adjustments and adaptations. For instance, N. T. Wright has conceived of the biblical metanarrative as a five-act play, involving Creation, Fall, Israel, Jesus, and New Creation in *New Testament and the People of God*, 140–41.

[3] N. T. Wright makes this connection between the symbolic elements of praxis and their inextricable relationship to both a metanarrative and a subsequent worldview. He writes, "It is a truth insufficiently acknowledged that a sensible worldview equipped with appropriate symbolic praxis must be in want of a story. ... Symbols and actions mean what they mean within a worldview." Wright, *Paul and the Faithfulness of God*, 456.

[4] See the argument in Hiebert, *Transforming Worldviews*, 265–305.

creation by the agency of his Son, through whom he has also communicated himself to the world (Heb 1:1–4).

Perhaps an account of the divine creation of the world does not automatically stand in opposition to the stories told by other religions. However, even in this brief reference, the first chapter of Hebrews distinguishes biblical creation from other origin myths by introducing the divine Son as the agent of creation, as the sustainer of creation, and as the purifier of sinful creatures: "He upholds the universe by the word of his power. After making purification for sins, he sat down at the right hand of the Majesty on high" (Heb 1:3 ESV).

The power of this divine Son, then, is not limited to creation or communication, but includes the capacity to accomplish purification.[5] In this initial introduction of the Son through whom God has created and spoken, we begin to glimpse the christological focus and imagery that will be sustained throughout the rest of the book: Jesus is the Son, the Lord, and the High Priest.[6]

Thus, the author of Hebrews presents a unique creator, referred to as God, who at the same time is distinguished from the creator referred to as the Son. This Son is further presented as having both a divine identity and a human identity.[7] Hebrews presents a God who is over and above creation as its creator, but also one who, through the Son, has entered sympathetically into the human condition. The rationale for this is given as one considers the second aspect of the biblical metanarrative that the author of Hebrews attends to: the separation between humanity and God due to sin.

Sin: Death, Guilt, Impurity, Separation

Prior to considering how Jesus achieves salvation on behalf of humanity, however, it is necessary to consider how the author presents the problem that sin creates and from which salvation is necessary. Throughout Hebrews, the author is keen to highlight at least four results of sin which carry forward the biblical storyline from Genesis through to Christ: Sin is that which produces death, guilt, impurity, and separation. For Jesus to resolve sin, he must be able to turn back these four effects.

---

5 Wright, "Seal of Approval," 145. Showing the narrative continuity of Christ as creator but also as the fulfillment of ancient Israel's sacrificial cult, Wright writes, "Hebrews demonstrates that although we are to acknowledge the Son's role in the act of creation, his priestly work of purification and intercession is that which properly sustains creation in the cultic framework Hebrews adopts."

6 Bauckham, "Divinity of Jesus Christ," 18–19.

7 Bauckham, 18. Bauckham contends that this threefold presentation of Jesus as Son, Lord, and High Priest reinforces both his divine identity and his human identity.

We see the author intentionally identifying these four effects throughout his letter. For instance, in Hebrews 2:9 Jesus is viewed as the forerunner of rescue from death:

> We see him who for a little while was made lower than the angels, namely Jesus, crowned with glory and honor because of the suffering of death, so that by the grace of God he might taste death for everyone. (ESV)

Jesus's vicarious death is likewise cited later in Hebrews 9:24–28 as the once-for-all sacrifice, whereby he has "put away sin by the sacrifice of himself" (v. 26 ESV). The reader is reminded of the biblical story in which death stands as an obstacle between humans and God as a consequence of sin.

Furthermore, in Hebrews 2:1–3 the author reminds the reader of what has been written in the past, warning that if "every transgression or disobedience received a just retribution, how shall we escape if we neglect such a great salvation?" (ESV). Transgressions of the law bring about guilt that requires forgiveness. The guilty state of sinners is reinforced by Hebrews 10:18, which states, "Where there is forgiveness of [sins and lawless deeds], there is no longer any offering for sin" (ESV). Thus sin is conceived of as transgression of law, and sinners obtain the status of guilt.

But death and guilt are not the only conditions caused by sin. The author of Hebrews reinforces what Leviticus teaches regarding sin, the consequences of a sin-stained world, and ritual impurity. Leviticus repeatedly demonstrates that sinners are in a state of guilt *and* impurity—both of which endanger a worshiper in the presence of a holy and righteous God.[8] Therefore sin—which causes both guilt and impurity—separates God from humanity.

The author highlights this separation, pointing out that even the tabernacle as the meeting place of God and the high priestly representative of his people is marked by a curtain that reinforces divine-human separation (Heb 9:1–10). Here the author reflects on the curtain as a symbol of division that disrupts the biblical story of a God who intends to dwell among his people yet whose holy and righteous presence poses a danger to his sin-stained people. Fortunately, Hebrews relates the history of God's merciful provision of a remedy for sin and separation through the biblical concept of atonement.

Atonement: Life, Righteousness, Purification, Restoration

While one might look at various places in Scripture to consider the biblical teaching on atonement, the Day of Atonement, recorded in Leviticus 16, provides the clearest basis for analysis. There, through a series of prescribed sacrifices, washings, and the presentation of blood in the innermost places of

---

[8] Sklar, *Sin, Impurity, Sacrifice, Atonement*, 182.

the tabernacle, God provides the mechanism by which to effect atonement. In Israel's story, it is this ritual that allows God to remain in the midst of the people despite their imperfection and impurity.

Whereas Leviticus sets the stage in the Hebrew Scriptures for a proper understanding of the separation between sin-stained creatures and a holy and righteous God, Hebrews both upholds and extends that narrative by demonstrating the inability of the previous system to satisfy the perpetual need for atonement. If sinful creatures are to be eternally restored to a condition proper to the presence of God, the annual Levitical prescriptions are wanting for permanence. Hebrews presents Jesus as the substance of which Leviticus was but a shadow because he is able to turn back the effects of sin through his once-for-all vicarious work as substitutionary sacrifice and eternal high priest.

Still, for some unfamiliar with the biblical concept of atonement, Jesus's death and resurrection may seem extraneous to his ability to serve as an intercessor for his people. We will consider the logic and necessity of the crucifixion and resurrection as the natural extension of the Levitical system of atonement in the following section. But before turning attention to Christ's satisfaction of sacrifice, we must also see how the book of Hebrews includes the final act of the biblical metanarrative in its argument.

New Kingdom: "Outside the camp" and "The city that is to come"
While the author of Hebrews spends most of the book discussing the Levitical sacrificial system as completed in Jesus, there is throughout a consistent reminder that Christ's atonement is not merely an end in and of itself. Rather, it provides an eternal hope of an age that is to come. That age is marked by being invited into God's eternal rest: a rest marked by God's very presence.

First, in Hebrews 3:7–4:13 the author provides a biblical overview of the concept of rest, from Genesis's creation account through to the wilderness generation. Extending this concept into the present via reference to Psalm 95, the author warns contemporary readers to enter God's rest "today." Since Psalm 95 was written long after Joshua's conquest, the author of Hebrews argues that there must be a future rest yet to come—one which Jesus has now inaugurated.

Rest is not the only promise that the author holds out for the reader. In Hebrews 10:19–22, for instance, the reader is offered entrance into the holy place of God's presence via the body of Christ that has opened the way to God. The reader is given assurance that by faith one can draw near in confidence, and in Hebrews 12:18–24 there is an invitation to enter into—

without fear, thanks to the perfecting work of Christ—the festal gathering of the angelic host.

And again, in Hebrews 13:12–14, the author calls the faithful to join Jesus "outside the camp"—in his suffering—in order to await the coming city that will last eternally. Whatever else the age to come may hold, the author of Hebrews is intent on reminding the reader that it is marked by believers drawing near to God in the confidence of faith in Jesus's work as our great high priest.

The Metanarrative
Though sketched in brief, the preceding section has sufficiently demonstrated that the book of Hebrews gives at least some attention to the major elements that compose the biblical metanarrative. It speaks of a God who has created in order to dwell with his people, yet it acknowledges the separation between them and God caused by human sin. The problem of sin, however, has a remedy promised for ages in Israel's religious cult and finally realized in Jesus's atoning death, resurrection, and ascension.[9] In addition, the author recognizes that Jesus's accomplishment makes possible the anticipated end of the biblical storyline wherein humanity and God are restored to fellowship in the city that is yet to come.

This story is necessary for understanding the divine intention to dwell with his people and also to demonstrate the problem posed by sin. It does not, on its own, however, suffice to answer the question, "Why does Jesus's death, resurrection, and ascension have any bearing on human sin?" For that, we must consider how the author of Hebrews specifically views the sacrificial atonement of the Levitical system through the lens of Christ.

Cult & Christ: The Shadow and the Substance

At the center of non-Christian misunderstanding of Jesus's death and resurrection may often be a lack of understanding of the Israelite sacrificial cult and its connection to atonement. The narrative backdrop sketched throughout Hebrews allows the author to focus on the sacrificial cult within the context of this overarching storyline. It is this storied attention to the sacrificial cult that provides the most helpful contribution of the book to explaining the relationship between atonement and Christ's sacrificial death and victorious resurrection and ascension.

---

9 Including the resurrection here might cause some to protest that Hebrews does not spend much time discussing the resurrection. While the weight of attention given to Christ's high priestly role does overshadow that which is devoted to the resurrection, David Moffitt has argued convincingly of the importance of the concept of resurrection in his book, *Atonement and the Logic of Resurrection in the Epistle to the Hebrews*.

To elucidate a biblical understanding of atonement in Christ, we must be clear on how the author of Hebrews carries forward the various elements of Levitical atonement. We might do so by considering some of the likely questions our non-Christian audience might be asking.

Why So Much Death?
Animal sacrifice is a common practice in many of the world's religions. However, the biblical concept of atonement utilizes sacrifice as but one component in a more multifaceted process of reconciling creatures to their creator. It behooves us to consider two of the questions that might occur to non-Christians as they observe the Levitical process of making atonement and encounter the treatment of it in Hebrews. First, why is there so much death?

As indicated above, the biblical worldview presents a perfect and holy creator who intends to dwell with his people. Yet according to God's warning in Genesis 2:17, sin results in death. Affirming this death penalty, Hebrews 2:2 reminds the reader that the consequences of sin are inescapable. Yet Hebrews 2:9 describes Jesus as vicariously tasting death for those who deserve to die.[10] Jesus's death is effective only because the logic of biblical atonement allows a vicarious, sacrificial death to serve as a ransom (Hebrew *kōpēr*) for the lives forfeited by sinners.[11]

The logic of this ransom concept and its relationship to atonement is helpfully explained by Old Testament scholar Jay Sklar. In particular, Sklar explains the ransom concept as it appears in Exodus 21:28–32. There the reader encounters laws concerning the owner of an ox that gores someone to death and consequently becomes culpable. Exodus prescribes two alternatives: (a) the family of the ox's victim can demand the life of the ox's owner, or (b) the family and the ox's owner can come to an agreement involving a ransom exchange.

Sklar summarizes the situation thus: "The life of the ox-owner has been forfeited through their wrong into the hands of the family of the slain and their only hope of deliverance is for that family to choose to place a [ransom] upon them."[12] It is the prerogative of the offended family to choose to offer a ransom, which functions as a lesser penalty than the forfeited life of the offender. If offered and accepted, this ransom provides restitution and interpersonal restoration between the parties.[13]

---

10 Lane, *Hebrews 1–8*, 37.

11 Though focusing on Pauline writings and not Hebrews, one might also consult the convincing treatment of the exegetical case for substitution in biblical atonement in Gathercole, *Defending Substitution*.

12 Sklar, *Sin, Impurity, Sacrifice, Atonement*, 51.

13 Sklar, 52.

Applying this ransom logic to the standing of sinners before God, one sees God as the offended party who has, through the sacrificial system, agreed to the vicarious, ransoming death of sacrificial animals in the place of sinners. However, as the author of Hebrews points out, these animals, repeatedly offered year after year, were never able to perfect those who were seeking to draw near to God (Heb 10:1–2). Thus, even this system of ransom points toward a day when God's justice will be fully and completely—or, as Hebrews puts it, once-for-all—satisfied.

In the Levitical system, then, sin-guilt is atoned for by the acceptance of the deaths of sacrificial animals in the place of sinners. In the New Testament, Jesus serves as the spotless God-man in whom the shadow that is the sacrificial system finds its eternal form and substance.[14] The author of Hebrews confirms this completion, as he states, "But when Christ had offered for all time a single sacrifice for sins, he sat down at the right hand of God. ... For by a single offering he has perfected for all time those who are being sanctified" (Heb 10:12–14 ESV). The death of Jesus serves as an atoning ransom for sinners, exhausting God's righteous wrath against sin.

Yet the vicarious death is not the end of the atonement process. Both in Leviticus and in Christ's ministry there is yet more to the process of atonement. In Leviticus 16 the high priest must yet collect the blood of the sacrifice and bring it into the Holy Place in order to present it before the presence of God in the Holy Place. It behooves us, then, to consider a second question that might be raised by non-Christians: Why does atonement require the presentation of blood?

Why So Much Blood?
The role of blood in biblical atonement is vitally important, though again, it is not necessarily unique that blood manipulation should feature in the cult of a particular religion. For example, in Egypt it is common for participants in the annual Islamic sacrifice, *'Id al Adha*, to dip their hands in the blood of the sacrifice and apply bloody handprints to the doorframes of their homes, businesses, or vehicles. However, rather than effecting atonement, this practice is usually associated with a symbol of good luck or a way of warding off spirits.

According to the biblical instructions, however, the application of blood is immediately connected to the extended process of making atonement. It is presented before the very presence of God in the holy of holies, and it

---

14 Torrance, *Atonement*, 33. Torrance summarizes the biblical concept of *kipper* by explaining that it envisions and effects "redemption as the actual wiping out of sin and guilt, and so of effecting propitiation between man and God." This atonement is foreshadowed in the Levitical system as a shadow, but fulfilled permanently in Christ as the shadow's true form.

is connected to the concept of purifying and cleansing the temple and the camp.[15] This purifying agency is connected to the fact that Leviticus 17:11 explicitly clarifies that blood serves as a symbol of life, with the power to purify: "The life of a creature is in the blood, and I have appointed it to you to make atonement on the altar for your lives, since it is the lifeblood that makes atonement" (CSB). Whereas contact with death causes defilement, contact with this symbol of life serves as a cleansing agent.

Prior to this explanation of what blood symbolizes, Leviticus 16:16 connects the presentation of blood to the cleansing of the tabernacle from impurity. Such an explanation helps to clarify an otherwise confusing aspect of the concept of atonement in Leviticus. That is, the process of atonement is called for both in situations of sin-guilt and in situations of ritual impurity.[16] Interpreters have at times viewed these apparently discrete situations as requiring separate treatments to the degree that they have proposed two different translations of *kipper* language—one in situations of guilt and another in situations of impurity.[17]

However, Sklar has conclusively demonstrated that situations of impurity and sin both require atonement according to the biblical logic. Sklar reconciles these apparently different situations of guilt and impurity through an exhaustive study of atonement, concluding,

> The end point of sin and impurity is the same: both endanger (requiring ransom) and both pollute (requiring purgation). As a result, it is not simply [ransom] that is needed in some instances and purgation that is needed in others, but [ransom]-purgation that is needed in both. … The verb that describes this dual event is [*kipper*], and the ability of the [*kipper*]-rite to accomplish this dual event is due to the blood of the sacrifice which both ransoms and purifies.[18]

Atonement, then, is a complex process whereby sinners are reconciled to God by having their guilt removed and their impurity purged. The sacrificial animal dies in the stead of the sinning community, who by their sin have

---

15 Sklar, *Leviticus*, 206–15.

16 Compare Leviticus 15:30 (atonement required for impurity) with 16:6 (atonement required for sin); see also the dual function of atonement in removing impurity and forgiving guilt in Leviticus 16:16.

17 See Wenham, *Book of Leviticus*, 59, who writes, "to make atonement (*kipper*) has two different meanings in Hebrew, 'to wipe clean' or 'to pay a ransom.'"

18 Sklar, *Sin, Impurity, Sacrifice, Atonement*, 182.

forfeited their lives. Its blood, presented as a symbol of life, purges the impurities that accumulate as people stained by death conduct their lives.[19]

In the end, if human sinners find themselves both guilty and defiled, they cannot hope to enter the presence of a righteous and holy God without meeting the same fate as Nadab and Abihu did when they attempted to approach God in an unprescribed manner (Lev 10:1–7). Commenting on the atonement process prescribed in Leviticus, Mark Boda writes:

> What the priestly legislation provided then was an intricate theological-symbolic world designed to preserve God's presence in the midst of his people. The people were constantly reminded of his holy character through their failure to follow his commands but at the same time experienced his gracious character as they received atonement for both cleansing and forgiveness.[20]

Rather than two processes—one to deal with impurity and another to handle guilt—God provides a single, complex ritual that involves a ransoming, substitutionary death and a purgation of impurity effected by the presentation of blood in the holy place by an appointed representative of the faithful community. This ritual allows the Israelites to retain the presence of their God in their midst, despite their sin-guilt and the ever-encroaching defilement that their sins brought into the camp.

---

19 It should be noted that the discussion regarding the role of blood as a symbol of life is contested. For example, Hermann Kuma, in *Centrality of Αἷμα (Blood)*, argues that *haima* can carry the meaning of both death and life, though the author of Hebrews seems more interested in its role as a symbol of life. In his critique of Kuma's work, Matthew Emadi contests Kuma's position, arguing that blood should be understood as symbolic of Christ's atoning death. Emadi writes in his review:

> The fact remains however, that the life that is possible for the believer is possible only as a result of the blood spilt in sacrifice. The shed blood of Christ represents a life that was surrendered. The sacrifice of Christ's blood necessarily refers to his death at Calvary. It therefore appears that Kuma overemphasizes the effect of Christ's blood and underemphasizes its actual referent, namely, sacrificial death. (Matthew Emadi, review of *Centrality of Αἷμα (Blood)*, 107)

Emadi is certainly correct in noting that sacrificial blood cannot be procured apart from sacrificial death. However, I believe that the prescriptions and descriptions given for the ritual use of blood as described in the Levitical sacrificial system (see Lev 17:11, 14) are clearly intent on viewing blood as a symbol of life and an agent of purification from defilement. Furthermore, according to the Levitical conventions, contact with death brings about defilement. Thus, it would seem inconceivable for the high priest to be instructed to bring a symbol of death into the holy presence of the author of life. Therefore, contra Emadi, I believe the author of Hebrews has blood-as-life in view as his presentation of Christ as the eternal high priest unfolds.

20 Boda, *Severe Mercy*, 76.

Why Does Jesus Satisfy the Cycle?

Turning to Hebrews, then, one sees the completion of this complex process established in the spotless life of Jesus, his substitutionary death, his victorious resurrection, and finally through his appearance as the great high priest who is able to plead his own living blood in order to provide an eternal cleansing atonement for those to whom it is applied by faith. Thus, the author of Hebrews writes, "For by a single offering he has perfected for all time those who are being sanctified" (Heb 10:14 ESV). And a few verses later, he connects Jesus's atonement with forgiveness of sins and purification mediated eternally by his blood:

> Therefore brothers, since we have confidence to enter the holy places by the blood of Jesus, by the new and living way that he opened for us through the curtain, that is, through his flesh, and since we have a great priest over the house of God, let us draw near with a true heart in full assurance of faith, with our hearts sprinkled clean from an evil conscience and our bodies washed with pure water. (Heb 10:19–22 ESV)

In other words, Levitical atonement reaches its apogee in Jesus's once-for-all sacrifice that puts away human sin (Heb 9:26), his resurrection that inaugurates his eternal priesthood (Heb 7:24), and his ascension that allows him to cleanse the consciences of his people (Heb 9:13–14).

In all this, then, Hebrews demonstrates that the Levitical system of atonement was but the shadow prophetically anticipating Jesus as the image and substance toward which it pointed. For those unfamiliar with the Levitical sacrificial system, this background information is necessary to make sense of Paul's claim that "Christ died for our sins." Thus, Hebrews is particularly helpful as it situates the explanation for Jesus's death, resurrection, and ascension within the thickness of the biblical storyline and its anticipation of a lasting means of atonement.

The final section of this chapter will attempt to display how Hebrews explains the content of Paul's 1 Corinthians 15:1–5 gospel to those of a non-Christian background using Islam as a case study.

Continuity and Contrast: Islam as a Case Study

The previous sections aimed to show how the book of Hebrews provides a clear connection between the biblical storyline, Levitical atonement, and Jesus's death, resurrection, and his ascended session as high priest. For those who have little understanding of the Old Testament and ancient Israel's sacrificial cult, Hebrews both extends and renarrates Israel's story in Christ.[21] Such a demonstration of continuity between the Old Testament and Christ is helpful in general for showcasing the unbroken storyline of the biblical metanarrative to non-Christians. It is of special importance in explaining biblical atonement in Christ to Muslims.

Barriers to Communicating Christ's Atonement to Muslims

Islamic theology presents several unique barriers to the meaningful communication of biblical atonement. The first complication is linguistic. The Qur'an uses the Arabic word *kaffara* to translate the Hebrew word for atonement (*kipper*). The preceding argument has shown *kipper* to be a complex concept aimed at retaining the presence of God among his people by effecting both purification and forgiveness. This is accomplished by means of substitutionary sacrifice and blood manipulation. The problem this poses for communicating the gospel in Christ to Muslims arises because this word also appears in the Qur'an, but where it plays a reduced role—having no relation to blood, only glancing connection with sacrifice, and perhaps best understood as a covering-over of sins.[22]

Further complicating communication, Islam includes the individual components of biblical atonement—sin, impurity, sacrifice, and *kaffara* language—though without the same meaning or connection to one another. For instance, sacrifice continues within Islam, though its function is to validate Islam as a heavenly religion.[23] Likewise, Islam includes distinct prescriptions for how one might appeal to God for forgiveness and also ways that one might seek and effect purification. Yet, whereas biblical forgiveness, purification, sacrifice, and blood manipulation are all bound together in the single concept-cluster called atonement, Islam presents each of these elements distinctly from and unrelated to one another. For a Muslim audience, then, a superficial discussion surrounding atonement in Christ might present itself as illogical and unnecessary on the basis of the availability of the same offerings within Islam.

However, Islam repeatedly claims to extend the revelation of the prior Scriptures despite proclaiming a God who neither speaks of an intention

---

21 Many have claimed that Hebrews provides an argument for Christianity's supersession of Judaism. However, I find Hays, "Here We Have No Lasting City," 151–73, to be quite convincing that Hebrews should be read as an extension and transformation of Israel's story rather than a distinct rejection, replacement, or supersession thereof.

22 Space prohibits a full treatment of the concept of atonement in the Qur'an, but for those interested in deeper study, see Bennett, *Narratives in Conflict*.

23 The Qur'an teaches that each community that has received revelation from the heavenly book (Jews, Christians, and Muslims) has also been given a ritual, sacrifice, or sign to validate their practices. See Qur'an 22:67: "For every community we have appointed a ritual which they practice. So let them not argue with you about the matter, but call (them) to your Lord. Surely you are indeed on a straight guidance" (cf. Qur'an 22:34).

to dwell among his people nor provides a system of substitutionary atonement. Both of these ideas are challenged by Hebrews, and Hebrews also demonstrates the necessity of Christ's atonement, if God does in fact intend to dwell with his creatures. It is worth unpacking these ideas briefly below before considering how Hebrews might provide both an explanation for Muslims and a challenge to the Islamic claim to inherit and continue prior biblical revelation.

Sin, Impurity, and *Kaffara* in Islam
Superficially, one might consider the idea of sin as basic to most religions. Nearly all faiths employ a norming system of ethics that aims to help adherents identify and avoid vices while commending and pursuing virtues. The language of sin is often applied as a general reference to violation of these religious norms. Islam is no exception to this religious impulse. However, where Christianity views sin—resulting in death, guilt, and impurity—as causing a rupture in an otherwise intimate relationship between creator and creature, Islam views both sin and the relationship between God and creatures differently.

As noted above, biblical atonement involves an intercessory priest engaging in a single-yet-multifaceted atonement process resulting in the corporate forgiveness of guilt and purgation of impurity. This atonement is achieved through substitutionary sacrifice and the presentation of purifying blood before the presence of God. Islam, on the other hand, offers forgiveness directly to repentant sinners without intercession, sacrifice, or substitution. Likewise, though Islam recognizes impurity as a condition requiring remedy, one can effect purification for oneself by way of ritual water-washing. Forgiveness and purification are made available in Islam, yet they are divorced from the intimately related concept cluster of atonement found in the Bible.

If, then, Muslims have access to forgiveness and purification via different pathways, perhaps a gospel message of Christ crucified—a fact that Islamic theology denies—and resurrected vicariously—another fact denied by Islam—will seem to offer a solution to a problem that Islam does not face. Yet there remain two distinct elements of Islamic teaching that require more than the provision of an alternative means of achieving forgiveness and purification: (a) the concept of God's presence, and (b) the claim of continuity.

The Remote Presence of God in Islam
If Islam proposes a forgiveness that does not eradicate sin or expunge it from the sinner's account, the sin remains even if it is overlooked or forgiven. For a

Christian who anticipates dwelling in the immediate and unmediated presence of a holy and righteous God, this poses the significant problem faced by Nadab and Abihu, who drew near to God while still in their sin (Lev 10:1–7).[24] However, on the basis of the Islamic doctrine of *tawhid*—the monadic oneness of God—there is little expectation for humans to enter the presence of God or for God to draw near in an immediate fashion. If God remains remote, humans can have their sins overlooked without either requiring wrath against sin to be propitiated or impurity to be eradicated.

Yet, in order to view God as ever-transcendent, Islam must make a radical break with the repeated biblical affirmations that God intends to dwell with his people and in their midst.[25] Since the Qur'an regularly affirms its continuity with prior revelation, this departure poses a significant problem whereby the Muslim must either (a) affirm the untenable position that all of the biblical verses referring to God's presence dwelling with his people are corruptions of the original text of the Bible, or (b) deal with the fact that the Torah prescribes substitutionary atonement that the Qur'an omits and even rejects.[26] The book of Hebrews, on the other hand, presents Christ as a natural continuation of the Torah's teaching regarding God's intention to dwell with his people and the need for substitutionary atonement.

Departure of Islam and Continuity in Christ

In contrast to the claims that Islam continues the story told through prior Scripture, the author of Hebrews demonstrates narrative, ritual, and worldview continuity as he argues that the Palestinian man named Jesus— who lived, was crucified, and rose again in the first century—was not the invention or innovation of a new, late-in-time religious community. Rather, this Messiah is the natural and fitting culmination of what God purposed in drawing near, promised in covenant, and pointed toward in the sacrificial

---

24 In fact, since Leviticus 16 begins with a reminder of what happened to Aaron's sons, it appears that the biblical prescription for the Day of Atonement rituals is given as a recognition that the presence of God cannot be trifled with, nor can any unfit creature bear up before it without a radical atonement.

25 Examples include Exod 29:45–46; Lev 26:11; Num 5:3; 1 Kgs 6:13; Ezek 37:27; Zech 2:10–11; Rev 21:3.

26 This position is untenable at the very least because the Qur'an endorses the texts that are "between the hands" of its Jewish and Christian audiences in the seventh century. Consultation of biblical manuscripts from two centuries prior to the rise of Islam demonstrates the presence of such verses at the time of the Qur'an's commendation. Furthermore, the Qur'an does not actually affirm any textual corruption of the *tawrat*, *zabur*, or *injil*. It simply accuses the Jews and Christians of misinterpreting or obscuring their scriptures. Later tradition teaches the textual corruption more clearly, though without qur'anic warrant. See Gabriel Said Reynolds, "On the Qur'anic Accusation of Scriptural Falsification," 189–202.

cult. Jesus is the Messiah anticipated both by prophecy and by cult. Indeed, the author concludes, in multiple places, that "it is fitting" that the Christ should be made perfect through suffering (Heb 2:10).

Hebrews thus challenges the Islamic claim to continuity by showing how those trusting in Christ find him satisfying the ritual need of sinners before a holy God, naturally extend the story of ancient Israel, and maintain the same worldview-level expectations that God intends to dwell among his people, and therefore must find a way to eradicate their sins and impurities. Drawing on John Owen's insights into the book of Hebrews, Kelly Kapic states Jesus's continuity with Old Testament expectations and storyline this way:

> To know Messiah, one must understand the Old Testament. It was the soil that produced the expectations and shape of Messianic understanding. The New Testament was not to be pitted against the Old Testament, precisely because it is the great shining sun that illumines the rooms, through which people had been walking in darkness.[27]

In other words, the author of Hebrews presents a compelling claim to continuity in the person and work of Jesus the Messiah. His once-for-all sacrifice and eternal priesthood is not anomalous, but fitting to the narrative and worldview produced by the Old Testament. In presenting such continuity, Hebrews not only explains the gospel of Christ but implicitly challenges the Islamic claim to inheriting the biblical storyline; and it highlights the discrepancies between an Islamic conception of God who remains transcendent and the biblical portrait of a God who would draw near.

Given the particular barriers to communication that arise uniquely from a faith that claims to inherit and complete shared Scriptures and concepts, Islam represents perhaps one of the most difficult audiences with which to truly communicate Christ's atonement. Yet by providing the storied framework and worldview for biblical atonement, Hebrews demonstrates a robust continuity between Israel's ritual pursuit of atonement and Christ's provision thereof. Not only does this help to communicate atonement in Christ to a Muslim audience, but it also implicitly challenges Islam's claim to continuing the story and worldview of the prior Scriptures. In the end, though, within this case study focused on Islam, Hebrews' presentation of the component parts of story, worldview, and ritual offer an explanatory frame by which to explain Christ to those of other faiths and to offer a comprehensive and compelling story of the world and the place of humanity in it.

---

27 Kapic, "John Owen's Theological Reading of Hebrews," 141.

Conclusion: A More Compelling Story

At the beginning of this chapter, I noted that those who are unfamiliar with the biblical teaching on sacrificial atonement might view the death and resurrection of Jesus as an interesting story, but not one that is at all clearly connected to the remission of sins. We have seen, however, that Hebrews provides clarity for the uninitiated by retelling the biblical metanarrative that speaks of a creator God whose intention is to dwell among his people and who, despite human sinfulness and impurity, has promised a restoration through a process called atonement.

As the author of Hebrews explains Jesus's messianic role as the fulfillment of the preparatory sacrificial system, the reader understands that Jesus's death, resurrection, and ascension are connected to the atonement necessary for humans to dwell in God's presence. David Moffitt summarizes the whole atonement process:

> Blood/life stands at the center of the process that results in atonement, since the life in the blood is the agent that has the power to redeem and purify. Because blood has these properties, blood offering both ameliorates the punitive danger the people face *and* enables the divine present to continue to dwell among the people in the tabernacle's inner sanctum.[28]

For the author of Hebrews, then, the once-for-all sacrifice of Jesus and his presentation of eternal blood in the true holy place of God's heavenly presence is that which eternally purifies, redeems, and allows humans to approach the presence of the Almighty without fear.

Hebrews provides an extended explanation of the gospel that reaches back into Israel's story, cult, and worldview in order to trace the contours of the shadow onto the person and work of Christ. In so doing, Hebrews tells Israel's story in a new and fulfilled way that both extends it and explains how Jesus could claim that all the writings and prophets pointed to him and his work.

In other words, Hebrews provides the explanation of the Scriptures with which Paul says Jesus's death and resurrection for sins accord. For non-Christians unfamiliar with those Scriptures, their story, and the worldview that expects God to dwell among his people, Hebrews explains Paul's shorthand gospel with clarity. As such, Hebrews exhibits unique missional value in renarrating the world in and according to Christ.

---

28 Moffitt, *Atonement*, 265.

Bibliography

Bauckham, Richard. "The Divinity of Jesus Christ in the Epistle to the Hebrews." In *The Epistle to the Hebrews and Christian Theology*, edited by Richard Bauckham, Daniel Driver, Trevor Hart, and Nathan MacDonald, 15–36. Grand Rapids: Eerdmans, 2009.

Bennett, Matthew. *Narratives in Conflict: Atonement in Hebrews and the Qur'an*. Eugene: Pickwick, 2019.

Boda, Mark. *A Severe Mercy: Sin and Its Remedy in the Old Testament*. Winona Lake: Eisenbrauns, 2009.

Curry, Theodore. "Mission to Muslims." In *Theology and Practice of Mission*, edited by Bruce Ashford, 222–51. Nashville: B&H, 2011.

Emadi, Matthew. Review of *The Centrality of Αἷμα (Blood) in the Theology of the Epistle to the Hebrews: An Exegetical and Philological Study*, by Hermann Kuma. *Themelios* 38, no. 1 (2013): 106–8.

Gathercole, Simon. *Defending Substitution*. Grand Rapids: Baker, 2015.

Hays, Richard. "Here We Have No Lasting City: New Covenantalism in Hebrews." In *The Epistle to the Hebrews and Christian Theology*, edited by Richard Bauckham, Daniel Driver, Trevor Hart, and Nathan MacDonald, 151–73. Grand Rapids: Eerdmans, 2009.

Hiebert, Paul. *Transforming Worldviews*. Grand Rapids: Baker, 2008.

Kapic, Kelly. "John Owen's Theological Reading of Hebrews." In *Christology, Hermeneutics, and Hebrews*, edited by Jon Laansma and Daniel Treier, 135–54. New York: T&T Clark, 2013.

Kuma, Hermann. *The Centrality of Αἷμα (Blood) in the Theology of the Epistle to the Hebrews: An Exegetical and Philological Study*. Lewiston: Edwin Mellen, 2012.

Lane, William L. *Hebrews 1–8*. Word Biblical Commentary 47a. Dallas: Word, 1991.

Moffitt, David. *Atonement and the Logic of Resurrection in the Epistle to the Hebrews*. Novum Testamentum Supplements 141. Leiden: Brill, 2011.

Reynolds, Gabriel Said. "On the Qur'anic Accusation of Scriptural Falsification (*tahrif*) and Christian Anti-Jewish Polemic." *Journal of the American Oriental Society* 130 (2010): 189–202.

Sklar, Jay. *Leviticus*. Downers Grove: IVP Academic, 2014.

Sklar, Jay. *Sin, Impurity, Sacrifice, Atonement*. Sheffield, UK: Sheffield Phoenix, 2015.

Torrance, T. F. *Atonement*. Edited by Robert T. Walker. Downers Grove: IVP Academic, 2009.

Wenham, Gordon. *The Book of Leviticus*. Grand Rapids: Eerdmans, 1979.

Wright, N. T. *The New Testament and the People of God*. Minneapolis: Fortress, 1991.

Wright, N. T. *Paul and the Faithfulness of God*. Minneapolis: Fortress, 2013.

Wright, Terry. "The Seal of Approval: An Interpretation of the Sons, Sustaining Action in Hebrews 1:3." In *The Epistle to the Hebrews and Christian Theology*, edited by Richard Bauckham, Daniel Driver, Trevor Hart, and Nathan MacDonald, 140–48. Grand Rapids: Eerdmans, 2009.

Chapter 2

Missio Dei as the Grand Narrative in the Epistle to the Hebrews

Linda P. Saunders

The book of Hebrews is most often classified as a theological exposé about God's supreme sacrifice and the work of Jesus Christ's atonement; too often, though, the missiological framework for this book is overlooked. In their article, "A Fruitful Missional Exegesis for a Missional Hermeneutic and Missiology," Timothy M. Van Aarde and Lygunda Li-M contend that "a gap exists between the art of theological or biblical scholarship and the missiological vocation."[1] They further assert that "a failed marriage has taken place between biblical scholarship and missiology."[2] While Van Aarde and Li-M's article focuses on evangelical and ecumenical theologians regarding their respective approaches to missiology and theology, they identify a missing link in many theological exegetical exposés of Scripture—that missing link is the missiological framework in theological exegetical work.

In Hebrews 1:3, Jesus Christ is introduced as God's divine help, God's "express image" (χαρακτήρ, *charactēr*),[3] the supreme sacrifice; and it is this thesis that illuminates the *missio Dei* and God's atoning work through the blood of Jesus Christ in the context of the grand narrative of God's redemptive plan. Moreover, the author of the book of Hebrews affirms Jesus Christ as the seed of Abraham (Heb 2:16).[4] From this perspective, the author of Hebrews articulates a cohesive and cogent case to demonstrate how the seed of the woman in Genesis 3:15—the ultimate substitutionary atonement for the sin of humanity—is the seed of Abraham and is inextricably and unequivocally linked to the *missio Dei*.[5]

A thorough and proper exegesis of the book of Hebrews will reveal God's missionary plan—which he set in motion before he laid the world's foundation—and this is the same theme interwoven into God's ultimate mission, to reconcile the world to himself through the redemptive work accomplished at Calvary (2 Cor 5:18–19). The Scriptures are replete with

---

[1] Van Aarde and Li-M, "Fruitful Missional Exegesis," 1–10.
[2] Van Aarde and Li-M, "Fruitful Missional Exegesis."
[3] All Scripture references are quoted from the KJV unless otherwise noted.
[4] This chapter is written with the understanding the audience had a thorough knowledge about the Jewish heritage and Jewish laws and customs.
[5] *Missio Dei* is a Latin phrase used to denote the singular mission of God, which is to seek—ever since the fall of humanity (Gen 3)—and to save lost humanity (Luke 19:10).

reminders that God created a way of escape from sin through Jesus Christ. John 1:1 and 1:14 emphasize Christ's incarnation—the Son of God robed himself in flesh to fulfill the prophecies pertaining to the redemption of humanity. We are reminded in Scripture how God stretched forth his arm when there was no one who could intervene (Isa 59:16). Scripture declares that God was fully aware that there was no one who was worthy to atone for the salvation of humanity (Isa 63:5); and from the beginning, God spoke the first prophecy, which pointed to the *missio Dei* (Gen 3:15).

Beginning in chapter 1, the author of Hebrews captures the essence of the missiological work of the Cross—by recognizing Jesus's role in creation, his sonship, and his priesthood. The author of Hebrews is familiar with his first-century Jewish audience; therefore, the book is written from their perspective.[6] Because his audience was familiar with Abraham, the covenants, and the law, the author of Hebrews uses this Jewish cultural backdrop to paint a vivid picture about God's ultimate mission. Thus, the book of Hebrews delineates the theme of the grand narrative by illustrating the role of Jesus as Abraham's seed, the high priest, and the redeeming Savior. By exegeting Hebrews 1:3 and 2:16 in this chapter, I will argue that Hebrews, a meticulously written theological exposition about the atoning work of Christ, is also a cogent and cohesive framework to communicate a clear and concise message about the *missio Dei*—the chief objective of the grand narrative.

God's Supreme Sacrifice in the Context of the *Missio Dei*

The grand narrative is a story about God's promised hope, and that hope was promised through God's divine plan of redemption, his salvation mission—the *missio Dei*. The author of Hebrews diligently outlays this narrative to demonstrate to the first-century Jews that Jesus was indeed the promised hope (Heb 3:6; 6:11, 18–19; 7:19), the culmination of God's mission that began centuries before with a promise to Abraham (Gen 12:1–3). Hebrews 1:3 introduces God's Son as God's identical likeness, the perfect expression of God's image. This verse also validates the perfected mission of God, and clarifies that it was Jesus Christ, God in flesh, who satisfied the demands of sin or completed the work of God's mission to reconcile fallen humanity. Arguably, verse 3 is the thesis for not just the book of Hebrews, but the

---

[6] While the author of the book of Hebrews does not explicitly state his audience, he writes with an understanding that his audience is intimately familiar with the OT Scriptures, the Jewish laws and covenants, and their place as heirs with Abraham's lineage. Theologians have not come to a consensus regarding this audience (Wright and Bird, *New Testament in Its World*, 715; Cockerill, *Epistle to the Hebrews*, 16–23). This chapter is limited to the missiological discussion in the book of Hebrews, and for that reason time and space is not given to discuss the authorship of Hebrews or its audience.

entire grand narrative of God's missional activity to redeem his creation and restore the ruptured relationship induced by Adam's disobedience.

To fully comprehend what the author of Hebrews is communicating to his audience, a brief word study will shed light on this concept. In the Greek, the term "express image" is χαρακτήρ (*character*), which means to make an impression of something. In Genesis 1:26, a similar concept is used to demonstrate humanity's relationship to God; human beings were made in God's image—meaning they were made in God's likeness—like God, but not identical or equal to God. Humanity cannot correctly claim to be Yahweh. However, in Hebrews, the author clearly sets apart the Son, as the one who is an identical replica of God—the one who shares God's glory because he is the "express image" of God's glory. "Since God's glory has impressed itself on Him [Jesus], as the One exalted by God, He is its reflection and image."[7]

Thus, this Greek term is critical to the exegesis of this text because it introduces the idea of an identical replica—a suitable substitution. The Greek New Testament New Revised Standard Version translates verse 3, "who being radiance of splendor and reproduction of the substance of him" (Heb 1:3 NRSV). Thus, the Greek word χαρακτήρ (*character*) clarifies the context in which the book of Hebrews identifies the person of Jesus Christ.

Building on the term "express image," there are three elements in Hebrews 1:3 that serve to position the book of Hebrews as the thesis of the grand narrative. First, the author of Hebrews establishes the identity of Jesus: he is the identical image of God and the brightness of God's glory. Second, the author recognizes Jesus's authority—as the one who is perfectly suited to stand in the gap as the propitiation for the sin of the world. Finally, the author identifies the work of atonement that Jesus wrought on behalf of sinful humanity.

These three elements (identity, authority, and work of atonement) meet the requisites to complete the *missio Dei*. God declared that there was no one to bridge the chasm caused by the fall and sin; therefore he would fill this void himself (Isa 63:5). The first part of Hebrews 1:3 satisfies this requisite, when the author of Hebrews identifies Jesus as the brightness of the Word in the flesh of the invisible God. Part b of this verse attributes both power and authority to Jesus, through God's Word, which is evidenced throughout the Gospels—Jesus was sent in his Father's name to do the work of his Father (cf. John 5:36; 9:4; 10:25; 14:10). Part c of verse 3 acknowledges the atoning work of Calvary. Jesus himself eradicated our sin by shedding his blood at Calvary, both as a sacrifice and as a priest. Jesus's atonement was not just

---

7 Wright and Bird, *New Testament in Its World*, 715; Wilckens and Kelber, "χαρακτήρ," 418, 421–22.

a purifying or cleansing to eradicate our individual actions of sin, but Jesus came to disavow and destroy sin (cf. Ps 51:5), so as both sacrifice and priest he accomplished this task.

God's Covenants and Laws in the Context of the *Missio Dei*

The author of Hebrews outlines God's redemption plan, including an explication for how the covenants and laws operated in the Old Testament (Exod 24:12; 20:22–23:19; Lev 6:9, 14, 25; 7:1, 7, 11, 37; 11:46; 12:7; Num 5:29–30; 6:13, 21; 10:29; 19:2; Deut 17:11, 18). The law was introduced as a means and measure for perfection in the priesthood. At this juncture, it is important to focus on the term "perfect," or "perfection," which is τελειόω (*teleioô*) in the Greek. It is also prudent to acknowledge the varying degrees for how this word is defined by theologians. Friberg, Friberg, and Miller contend, "In all its meanings [this Greek term] carries the component of a purpose that has been achieved."[8] David G. Peterson argues that the Greek term for "perfection" must be defined within the proper scriptural context— it cannot carry the same meaning in every context.[9]

One of the meanings for the Greek term τελειόω (*teleioô*) refers to the act of bringing an event or item to completion. Arguably, the Hebrews author uses this term to denote that there is nothing lacking or partial when referring to the atoning act of Jesus Christ. In Hebrews 2:10, 5:9, 7:11, 19, the author uses the Greek word τελειόω (*teleioô*) to vividly describe how the blood of Jesus Christ wrought a complete work to fulfill the requisites of the law and the demands of a just and righteous God. What the law lacked or what it could not accomplish or bring to completion—on behalf of humanity—Jesus achieved and accomplished (nothing was lacking) the work of salvation. "Being made perfect [τελειῶσαι], he became the author of eternal salvation unto all them that obey him" (Heb 5:9).

The law served as a measurement of obedience to God's ordinances and was given under the Levitical priesthood (Heb 7:11). Therefore the law, as well as the covenants God made with his people, served to usher in God's mission for redemption. In the Garden of Eden, Adam was instructed not to eat from the "tree of the knowledge of good and evil" (Gen 2:17). This command was given based upon the intimate relationship God and Adam shared. However, when Adam chose to disobey God's command, thereby severing his intimacy with God, the law became a necessary "substitution," although "the law made nothing perfect [complete]" (Heb 7:19). However, the law pointed toward God's supreme mission—his completed work. It is beneficial to note the Apostle Paul's response concerning the law.

---

8 Friberg, Friberg, and Miller, *Analytical Lexicon*, 377.
9 Peterson, *Hebrews and Perfection*, 22–24. Delling, "Τέλος κτλ," 49–51.

For God has done what the Law could not do, [its power] being weakened by the flesh [the entire nature of man without the Holy Spirit]. Sending His own Son in the guise of sinful flesh and as an offering for sin, [God] condemned sin in the flesh [subdued, overcame, deprived it of its power over all who accept that sacrifice]. (Rom 8:3 AMPCE)

This fact is echoed in Hebrews 7:19. The law was a temporary substitution; it was incomplete and weakened by the flesh (Heb 10:1). However, it served a purpose in the grand scheme of God's missionary endeavor. From the inception of the world's foundation, the law served as a prototype for God's perfect plan.

The covenants were created to point toward a greater task as well (Gen 17:7–8). If the old covenants were sufficient, the New Covenant would not have been necessary (Heb 8:6–8). To further expound upon this point to his Jewish audience, the author makes a cogent case by comparing the covenants God made with their forefathers to the New Covenant God created as part of his redemption plan—the covenant that would be written on the hearts of his people.

This New Covenant would not be written on stone. This New Covenant served as the means to perfection or completion for God's ultimate mission, to reconcile the world back to himself (2 Cor 5:18–19). Understanding both the law and the covenants paints a vivid picture about the intent of God's redemptive mission—a mission focused on right relationship between God and his people, a mission that cultivates reconciliation.

Redemption and Reconciliation in the Context of the *Missio Dei*

Reconciliation and redemption, key themes in the book of Hebrews, are key themes in the *missio Dei* as well. Ever since the fall in the Garden of Eden until today, God has sought to reconcile his relationship with his creation. Through his infinite wisdom, God ordained a way toward reconciliation through blood redemption (Heb 9:12–14, 18–25; 10:1, 4, 19–22). The author of Hebrews, knowing his Jewish audience understood the concept of redemption, explained the redemptive work of Christ in the context of the penal substitutionary codes because this was not a difficult concept to bridge.[10]

---

10 Shame/honor are part of Jewish cultural values, which is another concept reflected within the idea of redemption. Luke 15:11–32 (what many call the parable of the prodigal son) provides a perfect example of a vivid portrait of the honor/shame cultural value found within Jewish culture. While the exegesis of Luke 15:11–32 is outside the scope of this chapter, it is important to highlight the honor/shame motif found within the concept of redemption.

To set parameters around the concept of redemption, it is prudent to define this term in its first-century context. The Greek word for redemption in Hebrews 9:12 is λύτρωσις (*lutrosis*), which literally means to ransom.[11] It was the blood of Jesus that ransomed us from the penalty of sin and death. The Hebrew word for redemption is לִגְאֹל (*gaal*), which carries the same meaning in the Hebrew language as it does in the Greek language—to buy back, or to ransom, a slave.[12]

This term also signifies that the one who is next of kin is the only one who has the capacity to redeem, or to free from enslavement and bondage. For example, in Job 5:20, לִגְאֹל (*gaal*) is used to illustrate how God is our Redeemer—the only one who can buy us back from the grips of death. In Psalm 102:16–20, the psalmist declares that when God shall appear in his glory (Heb 1:3), he will redeem the prisoner from death (Isa 42:7; 61:1; Luke 4:18). The term לִגְאֹל (*gaal*) is used both when God is the subject and when sin is the subject.[13] It is important to emphasize this meaning because redemption (buying back what originally belonged to God) is arguably the impetus and purpose of the *missio Dei*.

In 9:12–15, the Hebrews writer marries the concept of redemption with the role of the covenant priest to flesh out the overarching purpose for God's mission—to rescue fallen humanity from the grips of sin and death (Heb 2:14–18). By so doing he demonstrates to his audience that this supernatural rescue could only take place through the redemptive work of a blood sacrifice (Heb 9:13–14). The author then reminds his audience about the times when their forefathers offered animal sacrifices for the atonement of sins (Heb 10:1–4). These sacrifices—which used the blood of animals—served a temporary purpose as an appeasement for remitting sin because the long-lasting effect for remission of sin was not yet available. The blood of a spotless, sinless, perfect lamb was necessary. Thus, God offered himself—through the person of Jesus Christ—to be the atonement and propitiation for the sin of humanity.

Hebrews 9:22 argues a compelling case for the sufficiency and potency of Jesus's blood. If the blood of bulls, goats, and other sacrificial animals could placate sin for a time, the blood of the perfect Lamb would be sufficient to serve as the ultimate sacrifice to redeem fallen humankind from the grips of sin and death. Jesus's blood would be the remedy to once and for all

---

11 Friberg, Friberg, and Miller, *Analytical Lexicon*, 249; Procksch, "λύτρωσις," 328–35.

12 Friberg, Friberg, and Miller, 70. The Greek verb λυτρόω (*lutroō*)—"to redeem"—means to buy back from slavery.

13 Procksch, "λύτρωσις," 333–35.

eradicate sin (Heb 7:22–27; 9:11–14). Moreover, the blood of Jesus points us toward the supreme purpose for the *missio Dei*: the divine help from God through the mission of God.

Divine Help from God: The *Missio Dei* and Its Purpose
The *missio Dei* has a singular focus and serves a singular purpose—i.e., to bridge the chasm caused by sin and usher in the way to reconciliation between God and his people. Divine help from God is at the center of the *missio Dei* and is interwoven throughout the grand narrative of God's salvation story. The writer of Hebrews makes it crystal clear that God's created are called-out and chosen. Because the New Covenant has been written on the hearts of God's people (not on stone tablets), his people—who are called by his name—have his laws written on their hearts (Heb 8:8–13; 10:16–18; cf. Jer 31:31–34). In this soteriology metanarrative, the author of Hebrews identifies three distinct roles—Abraham's seed, the people's priest, and their redemptive Savior—which posits Jesus as the one who fulfills the purpose of the *missio Dei*. These three distinctive descriptors clarify the purpose of the *missio Dei* and serve to clarify the process of the salvation story.

Jesus as Abraham's Seed
The promised seed prophesied in Genesis 3:15 is the same seed described in Hebrews 2:16. The writer acknowledges the human genealogy of Jesus Christ, which is the same seed from which the priest and redemptive Savior is born. Chapter 2 of the book of Hebrews is part of the author's introduction. Because the first-century Jews were familiar with their Jewish heritage and their Jewish ancestry, the author of Hebrews utilizes this familiarity to reveal how their Messiah was in fact the one spoken about in Genesis chapters 3 and 12.

The author builds rapport with his audience by reminding them that Jesus is from Abraham's lineage, and through Abraham they would receive the promised blessings. Moreover, the blessing promised to the heirs of Abraham is not just a temporal blessing of land and generational posterity, but the blessing promised to Abraham's offspring is a spiritual blessing, proven in the genealogy of Jesus (Matt 1:1–16; Heb 2:16; 6:13–16).[14]

Why is the blessing of Abraham an important part of this discourse? The blessing becomes inextricably tied to the promised seed because the New Covenant is directly linked to this future promise. Additionally, it is important to note how the idea of a covenant between God and humankind was "a radical innovation" because the pagan gods were only enforcers of

---
14 Cockerill, *Epistle to the Hebrews*, 148.

covenants—pagan gods were never parties in the covenants.[15] The author of Hebrews reasoned that if the Jews understood their connection to Abraham and the Abrahamic covenant, they would understand their connection to Jesus Christ and the importance of him being called Abraham's seed.

The Jews knew and accepted the idea that a Messiah was promised. They knew they were heirs to the promise given to their Father Abraham, however, the realization that Jesus Christ was that promised seed was not an idea readily accepted. Therefore, it was imperative for the author of Hebrews to articulate fully the idea that Jesus is the seed of Abraham, thereby opening the door for his audience to accept Jesus as the promised Messiah—the one for whom they had long awaited. It is this promise that gives substance to the author's claims in Hebrews 2:16.

In verse 16, is the author speaking only about the Jews? There are theologians who argue it is possible the author of Hebrews was not speaking only about the Jews, because in the complete context of Hebrews 6:12–16 the author "states his major concern for his hearers by urging them to assume their place as part of this faithful people destined for an eternal inheritance."[16] Gareth L. Cockerill further postulates that the author's "invitation extends to all who will hear."[17] The phrase "all who will hear" opens the door to future generations of hearers. From this perspective, it would be impossible to conclude the author was speaking only to the Jews.

Albeit it is safe to assert, the Jews understood Abraham's ancestry and the importance of this ancestral promise.[18] The author is willing to assure his audience that this promise was fulfilled in Jesus Christ because God is a God who cannot lie (Heb 6:17–18). Most importantly,

> Verse 16 begins by reaffirming the Son's commitment to them. Therefore, by calling "those who are about to inherit salvation" through Jesus Christ (1:14) the "seed of Abraham," the [author] affirms that they are the heirs of God's promise to Abraham.[19]

While demonstrating the connection to their father Abraham, the author continues to argue his case that Jesus is the focus of the *missio Dei* as he paints a portrait of Jesus in a priestly role. The author "uses every resource at his disposal to show the length to which God has gone in order to assure

---

15 Foster, "Missiology of Old Testament Covenant," 205–6.
16 Cockerill, *Epistle to the Hebrews*, 284.
17 Cockerill, 284.
18 Cockerill, 148, 283–84.
19 Cockerill, 148.

his people that his promise of salvation is reliable."[20] He then turns his audience's attention to Jesus's role as priest.

Jesus in a Priestly Role
Another critical part in the grand narrative is recognizing Jesus as the high priest. In the words of N. T. Wright and Michael Bird, Jesus "is the *priest* who accomplished a perfect work of purification."[21] Jesus was both the high priest and the sacrifice. He was both the high priest and the blameless lamb. How could one person perform the duties of both the priest and the sacrifice which the priest would offer? And what is the purpose of Jesus's role as high priest? First, it is prudent to define the term *priest* in the context of the Old Testament Jewish law. Second, the role the priests played in the Jewish sacrificial system will be briefly explored. Finally, this section will culminate with an explanation that explores Jesus's role as priest based on the homily the author of Hebrews presented to his first-century Jewish audience.

According to the Levitical law, the priests came from the tribe of Levi and were descendants of Aaron (Exod 28). The primary role of the priest was to make intercession for the people by offering sacrifices for the atonement of the sins of the people (Heb 5:1; Lev 16:20–22). While priests performed other administrative duties, for the sake of this discussion the focus will remain on the gifts and sacrifices offered by the priest. In the Old Testament context, priests represented the people when they stood before God to offer the sacrifice.

In this light, it is sometimes a difficult concept to grasp that Jesus was both the priest and the sacrifice. In her article, "Jesus the Interceding High Priest: A Fresh Look at Hebrews 7:25," Abiola Mbamalu emphasizes this point, and she also critiques J. Mauchline for his conflation of intercession and atonement. Mauchline conflates the issue of Jesus as both the intercessor and the atonement because he views the intercession of Jesus as a one-time event—a completed event.[22] Mbamalu, like the author of Hebrews, views Jesus's role as our atonement occurred once; however, his role as the intercessor is ongoing (Heb 7:25).

The author of Hebrews declares Jesus's role as high priest to be both a forensic event, an ongoing process, and a future event (Heb 7:25).

---

20 Cockerill, 148.
21 Wright and Bird, *New Testament in Its World*, 715. Wright and Bird emphasized the word *priest*.
22 Mbamalu, "Jesus the Interceding High Priest," 1. Nicholas J. Moore echoes Mbamalu's argument in his article and critiques David Moffitt's conflation of intercession and sacrifice. Moore, "Sacrifice, Session, and Intercession," 523–25. Mauchline, "Jesus Christ as Intercessor," 355–60. Moffitt, "Sacrifice, Session and Intercession," 523–24.

Jesus died as an act of the atonement; however, he lives to continue to intercede on behalf of his people (cf. Rom 8:34; 1 John 2:1). The distinct difference between the blood of bulls and goats and the blood of Jesus Christ—the blood of Jesus Christ is eternally efficacious (Heb 9:7, 12–14, 18–22, 25; 10:4, 19, 29). The Old Testament sacrificial system was limited, at best; nonetheless, it foreshadowed God's ultimate sacrificial plan for redemption. The Old Testament system used the blood of animals, which required yearly sacrifices offered by the high priest (Heb 7:26–27). It is in this light that we discuss the purpose for Jesus's role, which advances our knowledge and heightens our appreciation for the magnitude of Jesus's role in the *missio Dei.*

There is a twofold purpose for Jesus's role as high priest. Jesus is both the guarantor and the intercessor (Heb 7:20–25; Isa 59:16). In the Old Testament, the high priest was the intercessor, but he was not the guarantor for the sacrifice (Heb 7:20–22). In this context, the guarantor is the responsible party and the one held liable for the debt (Heb 7:22). When referring to the casualty in Eden, sin is the cause, the shedding of blood is the solution, but the liability rests on the guarantor, which is the blood of Jesus. For the author's audience, the high priest as the intercessor was comprehendible, but the high priest as the guarantor was a new ideology; therefore, it became necessary for the author to expound on Jesus's role as high priest.

Jesus's role as high priest in the context of intercessor was within the norms for the role played by the high priest in ancient biblical times. "In the Hebrew tradition one became high priest on the basis of law and performed one's high-priestly duties in accordance with law."[23] The author of the epistle points to Melchizedek's kingship and priesthood to further explain Jesus's role as high priest.

> Melchizedek's priesthood was beyond and above law; it was bestowed before the law was given and the covenant made. In his approach to and his exposition of a *christological* priesthood, the writer of the letter quotes the Psalmist's words "a priest forever, after the order of Melchizedek," or reproduces them with minor changes, no fewer than five times.[24]

T. K. Thomas is referencing how the author of Hebrews quotes Psalm 110 in Hebrews 5:6, 10; 6:20; and 7:11, 15–17 to better expound on this concept of Jesus as high priest. The author also references Genesis 14:18 in Hebrews 7:1–3. For the author of Hebrews, it is imperative to clearly identify these Scripture references. While Melchizedek could arguably be

---

23 Thomas, "Melchizedek, King and Priest," 404–5; Cockerill, *Epistle to the Hebrews*, 45.
24 Thomas, 405.

considered a mysterious biblical character, the first-century Jewish audience would recognize the name from their knowledge of the Psalms and the Pentateuch.[25]

It is the role as guarantor, though, that carried a more complex meaning for this Hebrews text. As guarantor, Jesus embodies the essence of the missiological framework found in the book of Hebrews. Not only is Jesus the mediator, or the one who stands in the gap as guarantor, but the Hebrews author attempts to convince his audience that this high priest is also the one responsible to pay the penalty for sin. Moreover, the law alone could not accomplish this task (Heb 7:19); the law required a perfect blameless sacrifice. Thus, the only remedy was to pronounce the oath of the priesthood upon the one who could intercede as well as serve as the substitution and therefore the guarantor.

> By concluding with the word "oath" the pastor leaves this word ringing in his hearers' ears as a reminder of God's assurance and an anticipation of the oath by which the Son is made "Guarantor" of the New Covenant (Ps 110:4 in Heb 7:20–22). The "unchangeable character" of God's promise is appropriate for a plan based on that "Guarantor's" "inviolable" priesthood (7:24) and effected by the "eternal spirit." (9:14)[26]

Jesus as a guarantor for the sin of humanity is a concept that harkens back to Genesis 3:15 and 12:7, God—through the person of his Son Jesus the Christ—promises a remedy to bridge the chasm caused by humanity's depravity. This remedy, or guarantor, is part of the divine and promised plan in the mind of God—the *missio Dei*. This remedy would also serve as the responsible party for the sin of humankind, while at the same time serving as the redemptive Savior.

Jesus as the Redemptive Savior

Jesus as the seed of Abraham operating in a priestly role sheds light on his position as the redemptive Savior. The quintessence of the *missio Dei* is that God would provide a plan for redemption—a means by which to pay the price for the penalty of sin—through which the process of reconciliation would be accomplished. In Hebrews 9:12, Jesus's work securing our eternal redemption speaks to his power and authority as the perfect Lamb. As previously discussed, the Old Testament sacrificial system required a blameless sacrifice, and the priest was required to make this offering

---

25 While Melchizedek is a key part of the Hebrews discussion, he is outside the scope of this discussion in the missiological context.

26 Cockerill, *Epistle to the Hebrews*, 287–88.

annually. Furthermore, the necessity for a perfect sacrifice is connected to this idea of redemption.

As set forth by God, the Jewish law for atonement required that blood be shed to make right or atone for the penalty of sin (Gen 3:21; Lev 17:11; Heb 9:22). As Wright and Bird contend, the Old Testament sacrificial system was set in motion for the cleansing and washing by blood which allows humanity the right to stand before a just God. However, " … the point here is not to enable people to come into God's presence (though from our point of view that appears part of it) but to enable the living God to dwell in us and with us."[27] This, then, is the purpose for Jesus's role as redemptive Savior—the only one suitable to buy back humanity from the enslavement of sin—and to set humanity free from the old covenant, thereby completing the process of reconciliation. For this reason, the author chose to expound on the covenants and the law.

By law, a just God demanded payment for sin. Because of love, a merciful God created an avenue by which to replace the Old Covenant with the New Covenant.

> As High Priest He does what the Old Covenant could not do by cleansing the heart from sin. As Mediator He undoes what the Old did, by removing the condemnation pronounced on the sinner.[28]

In his role as redeeming Savior, Jesus paid the price for sin and bought back humanity from the bondage of sin.

Conclusion

From the outset of his homily, the author of Hebrews captures the quintessence of the missiological framework found within the grand narrative. He gives his audience hope by reminding them of their heritage and their relationship to Abraham, and their knowledge about God's covenants with his people and the law. Through a meticulous exposé about the supreme work of redemption wrought through the person of Jesus Christ, the book of Hebrews articulates the missiological motif for the grand narrative by illustrating the role of Jesus as Abraham's seed, the high priest, and the redeeming Savior. In these roles, Abraham's seed speaks to the identity of Jesus, his role as high priest speaks to his authority, and his atoning work is glorified in his role as redeeming Savior.

---

27 Wright and Bird, *New Testament in Its World*, 723.
28 Cockerill, *Epistle to the Hebrews*, 403.

Sharing the identical theme found within the grand narrative, the atoning work of Jesus's blood, as outlined in the book of Hebrews, provides a cohesive framework to communicate a cogent and concise message about the *missio Dei*—the grand narrative's main objective. When all prophecies concerning Jesus's death had been fulfilled, Jesus accomplished what the law could not accomplish. He paid the penalty for sin and thereby reconciled the world back to God through the atoning power of his blood.

Because Jesus was the exact replica of God, he was able to accomplish the perfect mission: God's mission of reconciliation. Thus, to convince his audience that Jesus was the Messiah, the author of Hebrews drew inspiration from Old Testament Scriptures to illustrate how Jesus redeemed (bought back, ransomed) humanity, which was the express purpose for the *missio Dei*—the theme theologized in the epistle to the Hebrews.

Bibliography

Cockerill, Gareth Lee. *The Epistle to the Hebrews*. New International Commentary on the New Testament. Grand Rapids: Eerdmans, 2012.

Delling, Gerhard. "Τέλος κτλ." In *Theological Dictionary of the New Testament*, vol. 8. Edited by Gerhard Friedrich. Translated by Geoffrey W. Bromiley, 49–51. Grand Rapids: Eerdmans, 1964–76.

Foster, Stuart J. "The Missiology of Old Testament Covenant." *Journal of Spiritual Formation & Soul Care 2*, no. 2 (2009): 205–6. https://doi.org/10.1177/239693931003400404.

Friberg, Timothy, Barbara Friberg, and Neva F. Miller. *Analytical Lexicon of the Greek New Testament*. Victoria, BC: Trafford Publishing, 2005.

Mauchline, John. "Jesus Christ as Intercessor." *The Expository Times* 64, no. 12 (September 1953): 355–60. https://doi.org/10.1177/001452465306401202.

Mbamalu, Abiola. "Jesus the Interceding High Priest: A Fresh Look at Hebrews 7:25." *HTS Teologiese Studies/Theological Studies* 71, no. 1 (July 2015): 1–6.

Moffitt, David. "Sacrifice, Session and Intercession: The End of Christ's Offering in Hebrews: A Response to Nicholas Moore." *Journal for the Study of the New Testament* 42, no. 4 (June 2020): 521–41.

Moore, Nicholas J. "Sacrifice, Session, and Intercession: The End of Christ's Offering in Hebrews." *Journal for the Study of the New Testament* 42, no. 4 (June 2020): 521–541.

Peterson, David. *Hebrews and Perfection: An Examination of the Concept of Perfection in the Epistle to the Hebrews*. Society for New Testament Studies Monograph Series 47. Cambridge: Cambridge University Press, 1982.

Procksch, Otto. "λύτρωσις." In *Theological Dictionary of the New Testament*, vol. 4. Edited by Gerhard Friedrich. Translated by Geoffrey W. Bromiley, 328–37. Grand Rapids: Eerdmans, 1964–1976.

Thomas, T. K. "Melchizedek, King and Priest: An Ecumenical Paradigm?" *Bangalore Theological Forum* 31, no. 2 (1999): 403–9.

Van Aarde, Timothy M., and Lygunda Li-M. "A Fruitful Missional Exegesis for a Missional Hermeneutic and Missiology." In *die Skriflig* 51, no. 2a2235 (August 31, 2017): 1–10.

Wilckens, Ulrich, and W. H. Kelber." χαρακτήρ." In *Theological Dictionary of the New Testament*, vol. 9. Edited by Gerhard Friedrich. Translated by Geoffrey W. Bromiley, 418–19. Grand Rapids: Eerdmans, 1964–1976.

Wright, N. T., and Michael F. Bird. *The New Testament in Its World: An Introduction to the History, Literature, and Theology of the First Christians.* Grand Rapids: Zondervan Academic, 2019.

Chapter 3

Christ Outside the Gate
How Hebrews 13 and Galilee Locate Mission for Jesus and Relocate Mission for Us

Allen Yeh

Latin American liberation theology—similar to critical race theory (CRT) today—is often questioned for assuming that God "prefers" the poor and powerless. However, leaving aside some of the potentially negative implications of those movements, it can at least be said that Jesus himself set the example of doing mission from the margins by choosing Nazareth and Galilee (*not* Jerusalem) as his homes. Similarly, in the Old Testament era, Israel itself was the least among the nations and yet was chosen to showcase the Lord's splendor.

God delights in using the underside—the weak to shame the strong, the foolish to shame the wise, and, in Mary's Magnificat (Luke 1:46–55), he brings down arrogant rulers from their thrones. At the end of the day, God wields his power through the powerless to show that he is the one who accomplishes it, similar to how he whittled down Gideon's army (Judg 7:1–8). Hebrews represents a Judaic biblical worldview, and that in turn recenters mission. This kind of centripetal mission (the nations coming to Israel), as opposed to our more common centrifugal mission today (God's people going to the nations), is one that needs recovery. Especially needed is the perspective that Christ died outside the city gate—in the place of ignominy—for us. Hebrews 13:13 is explicit that living out the *imago Dei* comes with the injunction to join Christ in that outside wilderness and take upon ourselves the same dishonor and disgrace. This is nothing less than the ministry of the "wounded healer," which helps us keep God at the center and not have the focus on us.

The book of Hebrews might be considered the interpretive guide to the Old Testament. Though the author is unknown, he or she (the Apostle Paul has now been dismissed as the author, but some think his fellow tentmakers, Priscilla and Aquila, might have written the letter together) undoubtedly were Jews well-versed in the Torah. Because Hebrews is arguably the most Old-Testament-like book of the New Testament (with the possible exception of Revelation), it is not often seen as a source of robust missiology. This view is based, however, on the mistaken assumption that the Old Testament is not as missiological as the New Testament. If one can connect the dots between God's three strategies of mission throughout history, it can clearly be seen that these are not working against each other, but rather all are moving toward the same goal.

A Tripartite Salvation History

In his book *Announcing the Kingdom*, Arthur Glasser outlined that *Heilsgeschichte* (salvation history) is divided into three major parts:
- Part 1: Genesis 1–11: creation through Babel—God's action is universal, for all peoples.
- Part 2: Genesis 12—Acts 1: from Abraham to Jesus—the particular history of the Chosen People.
- Part 3: Acts 2—Revelation 22: the Holy Spirit and the church—back to universal history.[1]

This threefold division also seems to suggest the actions of the triune God: Part 1 focuses on God the Father, part 2 on God the Son, and part 3 on God the Holy Spirit. As such, the twofold division between Old and New Testaments is perhaps less helpful than, say, seeing Jesus as the end of part 2 rather than as the beginning of the New Testament. This makes sense of the observations of some theologians that John the Baptist is actually the last of the Old Testament prophets, and also the statement that Jesus came "only to the lost sheep of Israel" (Matt 15:24 NIV), and also that the church did not exist in the Gospels yet. Another caveat to add here is that part 3—while also universal—is not the same as the kind of universality found in part 1.

Certainly all of humanity can be included in part 1, as children of Adam and Eve, or of Noah and his wife. However, the kind of universality found in part 3 is actually more like chosenness in universality, or unity in diversity. The church—while not limited to an ethnicity any longer—is for the whole world, and yet still has a major qualifier for inclusion: being a follower of *Yeshua Hamashiach*, or Jesus the Christ. It is like a club which anyone (not based on race or gender or social class) can join, as long as one pays the membership fee. It just so happens that the membership fee is both entirely free and also the costliest price of all, because it demands your whole life!

The book of Hebrews is an interesting work in the sense that it is located in part 3 of the Bible but reads more like a part 2 book. This is something that makes it unique and actually quite necessary among the New Testament letters. Hebrews brings a Judaic biblical worldview which re-centers mission. One of the major differences is a Jewish centripetal mission (as opposed

---
1 Glasser, *Announcing the Kingdom*, 29–30.

to our more common Protestant centrifugal mission today).[2] A centrifuge, in a science lab, is a machine that spins chemicals, as the force of gravity drives them outward. Acts 1:8 exhibits a centrifugal mission as the disciples were commanded to go outward—in the power of the Holy Spirit—from "Jerusalem, and in all Judea and Samaria, and to the ends of the earth." However, we tend to forget the other model, which is a "drawing in."

Ralph Winter famously outlined the four stages of Protestant missions history, which were all centrifugal.[3] But Roman Catholics tended to opt for more of a centripetal type of mission through constructing mission stations.[4] The idea was to build a community that encompassed not just Christian education but holistic living. The twenty-one California missions[5] founded by the Franciscans were a prime example of this, as were the five San Antonio missions in Texas. This was a double-edged sword. On the one hand, learning agricultural techniques and literacy and music alongside the Bible was absolutely advanced compared to some "evangelism-only" efforts as seen today. However, the danger was importing one's culture: not just Christianizing them but in the process also Europeanizing them (missionaries of old often could not distinguish between the two).

The Jews struggled with the same pitfall, which seems to be the main weakness of centripetal mission. The Jerusalem Council recorded in Acts 15, in which James (the brother of Jesus) adjudicated between the Judaizers and Paul, illustrated this. The Judaizers wanted the new Gentile converts to accept Jewish culture along with the religion, but in the end James ruled in favor of Paul. Nonetheless, centrifugal mission also has its own host of problems. Obviously, the intention to respect local cultures is paramount: this is why the missionaries go to the target culture instead of expecting the nationals/locals to come to them. However, even centrifugal missions can be subject to the tendency toward imperialism (or even outright, explicit imperialism!) because the confusion between culture and Christianity is not absent there either. In fact, sometimes that is even worse because the imperialism can be conducted under the guise of contextualization.

---

2 Wright, *Mission of God*, 523–25.
3 Winter, "Four Men, Three Eras," 253–61.
4 To be fair, sometimes Protestants did this as well—e.g., Robert Moffat (the father-in-law of David Livingstone) set up a famous Kuruman mission station in southern Africa where he advocated teaching the "Bible and the plough." See Tucker, *From Jerusalem to Irian Jaya*, 147–51.
5 Yeh, "Significance of the California Missions," 71–98.

The Tension between Jewish and Gentile Missiology

This is where the book of Hebrews is essential reading for a more holistic missiology. The tension between Jewish and Gentile missions is something the Apostle Paul also felt, but tension is often where the truth lies. For example, some people may find the following to be irreconcilable "contradictions"—however, both mercy *and* judgment have to be characteristics of God simultaneously; both Jesus's divinity *and* humanity need to be present; both divine sovereignty *and* human responsibility are in operation at all times. Any tendency to only take one side, due to cognitive dissonance with these tensions coexisting, leads to heresy.

This is why the Apostle Paul is such essential missionary reading: he was a Jew of Jews (Phil 3:5–6 NIV: "circumcised on the eighth day, of the people of Israel, of the tribe of Benjamin, a Hebrew of Hebrews; in regard to the law, a Pharisee; as for zeal, persecuting the church; as for righteousness based on the law, faultless") and yet also "the apostle to the Gentiles" (Rom 11:13 NIV). He was a dual citizen of Israel and the Roman Empire, as exhibited by his two birth names of Saul and Paul (*not* a name change, as some mistakenly believe), which demonstrates his bicultural nature.

This has led to contemporary debates, such as the one between John Piper and N. T. Wright in regard to the traditional Protestant perspective on justification versus the New Perspective on Paul.[6] This is not the place to attempt to resolve such a controversy; however, it must be pointed out that the crux of the argument lies in how Greek versus Jewish the Apostle Paul is. The New Perspective says that Paul, contrary to the traditional Protestant perspective, is more Jewish than we give him credit for. Therefore, he is not so much creating a radical break with the Old Covenant, but rather is showing a continuation of it.

One might say that Paul is at heart a Jew, but really acts like a Gentile. (In 1 Corinthians 9, Paul writes like a master of contextualization, and he shifts to his Roman-citizen identity from his second missionary journey onward.) In perhaps the opposite way, the book of Hebrews is a Gentile [read: age of the church, or part 3] book, but reads like a Jewish / part 2 book. We need both Paul *and* Hebrews to frame a truly holistic mission, because both exhibit that necessary bicultural tension, but in opposite ways. The problem is, we've become mostly Pauline in our missiology, whereas maybe we need to be more Hebrews-like in our missiology as well.

The focus of the book of Hebrews is on the tabernacle and the temple, the Hebrew houses of worship. Unlike the church, which is polycentric

---

6 Wright, *What Saint Paul Really Said*; Piper, *Future of Justification*; Wright, *Justification*.

and centrifugal, a tabernacle/temple type of missiology is monocentric and centripetal. And yet, because a book-of-Hebrews kind of missiology is a hybrid (a Greek epistle with a Jewish heart), it is not just a "back-to-part-2" book. It is a renaissance, not a reformation. It is a missiology in which the emphasis is on the tabernacle (the poor, downtrodden sojourner) more than the temple (the glorious fulfillment of the Promised Land). This kind of "hybrid" missiology is not truly centripetal, because it has centrifugal tendencies.

The Abraham-Jesus ("Part 2") Connection in Hebrews

There are several factors that frame an Abraham-Jesus ("Jews for Gentiles") type of mission. First, there is ethnicity. The Abrahamic covenant, the beginning of part 2 of Glasser's tripartite divisions of salvation history, is the impetus for this kind of hybrid missiology. Unlike what Old Testament Israelites might have thought, Abraham was always for the Gentiles. He himself was born a Gentile, a pagan from Ur of the Chaldeans, who didn't even know the true name of God in his lifetime.[7] (Melchizedek just used the pagan word *El*, or perhaps *El Elyon*, in his fellowship with Abraham [Gen 14:18–20].) The author of Hebrews quotes Psalm 110:4 in calling Jesus "a priest forever, in the order of Melchizedek" (Heb 7:17 NIV), so there is a direct acknowledgement of this link. After all, Abraham and Jesus are the two bookends of part 2. Jesus himself is also emphasized to have Gentile blood in Matthew's genealogy (despite the fact that Matthew is supposed to be the Jewish Gospel!): Bathsheba the Hittite, Ruth the Moabite, and Rahab the Canaanite are all mentioned in his ancestry (Matt 1:1–17).[8]

Second, there is the target demographic. The Abrahamic covenant (developed in four parts: chapters 12, 15, 17, and 22 of Genesis) is about Abraham converting to God (from his pagan name Abram, in Genesis 17, so there was indeed a name change here, unlike with Paul). Abraham was given this promise by God:

> I will surely bless you and make your descendants as numerous as the stars in the sky and as the sand on the seashore. Your descendants will take possession of the cities of their enemies, and through your offspring all nations on earth will be blessed, because you have obeyed me. (Gen 22:17–18)

---

[7] The Jews were descendants of Judah, from which they derived their name. And Moses was the first one to be revealed the tetragrammaton—YHWH, the divine name—at the burning bush.

[8] And it is not simply that they were Gentiles; they were also women, and they also had questionable sexual mores. And yet Matthew saw fit to include them! This says something about God's regard for the socially marginalized.

God was so intent on this blessing to the nations that he swore it by himself (seen both in Genesis 22:16–17 and Hebrews 6:13–14, which are virtually identical in their wording). Again, Abraham was never just for the Jews—he was always setting his sights on the *nations*. In fact, my interpretation of the Hebrew words for "all the nations" in Genesis 12:3 ("... will be blessed through you") is *kol mishpehot*. The parallel is Jesus's utterance in Matthew 24:14—"And this gospel of the kingdom will be preached in the whole world as a testimony to all nations, and then the end will come"—which uses the Greek words *panta ta ethne*. At the first Lausanne Congress in 1974 in Switzerland, Ralph Winter famously redefined "nations" as ethno-linguistic groups, not political nations.[9] In other words, Abraham and Jesus ultimately wanted many ethnicities to come to the faith, even though Abraham was the father of monotheism (though not the father of Jews), and Jesus limited his mission mostly exclusively to Jews.

Third, there is the issue of location and social status. Both Abraham and Jesus are identified as pilgrims and sojourners (Abraham from Ur, Jesus to Egypt and back). And interestingly, both are compared to tents. This makes sense, because tents are mobile and fit with people who have no permanent home. The author of Hebrews wrote,

> By faith Abraham, when called to go to a place he would later receive as his inheritance, obeyed and went, even though he did not know where he was going. By faith he made his home in the promised land like a stranger in a foreign country; he lived in tents, as did Isaac and Jacob, who were heirs with him of the same promise. (Heb 11:8–9 NIV)[10]

Jesus, similarly, is described like this in Hebrews 9:11 (NIV):

> But when Christ came as high priest of the good things that are now already here, he went through the greater and more perfect tabernacle that is not made with human hands, that is to say, is not a part of this creation.

The comparison to the tabernacle (the tent version of the temple) is no accident. It implies that Abraham and Jesus's social locations were movable, and that they had not arrived at their destination. Abraham lived out Hebrews 11:13 (NIV):

---

9 Winter, "Highest Priority," 221.

10 And it wasn't just Abraham—note that Hebrews 11 catalogs the pre-Promised-Land people as the standouts, whereas the Promised-Land people were a footnote (vv. 32–33): "And what more shall I say? I do not have time to tell about Gideon, Barak, Samson and Jephthah, about David and Samuel and the prophets, who through faith conquered kingdoms, administered justice, and gained what was promised."

> All these people were still living by faith when they died. They did not receive the things promised; they only saw them and welcomed them from a distance, admitting that they were foreigners and strangers on earth.

In his incarnation on earth, Jesus lived out his sojourner mentality from the moment he was born—homeless in a manger in Bethlehem. And he continued that until the day he died, "outside the city gate" in Jerusalem (Heb 13:12 NIV). Though Bethlehem and Jerusalem are the two cities most associated with Jesus, neither was his home (he only went to the former for the census, and he only went to the latter in the last week of his life, for his Passion). Egypt and Nazareth and Galilee—truly marginal places—were his homes. Some say he spent over three years in Egypt as a child, perhaps about twenty-five years growing up being trained as a carpenter in Nazareth, and finally did three years of public ministry, with the town of Capernaum, in Galilee, as his headquarters much of the time. He did not arrive on earth as the cosmic Christ, but rather as a baby who had to grow "in wisdom and stature, and in favor with God and man" (Luke 2:52 NIV). The incarnation was, in essence, a pilgrimage.

The Marginalized as the New Center
"Can anything good come from Nazareth?" (John 1:46 NAB). This portable tent called the tabernacle, the not-so-glorious precursor to the splendor of Solomon's temple, is not only not honored, but is sometimes even disparaged. It does not attract, but rather "He had no beauty or majesty to attract us to him, nothing in his appearance that we should desire him" (Isa 53:2). He was born homeless, he was an international refugee as a child, he grew up in a backwater town, he chose as his ministry headquarters a place of multiethnic "riff-raff," and he died among the criminals. Our Lord and Savior himself re-centered the faith—not as the conquering hero that the Jews expected of their Messiah, but as the Suffering Servant who would die for them, coming into Jerusalem on a humble donkey. Ironically, though, many Christians today still have the same expectation as the Jews of the first century—namely, a faith of power rather than weakness.

First, there is social marginalization (where one is located). Christianity has historically been a minority, not just in numbers but in might. It is a wonder that Christians ever got to the place where prestige and centeredness became part of their makeup at all. Their status as a persecuted minority, until Constantine, was indicative of who they were. Some Christians have even gone so far as to say that Constantinianism (Christendom, or a top-down model of church in which Christianity is mandated by the state, leading to nominalism) is one of the worst things that ever happened to the faith. John Stott said,

> When I was ordained in the Church of England, evangelicals were a despised and rejected minority. ... Over the intervening 60 years, I've seen the evangelical movement in England grow in size, in maturity, certainly in scholarship, and therefore I think in influence and impact. We went from a ghetto to being on the ascendancy, which is a very dangerous place to be. Pride is the ever-present danger that faces all of us. In many ways, it is good for us to be despised and rejected. I think of Jesus' words, "Woe unto you when all men speak well of you."[11]

Second, there is orthodoxy (what one thinks). Theological development seems to have followed suit with the "Christianity as dictated by power" maxim. The original four ecumenical councils—Nicaea, Constantinople, Ephesus, and Chalcedon—were only ecumenical insofar as they were agreed-upon mostly just by Mediterranean (European, Middle Eastern, and certain North African) Christians, although there was one representative of Persia and India—John of Persia—who was present at the Council of Nicaea and signed the creed on behalf of them. Non-Chalcedonian Christians, such as the Coptic Christians, who were Jacobite Monophysites, were deemed heretics; and the Persian Christians, who were part of the Church of the East, were either deliberately written out of the pages of Western church history or simply forgotten.[12]

Yet these proved to be vibrant ecclesial communities who thrived for a thousand years and are still extant. Are they not to be considered Christians? What are the essentials of the faith that one must absolutely hold in order to be seen as part of the church proper, and what are the nonessential points of theology that are OK for Christians to disagree upon because they do not impinge upon their salvation or identity in Christ?[13]

Paul Hiebert argued, in "The Category *Christian* in the Mission Task,"[14] that for someone to be considered a Christian is less about what one knows and more about allegiance to Christ. And Andrew Walls wrote that if twentieth-century Pentecostal Nigerians are shown the Nicene Creed, "They accept the creed of Nicea [*sic*], but they display little interest in it: they appear somewhat vague about the relationship of the divine Son and the Holy Spirit."[15] Certainly Chalcedonian Christians, as well as Monophysites, Church of the East Christians, and Pentecostal Nigerians, believe that Jesus is God (unlike, say, Jehovah's Witnesses). They just disagree (or are less precise) about the nature of the relationship between the human and the

---

11 Stott, "Evangelism Plus," 96.
12 Jenkins, *Lost History of Christianity*, 57–58.
13 Yeh, "Majority World Theologies."
14 Hiebert, *Anthropological Reflections*, 107–36.
15 Walls, *Missionary Movement in Christian History*, 5.

divine. Must they leverage Greek terminology, like *hypostasis*, in order to be properly orthodox?

Hiebert tried to balance two potentially opposing tendencies: the welcoming of global theologies, while also not veering into syncretism. He came up with four "checks against syncretism": the Bible, the Holy Spirit, the global hermeneutical community, and creeds.[16] This is very much appreciated, but a caveat is in order: there must be equal footing and partnership for the global hermeneutical community and creeds to function properly. If the West holds the mouthpiece and the publishing most of the time, then there will be an imbalance. It is reminiscent of the African proverb, "Until the lion learns to write, every story will glorify the hunter."

Third, there is the way of ministry (how one does it). George Hunter III wrote a book called *The Celtic Way of Evangelism*. Celts were on the edge of Europe. They were outside the borders of the Roman Empire, and thus created their own identity—i.e., monasticism. This was a double-edged sword: on the one hand, they were not as missional as they could have been, had they been more open to cross-cultural contact.

Ireland is a solitary, windswept island on the edge of the Mediterranean world. On the other hand, they were left untouched to preserve the very best of Christianity. As a result, Ireland came to be known as "the island of saints and scholars." When Europe suffered through the Dark Ages and "civilization," as they knew it, fell, the Celts thrived and held their own; and in those monastic libraries they retained the glories of the faith—in theology, tradition, and history.

Hunter compared the prevalent Roman Christianity of the time to Celtic Christianity. He contends that the Celtic way of "belonging before believing" is better and more effective than the Roman way of "believing before belonging."[17] Unfortunately, it is the Roman way which has largely impacted the way we do Christianity today, due to the Roman church dominating the Celtic church following the Synod of Whitby in 664 AD and eventually the United States (which saw itself as the "New Rome"),[18] the richest and most powerful country in the history of the world, propagating this version of Christianity worldwide.

---

16 Hiebert, *Anthropological Reflections*, 91–92.
17 Hunter, *Celtic Way of Evangelism*, 45, 106.
18 The US has always been majority Protestant, not Catholic; nonetheless, the founding fathers modeled Washington DC on Greco-Roman architecture, set up their government (e.g., democracy, senate) on Greco-Roman ideals, "deified" their national heroes in shrines (e.g., the Lincoln Memorial looks like the Parthenon, the Jefferson Memorial looks like the Pantheon and they placed a painting in the Capitol dome called the "Apotheosis of George Washington"), and adopted the eagle (the symbol of Rome) as their national bird.

With all three of the above, there are examples throughout history in which the remnant holds the actual truth. Who is considered "Christian" or "orthodox" may actually be more of a matter of description than prescription. Sameer Yadav pointed out that orthodoxy—at any given moment—is basically whatever the majority or powerful deem it to be,[19] not so much what God deems it to be. Could it be that sometimes the majority of believers actually got it wrong, and a tiny minority actually got it right? The Christians in the first century would certainly claim that over and against the Jews. The Celts in the Dark Ages would certainly claim that over and against the Romans. The Protestants in the sixteenth century would certainly claim that over and against the Catholics—that the truth was lost for centuries until they got it right. N. T. Wright today sees his New Perspective on Paul as the correct view over and against the traditional Reformed Protestant perspective, even though it is the minority; and similarly, he believes that the truth was lost for centuries until he—or his precursor, E. P. Sanders—got it right.

This view is one that needs recovery. Especially needed is the perspective that Christ died outside the city gate—in the place of ignominy—for us, and Hebrews 13:13 is explicit that living out the *imago Dei* comes with the injunction to join Christ in that outside wilderness and to take upon ourselves the same dishonor and disgrace. This is nothing less than the ministry of the "wounded healer," which helps us keep God at the center and not have the focus on us.

David Bosch, in his magisterial *Transforming Mission*, is often considered one of the greatest—if not the greatest—missiologist of the twentieth century. One of his inestimable contributions is the idea of the *missio Dei* (God's mission), that mission should be located in the personhood of God (or more specifically, the Triune Godhead) and not in the church. Bosch wrote, "Mission is not primarily an activity of the church, but an attribute of God. God is a missionary God."[20] In other words, the *missiones ecclesiae* is secondary and flows from the *missio Dei*. Though he stated these words in the late twentieth century, it seems as if twenty-first century churches are still largely operating on a "might-is-right" or "power-is-proof" philosophy.

---

19 Sameer Yadav, *OnScript* podcast, "Theology, Race, and the Mystical Tradition," August 18, 2021.
20 Bosch, *Transforming Mission*, 389–90.

Latin America: Liberation Theology

Latin America is often relegated to the margins. The reasons for this have been outlined in my book *Polycentric Missiology*, with regard to its geographic location, its exclusion from various world conferences, and its religious status as not being deemed really "worthy" of being a recipient of missions, nor of being missionaries themselves.[21] Yet, its place in world Christianity is inestimable. Its Catholicism often causes Western evangelical missionaries to reject its contributions and conclusions—this despite the fact that not all Latinos are Catholic. This section will look at contributions from liberation theology, Orlando Costas, and Oscar Garcia-Johnson.

Liberation theology started as a grassroots movement in the Roman Catholic Church. Although the ideas were germinated by the Second Vatican Council of 1962–65, they were more fully initiated at the second Latin American Bishop's Congress (CELAM II) in 1968 in Medellín, Colombia. Vatican II advocated what were practically Protestant ideas, such as the affirmation of the Scriptures being translated into the vernacular, a more grassroots acknowledgement of the work of the laity, the ecumenical acceptance of non-Catholic Christians (Protestants, Orthodox) as "separated brethren," and more religious freedom done in local worship styles. CELAM II picked up on these ideas and furthered them, especially as espoused by a Dominican priest from Peru: Gustavo Gutiérrez, with his publication of *Teología de la liberación* (*A Theology of Liberation*, 1971).

Liberation theology was not strictly a Catholic idea, since Protestants Rubem Alves from Brazil and José Míguez Bonino from Argentina preceded Gutiérrez in some of these ideas. But it really got popularized through Catholics not only like him, but also the Boff brothers (Leonardo and Clodovis) from Brazil, Jon Sobrino from Spain, Óscar Romero from El Salvador, and others. Liberation theology was about God's "preferential option for the poor"—namely, the idea that theology can be done from the viewpoint of, by, and for the poor. This cohered well with a Catholic idea of the Virgin of Guadalupe, a Mariology that reflected well the perspective of those most marginalized in society, like women and indigenous.[22] Even in the Bible, Mary's blessedness affirms the centrality of women (or, at least, one particular woman) and her Magnificat sings explicitly, "He has brought down rulers from their thrones but has lifted up the humble. He has filled the hungry with good things but has sent the rich away empty" (Luke 1:52–53 NIV).

---

21 Yeh, *Polycentric Missiology*, 184–86.
22 Yeh and Olaguibel, "Virgin of Guadalupe."

It is sometimes said that heresy is the mother of orthodoxy, which is akin to the saying that "necessity is the mother of invention." Theology is *occasional*, which means it does not need to be codified until it encounters a situation which requires its firm articulation. As Latin Americans daily faced the reality of poverty, liberation theology naturally arose. In contrast, in the Mediterranean, Christianity instead developed doctrines like the Apostle's Creed and the Nicene Creed, which articulate a Hellenistic worldview designed to dialogue with a philosophizing culture. These creeds, while not having any errors of commission, perhaps had errors of omission. While they certainly emphasized Jesus's humanity in his birth, suffering under Pilate, crucifixion, and resurrection, they could have also included his thirty-three years of earthly life of being an international refugee, a carpenter, a rabbi, and his concomitant ministry like healing and feeding and miraculous signs.

These creeds could have also mentioned more Old Testament/Hebraic themes such as love—God's chief characteristic—and the greatest commandments, or the kingdom, which was the topic Jesus preached on most. In the Old Testament, Israel was the least among the nations and yet was chosen to showcase the Lord's splendor. In Jesus's upside-down kingdom, God delights in using the underside, the weak to shame the strong, the foolish to shame the wise, and the first shall be last. Jesus starts the Sermon on the Mount—the greatest sermon of all time—with the Beatitudes, which contend: blessed are the poor, blessed are those who hunger and thirst, and blessed are the meek. Liberation theology often focuses on the favor of God upon the poor, the oppressed, the powerless. The Mediterranean church on the ascendancy (so, not in the first couple of centuries, but post-Constantine i.e. from the Edict of Milan onward), in contrast, started caring more about power, so the favor of God became seen as on the Emperor, on the Pope/bishops, on the expansion of the Empire, on military might.

Latin America: Orlando Costas

Orlando Costas was a Puerto Rican theologian who lived from 1942–87. At the height of his career, he was one of the "Big Three" Latino evangelicals of the FTL (*Fraternidad Teológica Latinoamericana*), along with C. René Padilla of Ecuador and Samuel Escobar of Peru. Latin America never had a fundamentalist-modernist controversy like the United States did, so evangelicals never became hyper-conservative in response to liberalism. As such, Costas took what he deemed to be the best of liberation theology without accepting all of it. The two books in which he unpacked these ideas the most were *Christ Outside the Gate* (1982) and *Liberating News* (1989, published posthumously).

The first book, his magnum opus, took its title from Hebrews 13:12: "And so Jesus also suffered outside the city gate to make the people holy through his own blood" (NIV). But it is not enough to only focus on verse 12, to locate Jesus's identification with the marginalized, where he died among the criminals. Verses 13–14 is the injunction of where we are to be: "Let us, then, go to him outside the camp, bearing the disgrace he bore. For here we do not have an enduring city, but we are looking for the city that is to come" (NIV). Not only does Jesus call from the margins, but he redefines the center. Heaven is not where the world locates the center (namely, power); it is where Jesus locates the center (namely, powerlessness).

Today, the periphery is the non-Western, or Majority, world. Costas was not only writing from the perspective of Latin America, but also in solidarity with his colleagues in Asia, Africa, the Caribbean, and the Pacific. He and his fellow theologians of INFEMIT (International Fellowship of Evangelical Mission Theologians from the Two Thirds World) theologized together.[23]

For Costas, what was meant by "outside the gate" was not just social location; it was a hermeneutical method. He frequently spoke of theologizing *en el camino* ("on the road"), as opposed to "from the balcony." In fact, he had a line from Antonio Machado's famous poem inscribed on his tombstone: "*Caminante, no hay camino, se hace camino al andar*"[24] ("Traveler, there is no road, you make the road as you walk.")

This is very similar to Abraham's pilgrim existence, and to Jesus's tabernacle existence. Costas writes:

> The *planting and growth* of the church must not be thought of in terms of building sacred compounds but, rather, of sojourning (cf. Isa 19:23) communities, like Abraham who lived in tents sojourning "in the land of promise, as in a foreign land" (Heb 11:9). The church is to be a *paroikiai*, a temporary abode, a tent in the wilderness, not a fortress or an insulated castle.[25]

It is a missiological existence that necessitates movement: having the humility to move away from an anthropocentrism toward a Christocentrism. It is, in essence, what the father of the Protestant Reformation, Martin Luther, called *Reformata et semper reformanda* ("Reformed and always reforming"). Westerners almost always put the emphasis on the first part but neglect the second. This means that theology or missiology is reactive, not proactive, at

---

23 Now INFEMIT stands for International Fellowship for Mission as Transformation.
24 "Proverbios y cantares XXIX" ("Proverbs and Songs 29"), in Campos de Castilla (Fields of Castile).
25 Costas, *Christ Outside the Gate*, 192.

least initially. This is essentially the idea of theology being occasional. If the outcast, the minority, the periphery, is where Jesus is, then we always have to continue redefining ourselves over and against the majority, and perhaps the remnant is the place that holds the truth.

This is where Costas's final book, *Liberating News*, comes in. In this book, Costas develops the idea of evangelization from the periphery, with Galilee as a model. His argument was that the radical example of Jesus, from the Galilean periphery, must inform contemporary contextual evangelization. Namely, the periphery is the starting point of evangelization. When the periphery is evangelized, the ripples will be felt in the centers of power, not the other way around:

> If evangelization starts on the periphery of society, if it works from the bottom up, the good news of God's kingdom is vividly demonstrated and credibly announced as a message of liberating love, justice, and peace. … When evangelization begins at the centers of power, working from the top down, its content usually ends up being an easy and cheap accommodation of the vested interests of the mighty and wealthy. In such cases, evangelization suffers reduction, because the content of the gospel is truncated, turned into a private whitewash. … Evangelization is prophetic, and thus liberating, when it has a communal base, a basic, witnessing faith-community. Such a basic community is built from the periphery.[26]

The periphery is the poor, the oppressed, the disenfranchised—but also the minorities in the Majority World and those in the margins of society in Western nations. Costas saw himself as such a person, a Latino speaking to the United States from the periphery; but his journey *en el camino* was always an attempt at pushing toward those new centers as redefined by Christ.

The Holy Spirit-Church ("Part 3") Connection in Hebrews

Oscar García-Johnson wrote *Spirit Outside the Gate* as a follow-up book to Costas's *Christ Outside the Gate*, but he switched out the second for the third Person of the Trinity. What he meant by the title is "The Spirit Outside the Gate (or the trinitarian Spirit of Life, Love, and Justice) walks with subaltern communities sharing modern/colonial/imperial subjugations in their *missio Dei*, that is, theotopian decolonization in their struggle to make their life worthy and livable amid the most unfavorable conditions shaping their world-systems."[27] In other words, how hard it is for the rich (in this life) to enter the kingdom of heaven, but those who live out the marginalization on earth are the ones who will achieve heaven.

---

26 Costas, *Liberating News*, 62.
27 García-Johnson, *Spirit Outside the Gate*.

It was not Abraham himself (though he was commended for his great faith), but rather his descendant, Joshua, who got to enter the Promised Land. And yet even that was not enough, because Hebrews 4:8 (NIV) says, "For if Joshua had given them rest, God would not have spoken later about another day." Martin Luther, father of the Protestant Reformation, said: "There are only two days on my calendar: this day and That Day." And the New Jerusalem, the new heavens and the new earth, are That Day.

In "The Gospel as Prisoner and Liberator of Culture," Andrew Walls delineates the liminality (the bicultural/"between two worlds" characteristic) inherent in every Christian. There is always a tension between the Pilgrim Principle and the Indigenizing Principle, but Walls's description of the Pilgrim Principle really connects the dots: being aliens and strangers in this world means that Christians ultimately belong to the other world.[28] And this is the missiology of the church: not one which exists in colonial power or dominates the other, but one which works in powerlessness to show that God is the one who accomplishes it. It is nothing less than a Hebrews sensibility, one which shows God's grandeur because we ourselves get out of the way.

David Bosch and others would call this the *missio Dei* (as opposed to the *missiones ecclesiae*): it is God's mission, not our mission. We join him in it, but it does not belong to us. It is the way of the upside-down kingdom, the way of the sojourner, the way of the cross. It is not "might is right," but rather servant leadership. It is, as John the Baptist—often called the "last of the Old Testament prophets"—says: "He must increase, but I must decrease" (John 3:30 NASB). We must follow the Way in order to be truly missional in the Hebrews sense. So let us, therefore, go to where he is—outside the city gate—because Christ redefines the center and creates a new center, which is not of this world.

Conclusion

Hebrews is a roadmap for us to do this. It is not a centrifugal mission, which we are used to in the age of the church; it is more of a centripetal way of Jesus, drawing people to ourselves. However, it is not drawing people to ourselves through attractiveness or power, but rather through weakness and poverty of spirit, to the margins. This approach may seem counterintuitive, as it feels like we are going backward; but God's covenant is consistent, and it was his unfolding plan to map this blessing to the nations from Abraham to Jesus and beyond.

---

28 Walls, *Missionary Movement in Christian History*, 8–9.

Centripetal and centrifugal mission is not an either/or approach, but rather a both/and. As we rethink mission, it must remain authentically Trinitarian. Father, Son, and Holy Spirit do not supersede each other, but rather work together to enact a mission to the world that is consistent in the Godhead. There is a throughline that can be traced in the biblical narrative, which is clear if one has eyes to see it. In a way, this makes it parabolic.

Irenaeus, one of the early church fathers, famously theologized that the Son and the Spirit are like the two hands of the Father. With all due respect, that makes it so that there are two separate ways of salvation, either through the second or the third Person of the Trinity. Rather, there is only one way of salvation, and that is from the Father, through the cross of the Son, and then expressed in the power of the Holy Spirit (a better analogy might be to think of the Father as the head, the Son as the arm, and the Spirit as the hand). Skipping the weakness of the cross on the way to power is a formula for disaster. The Holy Spirit's power must be nurtured and developed in the crucible of suffering, in the margins of history, and on the periphery. This is the Hebrews way.

Bibliography

Bosch, David J. *Transforming Mission*. Maryknoll: Orbis, 1991.

Costas, Orlando E. *Christ Outside the Gate: Mission Beyond Christendom*. Maryknoll: Orbis, 1982.

Costas, Orlando E. *Liberating News: A Theology of Contextual Evangelization*. Grand Rapids: Eerdmans, 1989.

García-Johnson, Oscar. *Spirit Outside the Gate: Decolonial Pneumatologies of the American Global South*. Downers Grove: IVP Academic, 2019.

Glasser, Arthur F. *Announcing the Kingdom: The Story of God's Mission in the Bible*. Grand Rapids: Baker Academic, 2003.

Hiebert, Paul G. *Anthropological Reflections on Missiological Issues*. Grand Rapids: Baker, 1994.

Hunter, George G., III. *The Celtic Way of Evangelism: How Christianity Can Reach the West ... Again*. Nashville: Abingdon, 2010.

Jenkins, Philip. *The Lost History of Christianity: The Thousand-Year Golden Age of the Church in the Middle East, Africa, and Asia—and How It Died*. New York: HarperCollins, 2008.

Piper, John. *The Future of Justification: A Response to N. T. Wright*. Wheaton: Crossway, 2007.

Stott, John. "Evangelism Plus: John Stott Reflects on Where We've Been and Where We're Going." *Christianity Today* 50, no. 10 (October 2006): 94–99.

Tucker, Ruth A. *From Jerusalem to Irian Jaya: A Biographical History of Christian Missions*. Grand Rapids: Zondervan, 2004.

Walls, Andrew F. *The Missionary Movement in Christian History*. Maryknoll: Orbis, 2002.

Winter, Ralph D. "Four Men, Three Eras, Two Transitions: Modern Missions." In *Perspectives on the World Christian Movement*, edited by Ralph D. Winter and Steven C. Hawthorne, 33–44. Carlisle: William Carey Library, 1999.

Winter, Ralph D. "The Highest Priority: Cross-Cultural Evangelism." In *Let the Earth Hear His Voice: The Complete Papers from the International Congress on World Evangelization, Lausanne, Switzerland*, edited by J. D. Douglas. Minneapolis: World Wide Publications, 1975.

Wright, Christopher J. H. *The Mission of God: Unlocking the Bible's Grand Narrative*. Downers Grove: InterVarsity Press, 2006.

Wright, N. T. *What Saint Paul Really Said: Was Paul of Tarsus the Real Founder of Christianity?* Grand Rapids: Eerdmans, 1997.

Wright, N. T. *Justification: God's Plan & Paul's Vision*. London: SPCK, 2009.

Yadav, Sameer. *OnScript* podcast. "Theology, Race, and the Mystical Tradition." August 18, 2021.

Yeh, Allen. "Majority World Theologies." *Transformation: An International Journal of Holistic Mission Studies* 38, no. 3 (June 30, 2021): 197–211. https://doi.org/10.1177/02653788211027344.

Yeh, Allen. *Polycentric Missiology: 21st Century Missions from Everyone to Everywhere*. Downers Grove: IVP Academic, 2016.

Yeh, Allen. "The Significance of the California Missions to Californian Theology and Culture." In *Theology and California: Theological Refractions on California's Culture*, edited by Fred Sanders and Jason S. Sexton, 71–98. Surrey, UK: Ashgate, 2014.

Yeh, Allen, and Gabriela Olaguibel. "The Virgin of Guadalupe." *International Journal of Frontier Missiology* 28, no. 4 (October–December 2011): 169–77.

Chapter 4

The Incarnation and the Mission of God

Michael P. Naylor

The person and work of Christ is clearly a central concern in the epistle to the Hebrews. The author of this letter provides an exhortation to cling firmly to Jesus and warns his readers of the grave dangers of neglecting the salvation provided through Christ's priestly ministry. The author of Hebrews refers to the humanity of Christ throughout the letter,[1] and it does not appear that the true nature of the humanity of Jesus was in doubt.[2] Rather, the author is determined to demonstrate how God has achieved a better salvation through the work of his Son. This chapter will consider the necessity of the incarnation for accomplishing the mission of God. The first part of this essay will consider Christ's role as the promised Davidic heir, as demonstrated in the series of Old Testament quotations in Hebrews 1. Next, the author's use of Psalm 110 will be considered. Third, the wider scope of the priestly ministry of Jesus will be explored. Finally, implications for our understanding of the mission of God in Hebrews will be considered.

Jesus as Davidic Heir

Although references to David by name are not plentiful in Hebrews (see 4:7 and 11:32), the concern regarding Jesus as the Davidic heir is significant for the epistle's argument.[3] This concern emerges initially in chapter 1 in the catena of Old Testament quotations demonstrating the superiority of Jesus to the angels.[4] The series is introduced with a question: "For to which of the angels, did he ever say?"[5] This question is repeated at the conclusion of the

---

1 See, for example, Hebrews 2:9, 11, 14; 5:7–10; 7:14, 27; 9:12; 10:10, 20; 12:2; 13:12.
2 Unlike, for example, 1 John 1:1–2; 4:1–3.
3 The author of Hebrews stresses the high priestly role, rather than the kingship, which may account for the relative paucity of references to Davidic kingship. See Cockerill, *The Epistle to the Hebrews*, 104; Jamieson, *Paradox of Sonship*, 106–7; Brennan, *Divine Christology*, 193.
4 See Attridge, "Psalms in Hebrews," 197–212; Jipp, "Son's Entrance," 557–75. Lindars (*Theology of the Letter to the Hebrews*, 35) views this as a series of proof-texts identifying Jesus as Messiah. Some commentators identify Hebrews 1 as a response to angel veneration or angel Christology (see Attridge, *Epistle to the Hebrews*, 50–53), but the focus appears to be on the role of Messiah and the connection of angels with the Mosaic Law (see Heb 2:2; so Lane, *Hebrews*, 1:17). The author does, however, clearly distinguish between Jesus and the angels in his humiliation and exaltation (so Bauckham, "Monotheism and Christology," 170).
5 As Peeler (*You Are My Son*, 30) notes, the texts are configured as the speech of the Father to/concerning his Son. See also Pierce, *Divine Discourse*, 40–46.

catena in verse 13, albeit with some modification in the Greek text. The term *son* (υἱός) appears in several places in chapter 1 (see Heb 1:2, 5a, 5b, 8). The argument in Hebrews 1 doesn't hinge on whether the term *son*[6] is applied to the angels, as the author was likely aware of texts such as Job 38:7.[7] Rather, the concern seems to be with the unique role played by Jesus as the one born into the line of David in fulfillment of the promises concerning the Messiah.

The first quotation is from Psalm 2:7.[8] This psalm focuses on the king as the earthly representative of God who executes his justice in the context of the rebellious nations. The statement made in the quotation focuses on God's establishment of the king using the language of "Son" and "begotten."[9] With the introductory question in 1:5a, the author's use of Psalm 2:7 identifies a role that no angel could play: the earthly king who executes the rule of Yahweh.

The next quotation, in 1:5b, continues the Davidic focus and is drawn from 2 Samuel 7:14 (cf. Chr 17:13) LXX. Once again, the "father"/"son" language is highlighted as the text proclaims the promised relationship with God in the establishment of the Davidic line. Read in concert with Psalm 2:7, this text identifies God's choice of his anointed one, who executes his authority.[10]

The third quotation is introduced with a reference to the "firstborn" in verse 6. Although not a quotation of an OT text, the term warrants some consideration. Modern usage tends to utilize "firstborn" as a reference to birth order, but the term πρωτότοκος is also used to convey preeminence.[11] The term is likely an allusion to Psalm 89:27 (88:28 LXX),[12] where David is made to be the "firstborn."[13] If this is the case, this introductory formula provides yet another connection with the Davidic heir.

---

6   Either υἱός in the LXX or *bēn* in the MT.
7   Bruce, *Epistle to the Hebrews*, 53. See also Job 1:6; 2:1. In some interpretive traditions, Gen 6:1–4 may be considered here as well.
8   All quotations in Hebrews 1 follow the LXX.
9   The timing of the "begetting" is debated. Bauckham ("Divinity of Christ," 34) identifies this as dealing with the self-origination of God. Jamieson (*Paradox*, 104) suggests that the term is used with an "official," rather than biological, meaning concerning the installation of the king.
10 Peeler, *You Are My Son*, 37.
11 BDAG, 894.
12 So Bruce, *Hebrews*, 56.
13 And this is despite what is known concerning David and the other sons of Jesse (1 Sam 16:1–13).

The source of the next quotation in Hebrews 1:6b is debated. The most likely source is Deuteronomy 32:43d LXX, but Psalm 97:7 (96:7 LXX) is possible as well.[14] The context of Deuteronomy 32 addresses the uniqueness of God against the idols of the nations, and 32:43 speaks of the devotion of the heavenly beings to God. The author of Hebrews identifies the Father as the speaker ("And again,[15] when he brings the firstborn into the world, he says …"), thus identifying the "him" of 1:6b with the "firstborn" in 1:6a.

The next quotation comes from Psalm 104:4 (103:4 LXX) and provides an explicit statement concerning what the angels *are*. These heavenly beings, addressed in 104:4 (103:4 LXX), are made to be "winds" and "flames of fire," likely emphasizing their role in swiftly carrying out the will of God.[16]

The author turns his attention back to the Son in the next quotation from Psalm 45 (44 LXX). As noted in the opening verses of the psalm, the king is addressed as one blessed by God (vv. 1–2).[17] The quotation itself is drawn from verses 6–7 (vv. 7–8 LXX) and addresses God's establishment of the king.[18] The Hebrew text of 45:7 concerning "God" could be read as a possessive (i.e., "Your throne, God's, is forever);[19] in the LXX, however, the text would appear either to address God directly (interrupting the words addressed to the king) before returning to the king in 44:8b (LXX) or to identify the "you" addressed by the psalmist as "God."[20] The latter of these interpretations appears to be in view in Hebrews 1, as the quotation is introduced as being in reference "to the son."[21]

The penultimate quotation is taken from Psalm 102 (101 LXX) and deals with the eternality of God and his rule, despite the present experience

---

14 See Ellingworth, *Epistle to the Hebrews*, 118–19.
15 The term is best read with δέ introducing another quotation (see Harris, *Hebrews*, 24; Brennan, *Divine Christology*, 46; Attridge, *Epistle to the Hebrews*, 55; cf. Wis 14:1). Although this could be a reference to the incarnation (so Moffatt, *Critical and Exegetical Commentary*, 10–11) or to the parousia (so Westcott, *Epistle to the Hebrews*, 22), the exaltation of the Son is likely in view (so Caneday, "Eschatological World," 28–39; Brennan, *Divine Christology*, 46–47; Moffitt, *Atonement and the Logic*, 58–68; Schreiner, *Hebrews*, 68; Attridge, *Epistle to the Hebrews*, 56).
16 See Bauckham, "Monotheism and Christology," 179–81.
17 The setting of the psalm appears to be a wedding celebration.
18 This psalm appears to have been read messianically in the Aramaic targum of the psalm. See deClaissé-Walford, Jacobson, and Tanner, *Book of Psalms*, 416.
19 See Goldingay, *Psalms*, 53.
20 In the context of the psalm, the statement in verse 6 (v. 7 LXX) appears to address the king as "God," perhaps in reflection upon the role of the king as the representative of God on earth (see deClaissé-Walford, et. al., *Psalms*, 419–20).
21 So Bauckham, "Divinity of Jesus Christ," 25. He also notes the similar distinction between "the Lord" and "my Lord" in Psalm 110 (Bauckham, "Monotheism," 183; see also Attridge, "Psalms in Hebrews," 202).

of suffering on the part of the psalmist. In contrast to the transitory nature of creation, God's reign endures. In the context of the catena in Hebrews 1, the quotation serves to advance the enduring reign of God, especially in light of the establishment of the throne in the previous citation from Psalm 45 (44 LXX).

The final quotation is drawn from Psalm 110:1 (109:1 LXX). The author marks the end of the series of quotations with a similar question as in Psalm 1:5a, noting that this concluding statement likewise was spoken to no angel.[22] This quotation is the climax of the catena, and the author will spend significant time explicating the significance of this psalm in the rest of Hebrews. Given the centrality of this psalm in the argument of Hebrews, greater attention will be given to this psalm in Hebrews in the following section.

Although the title "Son of David" does not appear in Hebrews, the author is surely aware of this lineage.[23] It is through the incarnation into the line of David that these promises have come to the Son. Some interpreters identify a tension between the identification reflected in Hebrews 1:5–13 and the description of the Son in 1:1–3.[24] Caird attempts to resolve this by arguing that Jesus *becomes* "Son" by God's appointment after Jesus's faithful life.[25] The exordium, however, identifies the Son as heir and agent of creation prior to his work as high priest,[26] and the identification in 1:5 is better understood as a restatement of what is already true of Jesus.[27] Likewise, the suffering of Jesus is as a "son" (5:8).[28] At the same time, though, these promises are not fulfilled solely in the deity of the Son. Rather, Jesus's divine sonship necessitates his action in coming as a human born in the line of David.[29]

---

22 This also helps to tie together the statements from Ps 2 and Ps 110 (so Pierce, *Divine Discourse*, 60; Buchanan, *To the Hebrews*, 23).

23 The author identifies the descent of Jesus from the tribe of Judah (Heb 7:14), and the family heritage of Jesus was widely proclaimed in early Christianity (i.e., Matt 1:1–17; Luke 3:23–38; Rom 1:3; Rev 22:16).

24 See Attridge, *Hebrews*, 25, 47; Dunn, *Christology in the Making*, 208–9.

25 Caird, "Son by Appointment," 73–81; contra also Hurst, "Christology of Hebrews 1 and 2," 156, and Dunn, *Christology in the Making*, 208–9. On the deity of the Son in Hebrews, see Brennan, *Divine Christology*; Jamieson, *Paradox*; Bauckham, "Divinity of Jesus Christ."

26 Although a chiastic structure may be present in 1:2–4, there is still a narrative structure to these verses (Peeler, *You Are My Son*, 13–14). As such, 1:5ff should be seen as the outworking of his status as divine Son, perhaps conceived of as coming into his inheritance (Peeler, 46, 102).

27 Peeler, *You Are My Son*, 44–45; Brennan, *Divine Christology*, 180.

28 Lane, *Hebrews*, 1:121.

29 Rather than seeing this as becoming something he was not (see Jamieson, *Paradox*; and Milligan, *Theology of the Epistle to the Hebrews*, 73–74).

The promises to the Davidic heir, highlighted in 1:5–13, have thus been fulfilled, not by any angel but by the Son. God's determination to bring about this plan of redemption necessitated the promises to David.[30] It is not to any angel that these statements were made, as no angel could serve in this capacity. Only the Son of God, in the flesh, could do so.

Jesus, Priest according to the Order of Melchizedek

Psalm 110 looms large in the language and imagery within Hebrews. The psalm is unusual in the language used, and it poses several problems for the interpreter based on the terms, referents, and setting reflected in the psalm.[31] Psalm 110 is a royal psalm, centered again on the king as representative of God in executing God's judgment over his enemies (see vv. 2, 5–6).[32] This Davidic theme naturally coincides in Hebrews 1 with the quotation from Psalm 2 in 1:5.[33] Within Psalm 110, the first portion of the text is given as a divine oracle, with the LORD (*Yahweh*) speaking to "my Lord" (*Adonai*). The role of David in this psalm is debated as to whether he is to be regarded as the author of the psalm (a view taken apparently by NT authors) or as the recipient of the oracle via a prophet.

Also cryptic in this psalm is the reference to Melchizedek in the vow of verse 4. The introduction of this concern is a "surprising twist,"[34] and nothing is said in the OT about Melchizedek apart from Psalm 110 and the account in Genesis 14. King of Salem and priest of God Most High, Melchizedek meets Abram after the battle recounted in Genesis 14. The narrative is rather brief and does not return to Melchizedek again. Within Genesis, the text appears to serve as validation of God's blessing upon Abram.[35] The appointing of the king as high priest in Psalm 110, and a high priest according to the line

---

30 Schreiner, *Hebrews*, 66. Moffitt (*Atonement*, 142–44) stresses that it is the humanity of Christ that qualifies him for the exalted role over the angels. The humanity of Christ is surely in view, but the author's contention concerning the uniqueness of Jesus over the angels reflects the reality that only the divine Son, rather than any angel, could take on human flesh and fulfill these Davidic promises in accomplishing the mission of God (see Brennan, *Divine Christology*, 63).

31 See Ross, *Commentary on the Psalms*, 3:339–44; Mays, *Psalms*, 351–53; Allen, *Psalms* 101–50, 111–14.

32 Ross, *Psalms*, 3:339; Longman, *Psalms*, 15–16, 381; Brueggemann and Bellinger, *Psalms*, 479.

33 The placement of the psalm at this juncture in the psalter could indicate a prophetic purpose (concerning the Davidic Messiah) or a reaffirmation of God's continued faithfulness to the Davidic line following the earlier despair reflected in Psalm 89. See Ross, *Psalms*, 342–43; Brueggemann and Bellinger, *Psalms*, 480.

34 Longman, *Psalms*, 382.

35 See Hamilton, *The Book of Genesis*, 410–11.

of Melchizedek (rather than Aaron), is surprising.[36] Interpretations of the psalm as affirming the king's reign from Jerusalem or the role of the king as "sacred mediator"[37] are unconvincing.

The application of Psalm 110 to Jesus is not unique to Hebrews, and quotations and allusions to Psalm 110 can be seen in a variety of NT texts.[38] This identification appears to arise from Jesus's ministry in Jerusalem in the days leading to his crucifixion. Mark (12:35–37) and Luke (20:41–44) describe the teaching of Jesus related to the identity of the Messiah, and Matthew situates this in the series of controversies with the religious leaders during the passion week (Matt 22:41–46).[39]

The issue of identifying David's "Lord" as David's "son" proves to be the vexing question.[40] Although Jesus, according to the authors of the Synoptic Gospels, does not explicitly identify himself as Son of David in that context, the incarnation of the divine Son in David's line provides a lens for understanding the unusual language of Psalm 110.[41] The psalm is thus used by the NT authors to support the exaltation of Jesus, his present session at the right hand of God, and the identification of Jesus as the Christ.[42]

Even a cursory reading of Hebrews indicates that Psalm 110 is highly significant for the author's argument in the epistle.[43] In Jamieson's estimation,

---

[36] Apart from the reference to David's sons serving in some priestly capacity (2 Sam 8:18) and David's dancing in an ephod before the return of the ark (2 Sam 6:12–19), a king attempting to act in a priestly role was not supported (cf. 1 Sam 13:8–15; so Longman, *Psalms*, 382). The suggestion that this statement is uttered to Zadok (see Rowley, "Melchizedek and Zadok," 468–72) is unconvincing (so Anderson, *King-Priest*, 55; Ross, *Psalms*, 3:342).

[37] Allen, *Psalms, 101–50*, 116.

[38] On Psalm 110, see Anderson, *King-Priest*; Hay, *Glory at the Right Hand*. Hay (163–66) identifies the following allusions and quotations: To Psalm 110:1—Matt 22:44; 26:64; Mark 12:36; 14:62; [16:19]; Luke 20:42–43; 22:69; Acts 2:33, 34–35; 5:31; 7:55–56; Rom 8:34; 1 Cor 15:25; Eph 1:20; 2:6; Col 3:1; Heb 1:3, 13; 8:1; 10:12–13; 12:2; 1 Pet 3:22; Rev 3:21. To Psalm 110:4 – Heb 5:6, 10; 6:20; 7:3, 8, 11, 15–17, 21, 24–25, 28.

[39] The collocation of the language from Ps 110 and Dan 7 can be seen in Matt 26:62–65; Mark 14:62–64a; Luke 22:66–71 (see Anderson, *King-Priest*, 91–94).

[40] On Jewish interpretation of this psalm, see Hay, *Glory at the Right Hand*, 19–33. As Hay notes, Jesus does not challenge the identification of the Messiah as David's son. The Messiah's reign, more than just a restoration of the Davidic kingdom, would surpass that of David (see *Glory at the Right Hand*, 111).

[41] So Anderson, *King-Priest*, 89–91.

[42] See Hay, *Glory at the Right Hand*, 52–129.

[43] Buchanan identifies the psalm as the "primary text for the entire exposition, 1:1–12:29" (*Hebrews*, 8) and the book itself as a midrash on the psalm (xix). The latter identification is perhaps unwarranted, but the significance for the book is clear. Attridge (*Hebrews*, 23) rightly challenges Buchanan's assertion but identifies the psalm as a "red thread" throughout the work.

this text is the messianic "master key" for the author's view of Christ,[44] and especially as high priest.[45] Space does not allow an exhaustive exploration of the use of this psalm in Hebrews, but the author demonstrates, through his exegesis of Psalm 110, several significant points concerning the high priesthood of Jesus:[46]

- Not based on human descent (7:3)[47]
- Predicted and confirmed with an oath (7:20–22)
- A direct appointment to the priesthood (5:4–6, 10)
- Not predicated on the expectation of death (7:3, 16, 23–25)
- Not associated with the tribe of Levi or the line of Aaron (7:11–14)
- Associated with an eternal sanctuary and a new covenant (7:12; 8:2, 6, 13)
- Characterized by a completed sacrifice (7:27; 8:1–2; 10:11–14)[48]

As Jesus was born into the line of David, he is qualified for the role identified in Psalm 110. Jesus is able, then, to provide a better sacrifice, mediate a better covenant, and serve as a better high priest.

Jesus and the People of God

The focus on the incarnation in Hebrews moves beyond questions of the Davidic promises and the fulfillment of Psalm 110. While these are central concerns for the author, he also demonstrates how Jesus, on the basis of his humanity, is able to serve humanity effectively. In other words, the incarnation is not significant simply because it enabled Jesus to be connected to the Davidic line; it is necessary for Jesus to carry out the mission of God in providing a better salvation.

The Incarnation and the Sacrifice of Christ

One significant aspect of Jesus's role as high priest is the offering of himself as a sacrifice for sins (see 1:3b; 9:11–14; 10:10, 12, 14), and this particular concern is brought to the forefront in 9:11–10:18. The author demonstrates, in a variety of ways, the imperfection of the Levitical system of sacrifice

---

44 Jamieson, *Paradox*, 136.
45 Rom 8:34 could provide a potential exception in considering the intercession of Christ. See Hay, *Glory at the Right Hand*, 132.
46 On the use in Hebrews, see Anderson, *King-Priest*; Hay, 143–53.
47 The statement made by the author concerning the "father," "mother," and "genealogy" in 7:3 demonstrates that the priesthood of Melchizedek is not tied to a family line. See Lane, *Hebrews*, 1:166–67.
48 With the completion of this sacrifice, Jesus now intercedes for his people in the heavenly sanctuary (see Heb 7:25). See Moore, "Sacrifice, Session and Intercession," 531. See also Loader, "Christ at the Right Hand," 206.

(see 7:27–28; 9:6–10, 25–26; 10:1–4, 11). The deficiency of the system does not indicate a deficiency in God's redemptive work; rather, this system was intended to be temporary and to serve a typological role in anticipating the sacrifice of Christ (see 8:1–6; 10:1–4).

The atonement offered by Christ, however, was a one-time sacrifice (7:27; 9:12, 26). Like the sacrifices under the Old Covenant, though, Christ's sacrifice involved the shedding of blood.[49] In his discussion of the blood of Jesus, the author presupposes the reality of the incarnation as providing the means for Christ to offer his blood for the forgiveness of sin. In Hebrews 10, the author emphasizes, in light of Psalm 40 (39 LXX), the "body" prepared for Christ, a body obediently offered in atonement for sin.[50] Through the incarnation, then, Christ was able to offer himself as the anticipated sacrifice for sin.

The Incarnation and the Faithful Ministry of Our High Priest

In addition to the sacrifice offered by Christ, the author argues that the experience of the incarnation was necessary for Jesus to be qualified as our great high priest.

In Hebrews 2:10, the author of Hebrews asserts that Jesus has been "made perfect." Such a statement likely raises questions for those familiar with historic convictions concerning the sinlessness of Jesus. While the expression "made perfect" could appear to suggest moral perfection is in view,[51] usage in the LXX, particularly with regard to the priesthood, indicates a different meaning of the expression. This term occurs in the discussion of the ordination of Aaron and his sons as priests in the texts of Exodus, Leviticus, and Numbers.[52] With the connection in 2:10 between Jesus bringing salvation and the means of suffering, the author demonstrates the importance of the incarnation for achieving this salvation.[53]

The preparation for this role also involved "learn[ing] obedience from what he suffered" (5:8 NIV). Again, the author does not appear to argue that this involved growth from moral imperfection to perfection, as the author affirms that Jesus was without sin (4:15). The concern with obedience

---

49 The author indicates the instructive nature of the law in demonstrating the necessity of blood for forgiveness of sin (9:22).

50 See Ribbens, "Sacrifice God Desired," 284–304; Schreiner, *Hebrews*, 462–63.

51 David deSilva argues that this expresses the notion of being "brought to the final goal" (*Perseverance in Gratitude*, 198). See also Attridge, *Hebrews*, 84–87.

52 Exod 29:9, 29, 33, 35; Lev 4:5; 8:33; 16:32; 21:10; Num 3:3. The concern would then be vocational, not moral. See Peterson, *Hebrews and Perfection*, 66–73; Koester, *Hebrews*, 124. This may also reflect eschatological concerns (see Silva, "Perfection and Eschatology in Hebrews," 60–71).

53 So Peterson, *Hebrews and Perfection*, 66–73; Jamieson, *Paradox*, 90; Schreiner, *Hebrews*, 96–97; Lane, *Hebrews*, 1:122.

emerges again in 10:5–7 in the quotation of Psalm 40:6–8 (39:7–9 LXX). The psalm contrasts what is not desired (the mere offering of sacrifices) with the posture of obedience that God desires.[54] The author places these words on the lips of Jesus as he comes into the world (10:5), and in doing so, he links the incarnation with obedience to the will of God.[55] In what sense, then, might Jesus have "learned" obedience? A reasonable answer to this question is that his knowledge of obedience now includes experiential knowledge of human life.[56] As such, Jesus fully understands the experience of obeying God, and particularly amid suffering.

The author again asserts the importance of a high priest being chosen from among humans in Hebrews 5:1[57] and establishes the familial bond between Jesus and his people. As God accomplishes the "bringing [of] many sons to glory" (2:10), he does so through the incarnation, as both the "one who sanctifies" and "those who are sanctified" are of the same family.[58] Due to the children taking part in flesh and blood (2:14), it was necessary for Jesus also to share in them. Although depicted as a "champion" defeating the one who holds the power of death (2:14), Jesus does so through his suffering.[59]

These expressions suggest that the incarnation was essential to Jesus's role as high priest.[60] In Hebrews 2:18, the author states that Jesus is able to help those who are being tested[61] because he himself suffered when tempted. Although the specific nature of this aid is not described in this context, it is offered to humans, not to angels (2:16).[62] This help is offered in his capacity as high priest (2:17), and the incarnation has facilitated his ability to serve as a "merciful" and "faithful" high priest.

---

54 The inclusion of "body" in place of "ears" in 10:5 likely highlights the obedience, with the part replaced by the whole in Hebrews 10:5 (see Cockerill, *Hebrews*, 436; Schreiner, *Hebrews*, 297–98).

55 Jamieson, *Paradox*, 81; see Attridge, *Hebrews*, 273–74.

56 So Cockerill, *Hebrews*, 249; Attridge, 152–53.

57 So Schreiner, *Hebrews*, 158. Cockerill emphasizes this focus on "among men" to make clear the author's connection with the humanity of Christ (see *Hebrews*, 233).

58 See Brennan, *Divine Christology*, 189–93; Peeler, *You Are My Son*, 140–78.

59 See Lane, *Hebrews*, 1:56–57.s

60 So Brennan, *Divine Christology*, 127; Lane, *Hebrews*, 1:121; Peeler, *You Are My Son*, 108. This additionally suggests that Jesus became high priest at the time of his exaltation (so Jamieson, *Paradox*, 91–92). Although the humanity of Christ is an essential aspect of his qualification, such a conviction does not exclude the importance of the deity of Christ in serving in this role (see Brennan, *Divine Christology*, 128–44; contra Moffitt, *Atonement*, 208).

61 This likely includes both "temptation" as well as "testing." Hebrews affirms Jesus's complete faithfulness in this regard.

62 It is reasonable to conclude that this aid involves intercession on behalf of his people (cf. Heb 7:25).

The author develops this further in Hebrews 4. After describing Jesus as the great high priest who has gone through the heavens (4:14 ESV), the author pauses to comment on his ministry. The author states the initial assertion negatively: "We do not have a high priest who is unable to sympathize with our weaknesses." The heavenly context of Jesus's ministry does not render him unable to care for his people. Rather, Jesus has been tested in all ways and in the same manner that we are.[63] The incarnation, then, demonstrates his ability to relate to human beings in various kinds of suffering and difficulties. This ongoing ministry facilitates our access to the heavenly throne room in order to find the mercy and grace we need (Heb 4:16).

The Incarnation as the Eschatological Plan of God

Beyond the past offering of the Son and the present priestly ministry of the Son, the author of Hebrews identifies the role of the Son with respect to the future fulfillment of the mission of God. The central text is found in Hebrews 2.[64] Following a warning against "drifting away" in 2:1–4, the author returns to a discussion of Jesus and the angels in 2:5–9. Thematically, the concern with the authority of the Son persists from chapter 1 in considering the "subjection" of the world to come under his feet.

Previously, the author noted that the promise of Psalm 110:1 was given not to angels but to the Son (Heb 1:13). Now, in Hebrews 2:5–9, the author examines the language of Psalm 8:4–6.[65] This psalm provides a meditation on the relationship of humanity to the created order.[66] The author, however, reads the psalm Christologically in light of the incarnation.[67] The "all things" of Psalm 8:6 is understood comprehensively, likely in light of Psalm 110, rather than addressing only some aspects of the created order.[68]

The one to whom "all things" are subjected is one who is identified in Psalm 8:4 as a "man" and a "son of man." While it may be tempting to read "son of man" as a title, the author seems to focus on the class of human being as significant here.[69] It is to a human, who is lower than the angels,

---

63 As Lane notes, this capacity to care for us is directly tied to Jesus's humanity (*Hebrews*, 1:114).
64 Similar eschatological concerns can be seen in 6:5; 9:28; 10:13; 10:25; 11:10, 14, 16, 35; 12:22, 25–29; 13:14.
65 Ps 8 is then read in light of the prior reference to Ps 110. See Cockerill, *Hebrews*, 125, 128. See also 1 Cor 15:25–27 and Eph 1:20–23.
66 See Attridge, *Hebrews*, 203–5; Anderson, *King-Priest*, 170.
67 Bruce, *Hebrews*, 72–74.
68 So Peeler, *You Are My Son*, 67.
69 So Lindars, *Theology*, 39; Jamieson, *Paradox*, 78–79; Schreiner, *Hebrews*, 88; Attridge, *Hebrews*, 74.

that everything is subjected.[70] In his application of this psalm, the author identifies how Jesus was made lower than the angels. With this focus on the "world to come" (cf. also 1:6), the author of Hebrews demonstrates that it is through a human that this plan is accomplished.[71]

Conclusion: The Incarnation and the Mission of God

As demonstrated in the exploration of these themes in Hebrews, the divine Son has come in the flesh, and the incarnation was essential for him to fulfill the role of messianic heir and become our great high priest. The author of Hebrews articulates this in a narrative structure that recognizes the coming of Christ at a particular point in history as it involves his suffering, death, resurrection, and installation/enthronement as high priest.[72]

This plan was no last-ditch rescue effort or a "backup" plan due to an unexpected failure in the mission of God. At the very least, the author is at pains to demonstrate that the groundwork for this plan is clearly indicated in a careful reading of the Scriptures of Israel. Key figures and institutions, such as Abraham, Moses, the Old Covenant (including the priesthood, sanctuary, and sacrifices), God's promise of "rest," and so on, find their culmination in the work of Christ.

In the author's explanation of the incarnation, then, the divine design present in the wider scope of God's redemptive work can be seen. The author identifies the Son as the "heir of all things" prior to his identification of him as creator of the universe in 1:2. As Cockerill argues, this designation demonstrates God's determination for Christ to serve in this role prior to the act of creation, which thus indicates the divine purpose behind redemptive history.[73] As "heir" he takes on the role of messiah not to achieve the status as Son, but rather because of this status.[74] The author demonstrates, therefore, the essential nature of the incarnation both in terms of purpose (as necessary to accomplish the plan of redemption) and in terms of efficacy (for Jesus to be able to serve effectively as our high priest).[75]

---

70 "Little" could be understood positionally (see Cockerill, *Hebrews*, 133) or temporally (see Schreiner, *Hebrews*, 90; Attridge, *Hebrews*, 76). The latter best accords with the argument in the passage.
71 So Jipp, "Son's Entrance," 569–70, 575.
72 See Jamieson, *Paradox*, 76ff; 86ff.
73 Cockerill, *Hebrews*, 92.
74 So Webster, "One Who Is Son," 82; McCormack, "With Loud Cries and Tears," 62. In this way, there is no conflict between the convictions expressed concerning the deity (and personal preexistence) and humanity of Christ.
75 So deSilva, *Perseverance in Gratitude*, 121.

As indicated in the opening exordium, there is an essential continuity between God's "speaking" in the past and his "speaking" in these last days (1:1). The groundwork of these promises was established in God's work in the past, and the fulfillment has now arrived in the coming of Christ.[76] As the author asserts in 2:10 and 7:26, it was fitting for the people of God to have such a priest, not because of the deserving nature of God's people, but because of God's determination to accomplish his mission.[77]

Bibliography

Allen, Leslie C. *Psalms 101–150*. Rev. ed. Word Biblical Commentary 21. Nashville: Thomas Nelson, 2002.

Anderson, David R. *The King-Priest of Psalm 110 in Hebrews*. Studies in Biblical Literature 21. New York: Peter Lang, 2001.

Attridge, Harold W. *The Epistle to the Hebrews.* Hermeneia. Philadelphia: Fortress, 1989.

Attridge, Harold W. "The Psalms in Hebrews." In *The Psalms in the New Testament*, edited by Steve Moyise and Maarten J. J. Menken. The New Testament and the Scriptures of Israel, 197–212. London: T&T Clark, 2004.

Bauckham, Richard. "The Divinity of Jesus Christ in the Epistle to the Hebrews." In *The Epistle to the Hebrews and Christian Theology*, edited by Richard Bauckham, Daniel R. Driver, Trevor A. Hart, and Nathan MacDonald, 15–36. Grand Rapids: Eerdmans, 2009.

Bauckham, Richard. "Monotheism and Christology in Hebrews 1." In *Early Jewish and Christian Monotheism*, edited by Loren T. Stuckenbruck and Wendy E. S. North. Journal for the Study of the New Testament Supplement Series 263, 167–185. London: T&T Clark, 2004.

Bauer, W., F. W. Danker, W. F. Arndt, and F. W. Gingrich. *Greek-English Lexicon of the New Testament and Other Early Christian Literature*. 3rd ed. Chicago: University of Chicago Press 1999.

Brennan, Nick. *Divine Christology in the Epistle to the Hebrews: The Son as God*. Library of New Testament Studies 656. London: T&T Clark, 2022.

Bruce, F. F. *The Epistle to the Hebrews.* Rev. ed. New International Commentary on the New Testament. Grand Rapids: Eerdmans, 1997.

Brueggemann, Walter, and William H. Bellinger, Jr. *Psalms*. New Cambridge Bible Commentary. New York: Cambridge University Press, 2014.

Buchanan, George Wesley. *To the Hebrews*. Anchor Bible. Garden City: Doubleday, 1972.

---

76 See Schreiner, *Hebrews*, 30–33.
77 See Lane, *Hebrews*, 1:55.

Caird, G. B. "Son by Appointment." In Vol. 1 of *The New Testament Age: Essays in Honor of Bo Reicke*, edited by William C. Weinrich, 73–81. Macon: Mercer University Press, 1984.

Caneday, Ardel B. "The Eschatological World Already Subjected to the Son: The Οἰκουμένη of Hebrews 1.6 and the Son's Enthronement." In *A Cloud of Witnesses: The Theology of Hebrews in Its Ancient Contexts*. Library of New Testament Studies 387, edited by Richard Bauckham, Daniel Driver, Trevor Hart, and Nathan MacDonald, 28–39. London: T&T Clark, 2008.

Cockerill, Gareth Lee. *The Epistle to the Hebrews*. New International Commentary on the New Testament. Grand Rapids: Eerdmans, 2012.

deClaissé-Walford, Nancy L., Rolf A. Jacobson, and Beth LaNeel Tanner. *The Book of Psalms*. New International Commentary on the Old Testament. Grand Rapids: Eerdmans, 2014.

deSilva, David A. *Perseverance in Gratitude: A Socio-Rhetorical Commentary on the Epistle "to the Hebrews."* Grand Rapids: Eerdmans, 2000.

Dunn, James D. G. *Christology in the Making: A New Testament Inquiry into the Origins of the Doctrine of the Incarnation*. 2nd ed. Grand Rapids: Eerdmans, 1996.

Ellingworth, Paul. *The Epistle to the Hebrews: A Commentary on the Greek Text*. New International Greek Testament Commentary. Grand Rapids: Eerdmans, 1993.

Goldingay, John. *Psalms: Volume 2: Psalms 42–89*. Baker Commentary on the Old Testament Wisdom and Psalms. Grand Rapids: Baker, 2007.

Hamilton, Victor P. *The Book of Genesis: Chapters 1–17*. New International Commentary on the Old Testament. Grand Rapids: Eerdmans, 1990.

Harris, Dana M. *Hebrews*. Exegetical Guide to the Greek New Testament. Nashville: B&H, 2019.

Hay, David M. *Glory at the Right Hand: Psalm 110 in Early Christianity*. Society of Biblical Literature Monograph Series 18. Nashville: Abingdon, 1973.

Hurst, L. D. "The Christology of Hebrews 1 and 2." In *The Glory of Christ in the New Testament: Studies in Christology in Memory of George Bradford Caird*, edited by L. D. Hurst and N. T. Wright, 151–64. Oxford: Clarendon Press, 1987.

Jamieson, R. B. *The Paradox of Sonship: Christology in the Epistle to the Hebrews*. Studies in Christian Doctrine and Scripture. Downers Grove: InterVarsity Press, 2021.

Jipp, Joshua W. "The Son's Entrance into the Heavenly World: The Soteriological Necessity of the Scriptural Catena in Hebrews 1.5–14." *New Testament Studies* 56 (2010): 557–75.

Koester, Craig R. *Hebrews: A New Translation with Introduction and Commentary*. The Anchor Yale Bible. New York: Doubleday, 2001.

Lane, William L. *Hebrews*. 2 vols. Word Biblical Commentary. Dallas: Word, 1991.

Lindars, Barnabas. *The Theology of the Letter to the Hebrews*. New Testament Theology. Cambridge: Cambridge University Press, 1991.

Loader, W. R. G. "Christ at the Right Hand – Ps. CX.1 in the New Testament." *New Testament Studies* 24, no. 2 (1978): 199–217.

Longman, Tremper, III. *Psalms*. Tyndale Old Testament Commentaries. Vol. 15–16. Downers Grove: InterVarsity Press, 2014.

Mays, James L. *Psalms*. Interpretation. Louisville: John Knox, 1994.

McCormack, Bruce L. "'With Loud Cries and Tears': The Humanity of the Son in the Epistle to the Hebrews." In *The Epistle to the Hebrews and Christian Theology*, edited by Richard Bauckham, Daniel R. Driver, Trevor A. Hart, and Nathan MacDonald, 37–68. Grand Rapids: Eerdmans, 2009.

Milligan, George. *The Theology of the Epistle to the Hebrews*. Repr. Eugene: Wipf & Stock, 2000.

Moffatt, James. *A Critical and Exegetical Commentary on the Epistle to the Hebrews*. International Critical Commentary. Edinburgh: T&T Clark, 1963.

Moffitt, David M. Atonement and the Logic of Resurrection in the Epistle to the Hebrews. Novum Testamentum Supplements 141. Leiden: Brill, 2011.

Moore, Nicolas J. "Sacrifice, Session and Intercession: The End of Christ's Offering in Hebrews." *Journal for the Study of the New Testament* 42, no. 4 (2020): 521–41.

Peeler, Amy L. B. *You Are My Son: The Family of God in the Epistle to the Hebrews*. Library of New Testament Studies 486. London: Bloomsbury, 2014.

Peterson, David. *Hebrews and Perfection: An Examination of the Concept of Perfection in the "Epistle to the Hebrews."* Society for New Testament Studies Monograph Series 47. Cambridge: Cambridge University Press, 1982.

Pierce, Madison N. *Divine Discourse in the Epistle to the Hebrews: The Recontextualization of Spoken Quotations of Scripture*. Society for New Testament Studies Monograph Series 178. Cambridge: Cambridge University Press, 2020.

Ribbens, Benjamin J. "The Sacrifice God Desired: Psalm 40.6–8 in Hebrews 10." *New Testament Studies* 67 (2021): 284–304.

Ross, Allen P. *A Commentary on the Psalms*. 3 volumes. Kregel Exegetical Library. Grand Rapids: Kregel, 2016.

Rowley, H. H. "Melchizedek and Zadok (Gen 14 and Ps 110)." In *Festschrift für Alfred Bertholet zum* 80, edited by Walter Baumgartner, Otto Eissfeldt, Karl Elliger, and Leonhard Rost, 461–72. Tübingen: Mohr Siebeck, 1950.

Schreiner, Thomas R. *Hebrews*. Evangelical Biblical Theology Commentary. Bellingham: Lexham, 2020.

Silva, Moises. "Perfection and Eschatology in Hebrews." *Westminster Theological Journal* 39 (1977): 60–71.

Webster, John. "One Who Is Son: Theological Reflections on the Exordium to the Epistle to the Hebrews." In *The Epistle to the Hebrews and Christian Theology*, edited by Richard Bauckham, Daniel R. Driver, Trevor A. Hart, and Nathan MacDonald, 69–94. Grand Rapids: Eerdmans, 2009.

Westcott, Brooke Foss. *The Epistle to the Hebrews: The Greek Text with Notes and Essays*. Grand Rapids: Eerdmans, 1952.

Part 2
The Missionary Message of Hebrews

Chapter 5

Missional Hospitality in Hebrews
Welcoming God and Welcoming the Stranger

Edward L. Smither

Following a rich theological presentation on the supremacy of Christ, the author of Hebrews appears to close the letter with some miscellaneous practical admonitions. Among these, he writes: "Do not forget to show hospitality to strangers, for by so doing some people have shown hospitality to angels without knowing it" (Heb 13:2).[1] More than a random reminder to be good neighbors, I suggest that this admonition refers back to other themes within the letter and also connects to the theme of missional hospitality found throughout the Scriptures.[2]

In this chapter I first explore the meaning of biblical and missional hospitality through the paradigm of Abraham, through Israel's call to welcome the stranger, and through the ministry of Christ. After this broader look at biblical hospitality in mission, I aim to show that it is reinforced through the letter to the Hebrews. From this, we consider what it meant practically for first-century Jewish believers in Christ to be hospitable in mission and what it means for the church on mission in the contemporary world.

Mission and Hospitality

Let's begin by defining two important terms—*mission* and *hospitality*. By *mission* (*missio*), I mean *sending*. The first instance of sending in Scripture occurs just after the Fall, when the living God moves toward the fallen couple, posing a question, "Where are you?" (Gen 3:8). God covers their nakedness and shame with animal skins—a sacrifice that prefigured the redeeming work that Christ would accomplish at the cross. The unfolding narrative of Scripture abounds with God's initiative to send people and groups of people (Abraham, Israel, the prophets, Jesus, and the church) to announce his ways, his Messiah, and his message of redemption and reconciliation. Mission in Scripture is the mission of God.

---

[1] Unless otherwise noted, all Scripture in this chapter is taken from the New International Version (NIV).
[2] About the abrupt change in structure and tone in Hebrews 13, see Schreiner, *Hebrews*, 411.

As the church participates in God's mission, Christian mission means crossing boundaries between the *already* and the *not-yet* people of God, barriers between faith and non-faith. While mission can be a mono-cultural experience, Scripture resounds with the admonition to "Declare his glory among the nations, his marvelous deeds among all peoples" (Ps 96:3). The scope, or arena, of God's mission is the whole earth and among all cultural groups.

By *hospitality*, I mean loving the stranger (or another) and making room for them. In the New Testament (e.g., Heb 13:2), the word for hospitality, *philoxenia*, "combines the general word for love or affection for people who are connected by kinship or faith (*phileo*) and the word for stranger (*xenos*)."[3] Hans Boersma adds, "As the opposite of xenophobia (fear of foreigners), *philoxenia* is a virtue that counters our isolationist inclinations, which regularly coincide with nationalistic chauvinism and racial bigotry and feed into a hoarding mentality that neglects the poor and disadvantaged."[4]

In making room, we invite others, particularly strangers, to enter our space (our homes, our dinner tables), care for their physical needs by offering food and drink, and also care for their souls by listening and sharing our hope in Christ. Joshua Jipp writes, "Hospitality is the act or process whereby the identity of the stranger is transformed into that of guest."[5] Christine Pohl adds:

> Strangers ... are those who are disconnected from basic relationships that give persons a secure place in this world. ... When we offer hospitality to strangers, we welcome them into a place to which we are somehow connected ... a safe, personal, and comfortable place, a place of respect and acceptance and friendship.[6]

Abraham, Israel, and Jesus

Hospitality is a strong supporting motif in the mission of God and a thread that runs throughout the Scriptures.[7] Hospitality can be observed in the life of Abraham, in the story of Israel, and in the ministry of Christ.

Abraham. Abraham's journey presents a paradigm for hospitality that shapes our reading of the rest of Scripture. In Genesis 12:1–3, God tells Abraham:

---

3 Christine Pohl, *Making Room*, 31; see further Fermer, "Hospitality," 494.
4 Boersma, *Scripture as Real Presence*, 58.
5 Jipp, *Saved by Faith and Hospitality*, 2.
6 Pohl, *Making Room*, 13.
7 See my complete argument in Smither, *Mission as Hospitality*.

Go from your country, your people and your father's household to the land I will show you.

> I will make you into a great nation,
>   and I will bless you;
> I will make your name great,
>   and you will be a blessing.
> I will bless those who bless you,
>   and whoever curses you I will curse;
> and all peoples on earth
>   will be blessed through you.

Abraham is commanded to leave the comfort, security, and familiarity of his home in Ur, and to become a sojourner, relying on the goodwill and hospitality of others. While the outcome and fulfillment of his calling was to bless the nations, his work begins in vulnerability. Amos Yong notes that Abraham is the "sojourner-recipient of the hospitality of the Canaanites, the Egyptians, those in the Negeb and at Bethel, even of Melchizedek, king of Salem."[8]

In Genesis 18, Abraham welcomes and shows hospitality to others. Though he had been settled near the "great trees" of Mamre for some time (Gen 13:18), he continues to live in a tent—a temporary dwelling for a sojourner. In the beginning of Genesis 18, the writer indicates that God appeared to Abraham at the entrance to his tent during the heat of the day. Yet when Abraham looks up, he sees three men.

Ambrose of Milan (337–97), believed that the three visitors were the members of the Trinity, while Augustine (354–430) and Ephrem of Syria (306–73) thought they were angels. Some modern commentators argue that it was the preincarnate Christ with two angels.[9] Based on his reaction of bowing before the visitors and referring to them as "my Lord" (*Adonai*), Abraham believed that he was welcoming God in some form. In a sixth-century sermon, Caesarius of Arles (470–542) declared, "While blessed Abraham welcomed those men warmly, he merited to receive God in consideration of his hospitality."[10]

---

8 Yong, *Hospitality and the Other*, 109; see further Blomberg, *Contagious Holiness*, 34; and Brueggemann, *The Land*, 6.
9 See further Mark Sheridan, *Genesis 12–50*, 60–64; and Assohoto and Ngewa, "Genesis," 36.
10 Sheridan, *Genesis 12–50*, 64.

Following the pattern of Near Eastern hospitality, Abraham runs to meet his visitors and makes haste to care for their needs. He provides refreshment from the heat of the day by offering water to wash their feet and then provides them a place to rest. With the help of Sarah, who makes bread, and a servant, who slaughters and prepares a calf, Abraham offers a generous meal to these guests (Gen 18:4–8). Taking the posture of a servant, Abraham does not sit and dine with them. Instead, he stands by them as they eat (Gen 18:8). Once they have been welcomed and served, Abraham sends them on their way (Gen 18:16).[11]

Beyond a Near Eastern cultural custom, Abrahamic hospitality became a model and religious duty for the Jews. Philo of Alexandria (ca. 20 BC–ca. 40 AD) argued that Abraham's life and actions functioned as a law before the Law of Moses. Philo added that Abraham's care for his divine visitors symbolized the manner that believers welcome God.[12] Boersma adds that more than simply caring for the needs of his guests, Abraham's hospitality is a response to God's hospitality to him in the covenant (Gen 15).[13] Connecting Abraham's call (Gen 12) with his hospitability (Gen 18), Yong concludes: "[Abraham] is transformed into a paradigm of hospitality, both in his receiving of the divine guests ... and in his mediating God's redemptive hospitality ultimately (eschatologically) to all the nations of the world."[14]

Abraham's model of welcoming God in the act of showing hospitality to others is, of course, echoed in the words of Jesus in Matthew 25:35: "For I was hungry and you gave me something to eat, I was thirsty and you gave me something to drink, I was a stranger and you invited me in." To welcome a stranger is to welcome the Lord Jesus Christ, who is God.

Israel. Having received God's hospitality in Egypt and during their wilderness wandering, the Israelites were expected, after entering the Promised Land, to welcome strangers and sojourners. In Exodus 22:21, the Lord commands: "Do not mistreat or oppress a foreigner, for you were foreigners in Egypt." Similarly, Israel's published law in Leviticus 19:33–34 included this statute: "When a foreigner resides among you in your land, do not mistreat them. The foreigner residing among you must be treated as your native-born. Love them as yourself, for you were foreigners in Egypt." Christine Pohl summarizes:

---

11 See further Arterbury, *Entertaining Angels*, 60–61.
12 See Arterbury, 62, 70–71.
13 Boersma, *Scripture as Real Presence*, 70.
14 Yong, *Hospitality and the Other*, 117; see also Arterbury, *Entertaining Angels*, 59.

For the people of ancient Israel, understanding themselves as strangers and sojourners, with responsibility to care for vulnerable strangers in their midst, was part of what it meant to be the people of God.[15]

Like Israel in the wilderness, the strangers dwelling in Israel were "people without a place ... detached from basic, life-supporting institutions—family, work, polity, religious community."[16] According to Deuteronomy 10:18–19, they included the "fatherless and the widow" and the "foreigner."[17] They were landless, lacking an inheritance or the resources for thriving.[18] God called Israel to imitate his hospitality by caring practically for these guests by providing food, treating them fairly in court, offering fair work wages, and also including them in their religious festivals—such as the Sabbath, the Day of Atonement, and the Passover. Essentially, foreigners were to be treated as if they were citizens of Israel.[19] This inclusion in Israel's worship life also implied that many foreigners became believers in Israel's God.

The Israelites were called to be a light to the nations, especially as Gentiles passed through Israel, including those who lived among Israel. Remembering God's hospitality to them and effectively remaining sojourners at heart, the people of Israel discovered that a key aspect of their missionary witness to the nations was welcoming and showing hospitality to the strangers in her midst.[20]

Jesus. If Abraham was the paradigm for biblical hospitality in the Old Testament, then Jesus becomes that model in the New Testament.[21] Describing Jesus as a friend of sinners and tax collectors (Matt 11:19; Luke 7:34), Tim Chester writes: "*Why* did Jesus come? He came to serve, to give his life as a ransom to seek and sake the lost. ... *How* did Jesus come? He came eating and drinking."[22]

One of the most fascinating aspects of Jesus's missional hospitality was that he was at times host and at other times guest. Practically speaking, because Jesus did not have a home in which to welcome guests, his work as host was limited to public spaces (e.g., feeding of the five thousand and four

---

15 Pohl, *Making Room*, 5; see also Yong, *Hospitality and the Other*, 110.
16 Pohl, 87; see also Brueggemann, *Interpretation and Obedience*, 294.
17 See further Jipp, *Saved by Faith and Hospitality*, 137.
18 See further Pohl, *Making Room*, 28.
19 See further Jipp, *Saved by Faith and Hospitality*, 141; see also Exod 12:48–49; Lev 16:29; 19:9–10; 24:22; Num 9:14; 15:15–16; Deut 1:16–17; 5:14–15; 16:11–14; 23:22; 24:14–15, 19–22; 31:9–13.
20 See further Yong, *Hospitality and the Other*, 110; and Keifert, *Welcoming the Stranger*, 60.
21 See further Koenig, *New Testament Hospitality*, 15–16.
22 Chester, *Meal with Jesus*, 12.

thousand).[23] Throughout the Gospels, Jesus was the "exemplary recipient of hospitality," dependent on others from his birth, during his earthly ministry, and even in his burial.[24] While receiving the hospitality of others, the Lord often takes on the role of spiritual host through his preaching and bringing the kingdom of God. Yong notes, "Those who welcome Jesus into their homes become, in turn, guests of the redemptive hospitality of God."[25]

To illustrate Jesus's hospitality, let's consider one representative passage—Luke 7:36–50—in which a Jewish leader named Simon invites Jesus to his home.[26] What is not clear is whether Simon had invited the Lord so he could ask sincere questions or attempt to trap him. Accepting the invitation, Jesus demonstrates his willingness to dine with religious leaders, as well as "sinners."[27]

Although the meal takes place at Simon's home, an uninvited sinful woman from the town, possibly a prostitute, actually offers the Lord the most generous hospitality. Simon's home was structurally open, allowing passersby like this woman to see inside the home and even enter if they desired. Ceremonially unclean but desperate to see Jesus, she enters the home and anoints Jesus's feet with perfume, washes them with her tears, continually kisses them, and then dries them with her hair. Given the great cost of the perfume, she was either a woman of great means or, more likely, someone making a very generous sacrifice.[28]

When Simon points out the woman's sinful character to Jesus, the Lord switches from guest to host and begins to teach the Jewish leader. First, he tells Simon a brief parable illustrating the love and gratitude felt by those forgiven of great sins. Next, he rebukes Simon for not washing his feet, greeting him with a kiss, or anointing his head with oil, as a good host should do. Instead, he praises the sinful woman for acting as a gracious host in a home where she was not even invited. Finally, Jesus preaches the Kingdom of God to everyone present by announcing that the woman was forgiven of her sins and that she could go in peace. This account also shows that while Jesus was willing to share meals with Pharisees like Simon, "tax collectors and prostitutes [were] coming into the Kingdom of God ahead of Jewish leaders."[29]

---

23 See further Matt 14:13–21; 15:32–39; Mark 6:30–44; 8:1–10; Luke 9:10–17; John 6:1–15.
24 Yong, *Hospitality and the Other*, 101; see further Blomberg, *Contagious Holiness*, 99.
25 Yong, 102.
26 See further Smither, *Mission as Hospitality*, 32–44.
27 See further Arterbury, *Entertaining Angels*, 137–39; Chester, *Meal with Jesus*, 38.
28 See further Chester, 38–39; also Blomberg, *Contagious Holiness*, 132–33, 143.
29 Blomberg, *Contagious Holiness*, 162.

Though happy to receive the hospitality of sinners, Jesus still upholds God's law and a standard of holiness. As Rosaria Butterfield writes, "Jesus dined with sinners, but he didn't sin with sinners."[30] Through his hospitable mission, the Lord calls his hosts and table companions to faith and repentance. Craig Blomberg adds,

> Jesus' table fellowship with sinners reflects his willingness to associate with them at an intimate level, but not merely for the sake of defying convention or enjoying a party. ... Christ is indeed calling them to repentance and summoning them to become his followers.[31]

Imitating Israel in Hospitable Mission

The recipients of the letter to the Hebrews would have identified with the sojourning Israelites and their call to welcome the stranger. Though their congregation may have been a mix of Jewish and Gentile believers in Christ, given the themes in the letter, they would have had a significant grasp on the Old Testament and Jewish theology.[32] Due to family and social pressure, this group was tempted to forsake Christ and return to Judaism. Beyond this social pressure, this community of believers had also been persecuted for their faith, as we read in chapter 10:

> Remember those earlier days after you had received the light, when you endured in a great conflict full of suffering. Sometimes you were publicly exposed to insult and persecution; at other times you stood side by side with those who were so treated. You suffered along with those in prison and joyfully accepted the confiscation of your property, because you knew that you yourselves had better and lasting possessions. So do not throw away your confidence; it will be richly rewarded. (Heb 10:32–35)

In addition to facing persecution, the recipients of this letter were very likely diaspora believers; that is, they had migrated or become displaced because of persecution and pressure. William Lane supports this diaspora identity by arguing that "the roots of this Christian assembly are in a Diaspora Judaism."[33] In addition to this background, these believers, like the recipients of James and 1 Peter, were probably dispersed amid the persecution and hardships they were facing because of following Christ. The consensus of scholarship is that Hebrews was written to Christians in Rome.[34]

---

30 Butterfield, *Gospel Comes with a House Key*, 13.
31 Blomberg, *Contagious Holiness*, 167; see further Jipp, *Saved by Faith and Hospitality*, 23.
32 See further Jobes, *Survey of Hebrews*, 26; Lane, *Hebrews 1–8*, liv; and Schreiner, *Hebrews*, 6–7.
33 Lane, *Hebrews 1–8*, liv.
34 See further Witherington, *Letters and Homilies*, 19–20; Schreiner, *Hebrews*, 8–9; and Lane, *Hebrews 1–8*, lviii–lx.

While Jewish-background believers from Jerusalem had already experienced dispersion (Acts 8), Jewish Christians in Rome were also scattered. In what is probably the earliest reference to Christianity in Rome, the Roman historian Suetonius (ca. 69–ca. 122) wrote: "Since the Jews constantly made disturbances at the instigation of Chrestus, he [Emperor Claudius] expelled them from Rome."[35] In what is most likely a misspelling of *Christos* (Christ), Suetonius indicates that Jewish-background Christians were being dispersed, which very likely included the audience receiving what would become known as the letter to the Hebrews.[36]

With this context in mind, the admonition in Hebrews 13:2 to show hospitality is given to persecuted, oppressed, and even dispersed peoples who were being instructed to welcome strangers. They were to "remember those in prison as if you were together with them in prison, and those who are mistreated as if you yourselves were suffering" (Heb 13:3; see also Heb 10:32–34). Very much like sojourning Israel, they were to welcome and visit other strangers because they also had been strangers.[37]

Imitating the Patriarchs in Hospitable Mission

In addition to following Israel's call to welcome the stranger, the recipients of Hebrews were also invited, in chapter 11, to imitate the faith of a hall-of-fame group of Old Testament saints. Schreiner notes that through this survey "the author illustrates the character of the faith that saves."[38] Among this group of patriarchs were those who sojourned, receiving hospitality from others and also extending hospitality to others.

In this survey of saints, Abraham receives the most attention. The author writes:

> By faith Abraham, when called to go to a place he would later receive as his inheritance, obeyed and went, even though he did not know where he was going. By faith he made his home in the promised land like a stranger in a foreign country; he lived in tents, as did Isaac and Jacob, who were heirs with him of the same promise. For he was looking forward to the city with foundations, whose architect and builder is God. And by faith even Sarah, who was past childbearing age, was enabled to bear children because she considered him faithful who had made the promise. (Heb 11:8–11)

---

35 Suetonius, *Claudius* 25.4 cited in Jobes, *Letters to the Church*, 33.
36 See further Jobes, *Survey of Hebrews*, 32–34; also Witherington, *Letters and Homilies*, 26–30.
37 See further Schreiner, *Hebrews*, 332.
38 See further Schreiner, 349.

In describing Abraham's life, the author of Hebrews clearly points back to Genesis 12, wherein Abraham leaves his home and follows God's call toward an unknown destination.[39] As shown, Abraham relied on the hospitality of others in the Ancient Near Eastern world, but even as a sojourner he welcomed others, including the Lord. Sarah, whose faith was also commended, served alongside her husband in showing hospitality to the divine visitors. Though Abraham migrated in faith, he remained a sojourner, dwelling in tents. The same was true for Isaac and Jacob, whom Hebrews describes as "foreigners and strangers on earth" (Heb 11:13).[40]

The author of Hebrews also remembers Joseph. Sold by his own brothers into slavery, Joseph was a stranger in Egypt who was blessed by God and who brought blessing on the Egyptians and his fellow Israelites through his work of stockpiling and distributing grain. The writer adds that toward the end of Joseph's life he "spoke about the exodus of the Israelites from Egypt" (Heb 11:22). While Joseph desired that his bones be buried in Canaan (his earthly home), the author of Hebrews points his readers toward their home in the heavenly Canaan.[41]

Highlighting the life of Moses, the author of Hebrews adds:

> By faith he left Egypt, not fearing the king's anger; he persevered because he saw him who is invisible. By faith he kept the Passover and the application of blood, so that the destroyer of the firstborn would not touch the firstborn of Israel.
>
> By faith the people passed through the Red Sea as on dry land; but when the Egyptians tried to do so, they were drowned. (Heb 11:27–29)

Having fled Egypt and Pharoah, Moses initially sojourned in the wilderness before returning to Egypt to lead the Israelites out of slavery.[42] From there, Moses led them on their journey through the wilderness toward the land of promise where they would receive God's hospitality and the opportunity to flourish.

One interesting outlier among the Old Testament saints in Hebrews 11 is Rahab, the Gentile prostitute from Jericho who welcomed and protected the Israelite spies sent by Joshua (Josh 2:1–22). While extending hospitality to the men, she requested that when the Israelites took possession of the land they would "show kindness" and "spare the lives" of Rahab and her family (Josh 2:12–13). Her hospitable actions seem motivated by the fact that she

---

39 See further Lane, *Hebrews 9–13*, 355.
40 See further Schreiner, *Hebrews*, 349.
41 See further Schreiner, 359.
42 See further Schreiner, 364–65.

was becoming a believer in Israel's God. The authors of both Hebrews and James claim that her hospitality to the spies was a fruit of her faith:

> By faith the prostitute Rahab, because she welcomed the spies, was not killed with those who were disobedient. (Heb 11:31)
>
> You see that a person is considered righteous by what they do and not by faith alone.
>
> In the same way, was not even Rahab the prostitute considered righteous for what she did when she gave lodging to the spies and sent them off in a different direction? (James 2:24–25)[43]

Following the Israelites' conquest of Jericho, Joshua kept his promise to protect Rahab and her family, and she—a foreigner within Israel—became a part of Israel and worshiped the God of Israel (Josh 6:25).[44]

On an individual level, each of these patriarchs anticipated Israel's migration and experience as sojourners. In their own stories, each of them understood intimately what it meant to be a stranger in need of God's hospitality and the hospitality of others. This made them compassionate and willing to welcome strangers in their midst—a model that the people of Israel would follow and a model that first-century Hebrew Christians could also emulate.

Welcoming Strangers, God, and Christ

The recipients of the epistle were admonished to welcome strangers, because in doing so they were welcoming God. Of course, the text of Hebrews 13:2 states that they could have been welcoming "angels (*angelos*) without knowing it." Though angels are mentioned here, Ben Witherington argues for a strong connection to Genesis 18 and Abraham's act of welcoming the divine visitors. Witherington also makes a connection to Gideon's encounter with "the angel of the LORD" (Judg 6:11–13)—that is, the angel of the LORD who was God in some form. For Witherington, "welcoming angels" is another way of saying "welcoming God."[45]

Given the teaching on angels and the supremacy of Christ in Hebrews, the admonition in Hebrews 13:2 reminds the reader that to welcome a stranger is to welcome Christ. William Lane makes this argument by comparing the language structure in Hebrews 13:2–3 and Matthew 25:35–36.

---

43 See further Arterbury, *Entertaining Angels*, 77.
44 See further Schreiner, *Hebrews*, 366.
45 See further Witherington, *Letters and Homilies*, 354; also Bruce, *Epistle to the Hebrews*, 371.

Hebrews 13:2–3	Matthew 25:35–36
Do not forget to show hospitality to strangers, for by so doing some people have shown hospitality to angels without knowing it. Continue to remember those in prison as if you were together with them in prison, and those who are mistreated as if you yourselves were suffering.	For I was hungry and you gave me something to eat, I was thirsty and you gave me something to drink, I was a stranger and you invited me in, I needed clothes and you clothed me, I was sick and you looked after me, I was in prison and you came to visit me.

In each case, when a stranger is welcomed or a prisoner visited, Christ is welcomed. On one hand, Christ is welcomed because he is greater than the angels. On the other hand, angels also seem synonymous with divinity; so an angel and Christ are equivocal.[46]

Hospitality to Believers and Non-Believers

One of the strong theological themes in Hebrews is a Sabbath rest for the people of God. When God's people make room for others, offering refreshment through shelter, food, and presence, they are participating in and contributing to the Sabbath rest that Christ brings. This is particularly true when believers assemble for worship (Heb 10:24–25).[47] When first-century believers gathered to hear the Scriptures read and taught, to commune at the Lord's Supper, to sing hymns and spiritual songs, and to pray, their souls were refreshed in a Sabbath experience.

Of course, shared meals, as Andrew McGowan argues, were the glue that bound together the early Christian community and its liturgical gatherings.[48] Early Christians celebrated the Lord's Supper within the context of an actual meal. Since the habit of gathering for meals also supported the practice of meeting for worship, we can conclude that the early church was strengthened and expanded within an environment of hospitality.

Many commentators on Hebrews assume that the admonition to show hospitality in Hebrews 13:2 was limited to first-century believers' hospitality to believers who were "strangers" to them.[49] Indeed, Paul exhorts the church at Rome to "share with the Lord's people who are in need. Practice hospitality" (Rom 12:13). In his pastoral letters to Timothy and Titus, Paul

---

[46] See further Lane, *Hebrews 9–13*, 511; see also Jobes, *Letters to the Church*, 26.
[47] See further Jobes, *Survey of Hebrews*, 127–32.
[48] See further McGowan, *Ancient Christian Worship*, 19–20.
[49] For example, see Lane, *Hebrews 1–8*, liii; also Schreiner, *Hebrews*, 411.

also listed hospitality as a qualification for church leadership (1 Tim 3:2; Titus 1:8)—a ministry that would be carried out in the context of the church. Indeed, the ministries of Paul and other early-church itinerant evangelists were sustained by hospitable believers who opened up their homes to them.[50]

Though members of the early church were instructed to show hospitality to other believers, we cannot conclude that hospitality was limited to believers. The Gospels reveal many accounts where Jesus met non-believers around tables and in hospitable spaces, which proved to be missionary encounters where the kingdom of God was proclaimed. Of course, following the Day of Pentecost and the birth of the church, hospitality was a feature of the Jerusalem church—a community growing through conversion. Luke recounts:

> They devoted themselves to the apostles' teaching and to fellowship, to the breaking of bread and to prayer. Everyone was filled with awe at the many wonders and signs performed by the apostles. All the believers were together and had everything in common. They sold property and possessions to give to anyone who had need. Every day they continued to meet together in the temple courts. They broke bread in their homes and ate together with glad and sincere hearts, praising God and enjoying the favor of all the people. And the Lord added to their number daily those who were being saved. (Acts 2:42–47)

Finally, if our thesis holds that the recipients of this letter to the Hebrews were to emulate the people of Israel in welcoming the stranger, this would mean that many strangers the first-century church encountered were not believers. Like the Israelites, the Hebrews showed hospitality to others who were on the way to believing in Christ.

Conclusion

In this chapter I have endeavored to show that the command in Hebrews 13:2 to show hospitality was not merely a fragmented afterthought in relation to the rest of Hebrews. Rather, this teaching points the Hebrew Christians back to the hospitable models of Abraham, Israel, and Christ. The underlying biblical principle is that when we welcome a stranger, we welcome the Lord. While we minister to others in need, our service is first and foremost dedicated to God. When this first-century community, which was well-versed in the teachings and theology of the Old Testament, heard Hebrews 13:2, they would have made connections to Abraham and to Israel.

---

50 See Acts 16:13; 21:4–8; 28:14; 3 John 5–8; *Didache*, 11–12; see further Arterbury, *Entertaining Angels*, 94–107; and Jipp, *Saved by Faith and Hospitality*, 69–70.

What are the practical implications for showing hospitality and loving strangers in global mission today? First, God asks the vulnerable and even the poor to be hospitable. The people of Israel and the first-century Hebrew Christians were dispersed people. They welcomed strangers because they understood what it meant to be a stranger. While our material circumstances and life situation may improve, we do not have to reach a point of affluence in order to be hospitable. Poor believers in Christ from Brazil, the Philippines, and the nations of the Arab world demonstrate well how to welcome others from a posture of vulnerability and sacrifice.

Second, as we engage in mission in a diaspora world, it is good to follow the model of Jesus and receive the hospitality of others. Even as I write this chapter, I have been getting to know a refugee family who recently resettled in my city. While I have served them with rides to the grocery store, the doctor, and some fun outings, probably the most valuable thing I have done is visit them in their home, drinking tea and enjoying whatever food they put on the table. By receiving their hospitality, I have honored them and allowed them to be a blessing.

Third, hospitable spaces continue to be a place where dividing walls of hostility can be broken down. Sitting at the table for a meal, coffee, or tea is a great place for people from very different backgrounds to listen, learn, and share ideas: those with deeply polarized political allegiances; those from ethnic backgrounds where there has been a history of oppression or hostility; those with starkly different religious views; and those from warring nations. For believers in Christ, our future hope is a peaceable kingdom where people from every nation will sit together at the marriage supper of the lamb (Rev 19:7). In the now and not-yet of God's kingdom, initiating table fellowship with others from very different backgrounds—including where tensions exist—is a great way to practice the ministry of reconciliation.

Finally, amid the hard work and even the risks associated with offering hospitality (e.g., being taken advantage of, robbed, not appreciated), we are first and foremost welcoming God. In one sense, we welcome God by offering hospitality to those who bear his image. In another sense, we welcome God because he is worthy of our worship. And through our welcoming God, we witness to others about our life and hope in Christ.

Bibliography

Arterbury, Andrew. *Entertaining Angels: Early Christian Hospitality in Its Mediterranean Setting*. Sheffield, UK: University of Sheffield Press, 2005.

Assohoto, Barnabe, and Samuel Ngewa. "Genesis." In *African Bible Commentary: A One-Volume Commentary Written by 70 African Scholars*, edited by Tokunboh Adeyemo, 9–84. Grand Rapids: Zondervan, 2010.

Blomberg, Craig. *Contagious Holiness: Jesus' Meals with Sinners*. Downers Grove: IVP Academic, 2005.

Boersma, Hans. *Scripture as Real Presence: Sacramental Exegesis in the Early Church*. Grand Rapids: Baker Academic, 2017.

Bruce, F. F. *The Epistle to the Hebrews*. New International Commentary of the New Testament. Grand Rapids: Eerdmans, 1990.

Brueggemann, Walter. *Interpretation and Obedience: From Faithful Reading to Faithful Living*. Minneapolis: Fortress Press, 1991.

Brueggemann, Walter. *The Land: Place as Gift, Promise, and Challenge in Biblical Faith*. Minneapolis: Fortress Press, 2002.

Butterfield, Rosaria. *The Gospel Comes with a House Key: Practicing Radically Ordinary Hospitality in Our Post-Christian World*. Wheaton: Crossway, 2018.

Chester, Tim. *A Meal with Jesus: Discovering Grace, Community, and Mission around the Table*. Wheaton: Crossway, 2011.

Fermer, M. T. "Hospitality." Page 494, in *The New Bible Dictionary*, edited by I. Howard Marshall, et al. Downers Grove: IVP Academic, 1996.

Jipp, Joshua. *Saved by Faith and Hospitality*. Grand Rapids: Eerdmans, 2017.

Jobes, Karen H. *Letters to the Church: A Survey of Hebrews and the General Epistles*. Grand Rapids: Zondervan, 2011.

Keifert, Patrick R. *Welcoming the Stranger: A Public Theology of Worship and Evangelism*. Minneapolis: Fortress Press, 1992.

Koenig, John. *New Testament Hospitality: Partnership with Strangers as Promise and Mission*. Minneapolis: Fortress Press, 1985.

Lane, William L. *Hebrews 1–8*. Word Biblical Commentary 47A. Dallas: Word, 1991.

Lane, William L. *Hebrews 9–13*. Word Biblical Commentary 47B. Dallas: Word, 1991.

McGowan, Andrew B. *Ancient Christian Worship: Early Practices in Social, Historical, and Theological Perspective*. Grand Rapids: Baker, 2014.

Pohl, Christine. *Making Room: Recovering Hospitality as a Christian Tradition*. Grand Rapids: Eerdmans, 1999.

Schreiner, Thomas R. *Hebrews*. Evangelical Biblical Theological Commentary Bellingham: Lexham, 2020.

Sheridan, Mark. *Genesis 12–50*. Ancient Christian Commentary on Scripture: Old Testament, Vol. II. Downers Grove: IVP Academic, 2002.

Smither, Edward L. *Mission as Hospitality: Imitating the Hospitable God in Mission*. Eugene: Cascade, 2021.

Witherington, Ben, III. *Letters and Homilies for Jewish Christians: A Socio-Rhetorical Commentary on Hebrews, James and Jude.* Downers Grove: IVP Academic, 2007.

Yong, Amos. *Hospitality and the Other: Pentecost, Christian Practices, and the Neighbor.* Maryknoll: Orbis, 2008.

Chapter 6

Hope as an Anchor
The Missional Message of the Pilgrim People of God

Jessica A. Udall

We live in a world of people on the move. According to the UN Refugee Agency, in 2021, 89.3 million people worldwide were forced to flee their homes due to conflicts, violence, fear of persecution, and/or human-rights violations. "With millions of Ukrainians displaced and further displacement elsewhere in 2022," the UN reports, "total forced displacement now exceeds 100 million people."[1] For these men, women, and children, "sojourning and exile (caused by poverty, famine, political instability, tribal and racial discrimination, etc.) are the realities of daily life."[2] They may be called many things based upon the legalities of their journey—refugees, asylum seekers, or internally displaced persons—but a more old-fashioned word can apply to all of them: *pilgrims*.

Pilgrimage Identity in the Bible

Merriam-Webster defines *pilgrim* simply as "one who journeys in foreign lands."[3] The term often has spiritual connotations, referring to "a person who makes a trip, often a long and difficult one, to a special place for religious reasons."[4] In the New Testament, the Greek word παρεπίδημος (*parepidēmos*) gives the sense of being a stranger, or foreigner, who is "sojourning in a strange place." It is generally used metaphorically, with the understanding that heaven is the "native country" toward which believers are traveling while sojourning on earth.[5] The Christian understanding of the word *pilgrim*, then,

> denotes more than the physical experience of merely existing in a foreign land; it includes a sense of purpose and psycho-spiritual awareness that radically alters the quality of that existence … that although life on earth is temporary and fleeting, it also has a dimension of purpose that should inform everything the pilgrims do.[6]

---

1 "Global Trends: Global Forced Displacement," United Nations High Commissioner for Refugees (UNHCR), https://www.unhcr.org/flagship-reports/globaltrends/.
2 Arowele, "Pilgrim People of God," 438.
3 *Merriam-Webster Dictionary*, s.v. "pilgrim," https://www.merriam-webster.com/dictionary/pilgrim.
4 *Cambridge Dictionary*, s.v. "pilgrim," https://dictionary.cambridge.org/us/dictionary/english/pilgrim.
5 Thayer, *Thayer's Greek-English Lexicon of the New Testament*, 488.
6 Choge, "Ethic of Hospitality," xvii–xviii.

The instability of the world and the transience of humans has been a reality since the Fall, upon which Adam and Eve were sent out of their first garden home. Transience was particularly the experience of the Jewish people, whose father, Abraham, was called to leave his homeland and go where God would lead him. Although Abraham and his wife Sarah got to sojourn in the land of promise, their descendants migrated to Egypt due to famine. Eventually, they escaped their enslavement in Egypt through a dramatic exodus, wandered in the wilderness, entered new territories, were taken into exile in Assyria and Babylon, and by the time Jesus ministered on earth they were dispersed and scattered throughout the lands surrounding the Mediterranean.

During much of Israel's history, the ark of the LORD's covenant was housed in a glorified tent—the tabernacle—although the Israelites placed much significance upon the temple, which was built by Solomon during the zenith of Israel's temporary stability. But this symbol of belonging and place was destroyed in 586 BC. Psalm 137 was written in the context of the exile, and thus finds its authors longing for its eventual rebuilding in 515, centering their lament around homesickness for their city:

> By the waters of Babylon,
>> there we sat down and wept,
>> when we remembered Zion.
> On the willows there
>> we hung up our lyres.
> For there our captors
>> required of us songs,
> and our tormentors, mirth, saying,
>> "Sing us one of the songs of Zion!"
> How shall we sing the LORD's song
>> in a foreign land?
> If I forget you, O Jerusalem,
>> let my right hand forget its skill!
> Let my tongue stick to the roof of my mouth,
>> if I do not remember you,
> if I do not set Jerusalem
>> above my highest joy! (Ps 137:1–6 ESV)

Decades later, when some of the people returned to Jerusalem and rebuilt the temple, mingled with the sounds of joyful praises was the weeping of the older leaders who remembered the splendor of the first temple (Ezra 3:8–13). They wept because the splendor was gone. Perhaps they also wept for the sorrow of their long displacement and that their beloved city was now merely a shadow of its former days. Their hope in the stability of place and earthly peace was permanently shattered.

The ministry of Jesus was marked by instability as well; "Foxes have holes, and birds of the air have nests," he said, "but the Son of Man has nowhere to lay his head" (Matt 8:20 ESV). Early in the life of the first-century church, believers were scattered due to persecution (Acts 8:1). Paul and his coworkers spent their time in ministry on the move, sometimes deliberately and sometimes because they needed to escape their oppressors and those trying to snuff out their lives (Acts 14:19–20; 16:6–10; 2 Cor 11:33).

In the context of recording the persecution he had endured, Paul refers to his earthly body as a "tent" and describes his confidence that if the tent were destroyed, he would have "a building from God, a house not made with hands, eternal in the heavens" (2 Cor 5:1 ESV). Because of this confidence, he proclaims, "we are always of good courage ... as we look not to the things that are seen but to the things that are unseen. For the things that are seen are transient, but the things that are unseen are eternal" (2 Cor 5:6; 4:17–18).

Abraham's Pilgrim Identity in the Book of Hebrews

The author of Hebrews does not miss the opportunity to emphasize the pilgrim nature of the human experience in general and particularly of the walk of faith. The author references Abraham—someone familiar with sojourning—in chapter 6, using his life as an example of hope in the unchangeable purpose and promises of God in the face of changing, unstable, and difficult earthly circumstances.

> For when God made a promise to Abraham, since he had no one greater by whom to swear, he swore by himself, saying, "Surely I will bless you and multiply you." And thus Abraham, having patiently waited, obtained the promise. For people swear by something greater than themselves, and in all their disputes an oath is final for confirmation. So when God desired to show more convincingly to the heirs of the promise the unchangeable character of his purpose, he guaranteed it with an oath, so that by two unchangeable things, in which it is impossible for God to lie, we who have fled for refuge might have strong encouragement to hold fast to the hope set before us. We have this as a sure and steadfast anchor of the soul, a hope that enters into the inner place behind the curtain, where Jesus has gone as a forerunner on our behalf, having become a high priest forever after the order of Melchizedek. (Heb 6:13–20)

Trying to imagine Abraham's life brings one face to face with the enormity of the uncertainty and unsettledness he lived in for much of his life. First, there was the uncertainty of his location, when God promised to bless the world through him and told him to go to the lands that he would show him. Abraham left "a homeland in search of an unseen destination."[7]

---

7 Johnson, *Hebrews*, 169.

The destination was unknown and uncertain—at least to Abraham and those who accompanied him. They set off walking by faith, not by sight.

Even after settling in the land God had shown him, Abraham lived for decades wondering when and how God would fulfill his promise to give him a future through descendants. God repeated his promises and oath to Abraham several times (Gen 12:2–3; 15:5; 22:16) to encourage Abraham as he waited, as the fulfillment of the promises took many years. God behaves similarly with the "heirs of the promise" who came after Abraham and were also pilgrims in this world: he assures them with "his word of promise and his oath in confirmation of that word."[8]

Human promises and oaths are subject to the vagaries of the fallen world—our power is limited to fulfill any promise or to honor any oath—even if we intend to do so. Not so for God, however. His "purpose and intentions can be counted on."[9] He promises something and then swears by himself—"the source and sum of all that is true and trustworthy"[10]—because there is nothing higher by which to swear. Indeed, "God made his promise doubly secure, as it were, by an appeal to the infallible integrity of his own self."[11] God's deigning to bind himself in this way to prove the certainty of his promises "instills greater confidence in the readers" and "produces security in the believer" regarding the hope by which we anchor ourselves.[12]

Hope for Christian Pilgrims

The audience receiving the Epistle to the Hebrews needed hope. Through describing them as those who have "fled for refuge" (Heb 6:18), the author "provides a sharp image of readers who are not sure of their place in the world and are in need of what is stable and secure."[13] These mostly Jewish-background believers had been faithful and active in living out their newfound faith in the Messiah in the past, but their energy was waning, and they were having second thoughts. The threat of persecution loomed and many of them were wondering whether returning to Judaism would be better than continuing in the way of Jesus.

The author of Hebrews knew that "endurance [is] inspired by hope in our Lord Jesus Christ" (1 Thess 1:3); therefore, this epistle is filled with hope-giving reminders meant to revive and reorient those who felt they could no longer hold on to hope. The Old Testament is engaged and shown

---

8   Hughes, *Commentary on the Epistle to the Hebrews*, 233.
9   Mitchell, *Hebrews*, 133.
10 Hughes, *Commentary on the Epistle to the Hebrews*, 229.
11 Hughes, 230.
12 Hughes, 132.
13 Johnson, *Hebrews*, 171–72.

to point to a Great High Priest through whom "a better hope is introduced, through which we draw near to God" (Heb 7:19), and who is able to "save to the uttermost those who draw near to him" (Heb 7:25) to anchor their souls in the hope he provides.

This hope is not merely an abstract idea; it is "a sure and steadfast anchor of the soul" (Heb 6:19) to which we can "hold fast" (Heb 6:18). It creates an atmosphere for faith, which is "the assurance of things hoped for, the conviction of things not seen" (Heb 11:1)—another major theme in the book of Hebrews. Hope and faith always supernaturally grow together in the earthly tension of the already and not-yet, with faith living in the light of the hope of future realities in the present day. John Bunyan further explains the relationship of hope and faith with the imagery of a ship and anchor connected by the "rope" of the promises of God.

> Faith lays hold of that end of the promise that is next to us, to wit, as it is in the Bible; hope lays hold of that end of the promise that is fastened to the mercy-seat; for the promise is like a mighty cable, that is fastened by one end to a ship, and by the other to the anchor: the soul is the ship where faith is, and to which the hither end of this cable is fastened; but hope is the anchor that is at the other end of this cable, and which entereth into that within the veil. Thus faith and hope getting hold of both ends of the promise, they carry it safely ALL away.[14]

Thus, hope and faith are—if one will tolerate the mixing of metaphors—the two hands that allow believers to get a firm grasp on the promises of God and carry them close to their hearts as they traverse the storms of life. In light of the faith and hope which characterize the life of the growing believer, toward the end of the epistle the author of Hebrews proclaims, "Let us hold unswervingly to the hope we profess, for he who promised is faithful" (Heb 10:23).

Hope as a Unique Anchor

The author of Hebrews is no stranger to the mixing of metaphors. Indeed, immediately after mentioning hope as an anchor, he says that this hope enters like a priest into the Holy of Holies, following in the footsteps of Jesus, the great high priest who has become the forerunner. Alan C. Mitchell acknowledges that "the image of hope as an anchor conflicts with its movement into the sanctuary," since "anchors are fixed and are used to prevent movement."[15] Yet he suggests that "mixing the metaphors ... achieves the author's desired effect of placing the readers' solid hope in Jesus Christ" rather than in the shifting sands of this present world.[16] Attridge also

---

14 Bunyan, *Riches of Bunyan*, 293–94.
15 Mitchell, *Hebrews*, 136.
16 Mitchell, 136.

acknowledges that mixing the metaphors gives "dynamic connotations" to the typically understood static nature of an anchor.

When framing our discussion of Hebrews 6:13–20 in terms of our identity as spiritual refugees, it seems particularly appropriate that the anchor given to God's pilgrim people is somehow also moving and dynamic. It is unattached to any earthly thing, enabling movement through the world while being held by heavenly realities. In a sense, this anchor is cast upward,[17] something like a "grappling hook," finding a firm hold in the very person of Jesus, who has gone before us and "ever lives to intercede for us" (Heb 7:25).[18] Where he is, we will also someday be, and that will be our true home—"for here we have no lasting city, but we seek the city that is to come" (Heb 13:14).

Difficult life circumstances often provide an inflection point for humans. They are changed by their experiences, becoming harder and more closed or softer and more open. It may be that hardening happens when there is an absence of faith and hope, as can be seen in Hebrews 4 when the Israelites wandered in the wilderness and "the message they heard [good news from God] did not benefit them, because they were not united by faith with those who listened" and thus did not have hope that they would "enter [God's] rest" (Heb 4:2–3). The readers are then urged toward faith and hope in God, just as those wandering in the wilderness were. "Today, if you hear his voice, do not harden your hearts" (Heb 4:6).

Indeed, faith and hope are trusty tools for soft-hearted travelers in a fallen world, while love is an eternal reality of which we sojourners have only begun to grasp the outlines as we make our way toward our eternal, love-filled home. Andrew Peterson expresses the believer's relationship to faith, hope, and love in his song "No More Faith":

> I say faith is a burden, it's a weight to bear.
>> It's brave and bittersweet.
> And hope is hard to hold to
>> Lord, I believe, only help my unbelief.
> Till there's no more faith and no more hope,
>> I'll see your face and Lord I'll know
> That only love remains.[19]

---

17 In another sense, the anchor could be thought of as being dug deep into God's promises. Alexander Nairne (*Epistle of Priesthood*, 46–47) suggests that the ship is nearing land and the crew has dropped the anchor, while their captain (Jesus) has gone ashore and will call them soon. Abeneazer G. Urga ("Background and Nature of Jesus' Intercession," 267) comments that this sense of the metaphor brings home the fact that "believers are in the already-but-not-yet state of the faith journey."

18 Johnson, *Hebrews*, 173.

19 Andrew Peterson, "No More Faith," track 1 on *Clear to Venus*, Essential Records, 2001, compact disc.

This song riffs off 1 Corinthians 13, which conveys the mystery and longing of life in this fallen and unstable world.

> For now we see in a mirror dimly, but then face to face. Now I know in part; then I shall know fully, even as I have been fully known.
>
> So now faith, hope, and love abide, these three; but the greatest of these is love. (1 Cor 13:12–13)

Love, says Paul in this passage, "bears all things, believes all things [indicating faith], hopes all things, endures all things. Love never ends" (1 Cor 13:7–8).

Pilgrims as Spiritual Refugees
Faith, hope, and love are essential for believers if they are to persevere in their walk with Jesus. Leaning into their identity as spiritual refugees, Hebrews 6:18 is amplified: "We who have fled for refuge … ." Believers then learn to release their attachment to the comforts of an earthly home, acknowledging instead that they have hope in God's promises and choose to walk faithfully in the way of love.

Love is the main task of believers in the book of Hebrews. What does a hopeful, faith-filled life look like? It is filled with love, living in such a way that echoes the perfect love which we will someday experience fully. Chapter 13 contains a masterfully succinct explanation of the wide-ranging ways the love of God manifests itself when flowing through the lives of believers. It begins with, "Let brotherly love continue" (Heb 13:1).

Brotherly love is wonderful when times are good, but essential when hard times come. Abeneazer G. Urga points out that the true need for brotherly love and care "stems from the reality that the Christian life here on earth is not free of suffering." Indeed, "Brotherly love demonstrated through sharing, caring and fellowship enables Christians to persevere in the face of persecution and suffering."[20]

After instructing the Hebrews to love their brothers and sisters, outsiders are also clearly included in the circle of loving care: "Do not neglect to show hospitality to strangers, for thereby some have entertained angels unawares" (Heb 13:2). Thus, in just two verses believers have been shown that their love should be expressed both to those who are close to them and those who are outside their circles (*strangers*) and who are experiencing practically what is always true metaphorically (i.e., that we are far from home).

Next the readers are reminded of Jesus's stability in a tumultuous world. "Jesus Christ is the same yesterday, today and forever" (Heb 13:8).

---
20 Urga, "Possessions, Greed and the Christian Community."

This unchanging Savior to whom believers have fled and who has lovingly promised never to leave or forsake them is going somewhere in verse 12, and since he is our "forerunner" (Heb 6:20), he expects his followers to come with him.

> So Jesus also suffered outside the gate in order to sanctify the people through his own blood. Therefore let us go to him outside the camp and bear the reproach he endured. For here we have no lasting city, but we seek the city that is to come. (Heb 13:12–14)

When believers exit to find Jesus outside the camp, it "is not an escape from the world. ... Rather, it means that their earthly existence is predominated by the aspiration and yearning to be with Jesus in the heavenly home."[21] This life of "liminality" is a constant reminder that though we live in this world, it is not our ultimate home, for "it is here in this liminal place of living in the city while journeying outside the gate that we can 'run with perseverance the race that is set before us' (Heb 12:1) and, thereby, participate in and anticipate God's mission till Zion comes."[22]

Since Jesus was a Savior with no place to lay his head, he is leading his people on a pilgrimage outside the camp, where they will have opportunities to join in the mission of God—loving others and simultaneously encountering divine love in action while on the journey toward the full experience of perfect love when hope and faith fall away, no longer needed. We have already seen how hope propels mission, but it can also be said that mission reinvigorates hope, since "to see Christ coming in the human life, forgiving and transforming, is to be assured again and again of his coming in the clouds. We see this when we go forth to him outside the camp."[23]

As we walk through the world on the way to our heavenly home, pilgrims are given instructions for their journey.

> Through [Jesus] then let us continually offer up a sacrifice of praise to God, that is, the fruit of lips that acknowledge his name. Do not neglect to do good and to share what you have, for such sacrifices are pleasing to God. (Heb 13:15–16)

Loving service is made possible through faith-filled praises to God for the hope he holds out in the glorious gospel of grace. This gospel gives believers "strong encouragement to hold fast to the hope set before us" (Heb 6:18), and love compels us to share what we have. This hope is powerfully present, held fast by believers while they walk through the ever-changing,

---

21 Arowele, "Pilgrim People of God," 446.
22 Forney, "To the One Outside the Gate," 45–78, here 78.
23 Saunders, "'Outside the Camp': Hebrews 13," 23.

unstable world. Where believers are, there hope is; and it is a beautiful beacon of stability in the constant storms of life.

In Hebrews and in the Bible as a whole, "the word 'hope' is often synonymous with 'promise.'"[24] It involves three aspects that are emphasized at different times in Scripture: "expectation of the future, trust, and the patience of waiting"; and when "hope is fixed on God, it embraces at once the three elements."[25] In biblical usage, the word "never describes a subjective attitude (for example 'our hope' or 'hopefulness') but always denotes the objective content of our hope, consisting of present and future salvation" through Christ.[26]

If believers were to sum up the gospel message in one word, hope would be an apt choice, defined in the biblical sense. Indeed, elsewhere in the New Testament we see sharing the gospel described as giving "a reason for the hope that is in you" (1 Pet 3:15). Hope is the mystery kept hidden for ages but revealed in Christ. "God chose to make known how great among the Gentiles are the riches of the glory of this mystery, which is Christ in you, the hope of glory" (Col 1:27). Hope is the essence of the gospel, the message that we proclaim as followers of Jesus.

What could be more precious than hope in our current days of vitriol and contagion, uncertainty, and fear? In a general climate of dread trending toward despair about the state of our world, those who follow Jesus know where to flee for refuge, and they can invite others to do likewise. For those walking in the footsteps of Jesus, the book of Hebrews has good news, because the author acknowledges that faith in God does not need to be practiced in a particular or stationary geographical location. Rather, it is centered in the person of Jesus, who is omnipresent and who desires his followers to go to all nations with the Good News of his love. Christianity is a portable faith for a pilgrim people.

The fact that believers are referred to as those "who have fled for refuge" to God is significant because it reinforces the pilgrim motif in the book of Hebrews. Moreover, this reference seeks to shape the worldview of those enduring persecution by acknowledging the inherent instability of earthly existence, while contrasting it with the reality of the stability and certainty of God's love. Indeed, "those who are 'refugees' live without certainty … insecurity characterizes their existence."[27]

---

24 Attridge, *Hebrews*, 183.
25 Bultmann, "Ἐλπίς, Ἐλπίζω, Ἀπ-, Προελπίζω," 517–35, here 531.
26 Lane, *Hebrews 1–8*, 153.
27 Thompson, *Hebrews*, 139.

The allusion to believers being spiritual refugees (Heb 6:18) emphasizes the instability and danger of the fallen world, but the book of Hebrews is also infused with references to the redemptive identity of believers as pilgrims. Both refugees and pilgrims are travelers who are away from home, but refugees are escapees while pilgrims are purposefully walking to a highly anticipated destination "nearest to deity."[28] Hebrews 6:18 uses the past participle: "we who have fled for refuge." Those who have run to God have a sure hope for future rest, a place to belong and promises to hold fast to in faith; and they are also given purpose for their pilgrim walk through the world to love others and to share hope.

Earthly Refugees as Examples
It may be that those Jesus-followers who have literally fled for refuge yet held onto hope could lead the way in this regard: being a witness for the world as well as an example for brothers and sisters in Christ who have led more comfortable, stable lives. P. J. Arowele remarks,

> Ordinarily, the experiences of Christian minorities down the ages were a sufficient reminder of the exile status. But the hope, once, that Christianity would in time "conquer" the world often caused this exile character to be regarded as a transitory phenomenon. Now the realities of the modern world bring the realisation that the church is, after almost two thousand years, by no means at home on earth. ... Therefore, in acknowledging today to be an exile body on earth, the church is just being true to itself.
>
> No ecclesial groups appreciate this acknowledgement as much as those poor and oppressed minorities.[29]

Emily Jetepkeny Choge adds that because Christian refugees "are caught in that ongoing tension of the 'now and the not yet,' they are the ones who can best exemplify to Christians everywhere the essence and meaning of eschatological expectation."[30]

The book of Hebrews makes clear that while following a suffering Savior, persecution could necessitate the loss of all that was familiar and a fleeing for one's life to another place. Christian refugees and others who have had to flee their homes know what it means to leave the comfort and stability of home and most of their earthly possessions and decide that here they have no lasting city. They know the mental and emotional shift of losing one's grip on national identity to grasp even more firmly one's spiritual identity. They know the grief of walking away from an earthly home while

---

28 Johnsson, "Pilgrimage Motif in the Book of Hebrews," 239–51, here 245.
29 Arowele, "Pilgrim People of God," 449.
30 Choge, *Ethic of Hospitality*, xviii.

finding comfort in the reality of the heavenly home toward which they are going as they walk through the pilgrimage of this life. They are a pilgrim people who can instruct the rest of the church for whom this is—at least at this moment—only an abstract identity which can be hard to envision how to embody.

By looking to Christian refugees as examples and learning from them as teachers, other believers can gain a deeper understanding of hope during seasons of uncertainty. Refugees are those who have not been allowed to remain in denial about the evil in the world and the precarious nature of life and livelihood at any given time. They have been divested of the illusion of invincibility; they cannot unsee the knife's edge upon which every human walks simply by existing in a fallen world. But somehow, they do not despair, because they have found refuge. They have been allowed to live in a safer place physically (even if only a camp) and have been welcomed spiritually into citizenship in a "kingdom that cannot be shaken" (Heb 12:28).

Christians who were forced to flee their homes are

> not just refugees living a haphazard existence, but they are pilgrims journeying toward a specific destination. Most of them did not deliberately set out on the physical journey, but if they view their existence in this manner—not just as helpless victims who were pushed out of their land, but as purposeful pilgrims on a journey of faith, both literally and figuratively—then this brings an added dimension of purpose and meaning to their existence. It can transform the hopeless, dreary existence at the refugee camp to a life of hopeful expectation—not just for the durable solutions of the UNHCR, but for the ultimate manifestation of the kingdom of God.[31]

Many refugees who have the opportunity eventually to move out of the camps to a new country go through a season of depression after the initial "honeymoon" period. Though they are grateful to be in a location with more opportunities to settle down and build a life other than the life lived in the camps, they also come face to face with the fact that their host country is not a utopia either. They deal with culture shock, loneliness, hardship, and all too often are not warmly welcomed by locals. Any rosy expectations are usually dashed within the first few months.

But Christian refugees possess a potent antidote to this disillusionment, because they realize that hope is not geographical. Just as the book of Hebrews shows that faith does not have to be centered in a place (the tabernacle, the temple, Jerusalem, etc.), but instead is centered in an omnipresent person, believing refugees live out the fact that the Christian faith is portable and

---

31 Choge, xvii.

powerful regardless of where it is practiced. Christian refugees—whether literal, metaphorical, or both—have a God who is with them always, to the end of the age, and to the ends of the earth, as they share his hope with others (Matt 28:18–20).

Jesus gives hope in a motherland devolving into chaos, and he continues to give hope in a new land that may never quite feel like home. This is the only kind of hope that is powerful enough to counter the global spirit of heaviness and hopelessness that characterizes our current time. The refugee identity was a reminder to the Hebrews who were tempted toward lethargy and is a modern reminder to Christians in stable circumstances that earthly stability is illusory and can collapse at any time. The only sure hope and safety can be found in the unchangeable character and promises of God.

The message that a pilgrim people proclaim, then and now, is that God receives all refugees who run to him. And we are urged to look to the cloud of witnesses for encouragement to press on for our walk through this world. These witnesses include those listed in the book of Hebrews as well as faithful Christian refugees in the modern day. Toward this end, we will "not be sluggish, but imitators of those who through faith and patience inherit the promises" (Heb 6:12).

Conclusion

The book of Hebrews ends on a note of uncertainty. The author shares the good news that Timothy has been released from prison, but he does not know when or if Timothy will arrive or whether that arrival would be in time to accompany the author on his upcoming journey. It is evident that the author knew all too well that only God knew what tomorrow would bring. Likewise, in the modern day, refugees remind the wider church of the universal uncertainty of life, but of the certainty of hope.

It is pointless to try to make oneself secure. Circumstances can change unexpectedly and sometimes painfully, but God's character, purposes, and promises are unchangeable. At times, it can feel as though everything is shaky as believers struggle through life with the bodily "tent that is our earthly home" (2 Cor 5:1). However, they can hold on to "hope as an anchor for the soul, firm and secure" (Heb 6:19) as they look forward to "receiving a kingdom that cannot be shaken" and a "city that has foundations, whose designer and builder is God" (Heb 11:10). Believers are invited to "hold unswervingly to the hope we profess, for he who promised is faithful" (Heb 10:23). We join the great cloud of faithful witnesses, of whom it was said,

These all died in faith, not having received the things promised, but having seen them and greeted them from afar, and having acknowledged that they were strangers and exiles on earth. For people who speak thus make it clear that they are seeking a homeland. If they had been thinking about the land from which they had gone out, they would have had opportunity to return. But as it is, they desire a better country, that is, a heavenly one. Therefore God is not ashamed to be called their God, for he has prepared for them a city. (Heb 11:13–15)

In the already-but-not-yet times we live in, we can cope with uncertainty and change through faithful hope that works itself out in a love that creates echoes of heavenly realities by venturing with Jesus "outside the camp" to cultivate loving pilgrim communities that are committed to spurring one another on toward love and good deeds, standing in solidarity with and learning from the vulnerable (refugees), and always inviting strangers in to find and celebrate hope with us through worshiping Jesus our forerunner.

Bibliography

Arowele, P. J. "The Pilgrim People of God (An African's Reflections on the Motif of Sojourn in the Epistle to the Hebrews)." *The Asia Journal of Theology* 4, no. 2 (October 1990): 438–55.

Attridge, Harold W. *Hebrews*. Hermeneia. Minneapolis: Augsburg Fortress Publishers, 1989.

Bultmann, Rudolf. "Ἐλπίς, Ἐλπίζω, Ἀπ-, Προελπίζω." *Theological Dictionary of the New Testament* 2: 517–35. Grand Rapids: Zondervan, 1971.

Bunyan, John. *The Riches of Bunyan*. American Tract Society, 1850.

Choge, Emily Jeptepkeny. *An Ethic of Hospitality: The Pilgrim Motif in Hebrews and the Refugee Problem in Kenya*. Contrapuntal Readings in World Christianity. Eugene: Pickwick Publications, 2020.

Forney, David G. "To the One Outside the Gate: A Missional Approach to Polity." *Journal of Religious Leadership* 5:1–2 (Spring and Fall 2006): 45–78.

Hughes, Philip Edgcumbe. *A Commentary on the Epistle to the Hebrews*. Grand Rapids: Eerdmans, 1977.

Johnson, Luke Timothy. *Hebrews: A Commentary*. New Testament Library. Louisville: Westminster John Knox Press, 2006.

Johnsson, William G. "The Pilgrimage Motif in the Book of Hebrews." *Journal of Biblical Literature* 97, no. 2 (1978): 239–51.

Lane, William L. *Hebrews 1–8*. Word Biblical Commentary 47A. Grand Rapids: Zondervan, 1991.

Mitchell, Alan C. *Hebrews*. Sacra Pagina 13. Collegeville, MN: Liturgical Press, 2009.

Nairne, Alexander. *The Epistle of Priesthood; Studies in the Epistle to the Hebrews*. Edinburgh: T&T Clark, 1913.

Saunders, Landon. "'Outside the Camp': Hebrews 13." *Restoration Quarterly* 22 (1979), 19–24.

Thayer, Joseph H. *Thayer's Greek-English Lexicon of the New Testament: Coded with Strong's Concordance Numbers*. New York: Harper & Brothers, 1889.

Thompson, James P. *Hebrews*. Paideia Series. Grand Rapids: Baker Academic, 2008.

Urga, Abeneazer G. "The Background and Nature of Jesus' Intercession in Heaven as a High Priest for Believers in the Epistle to the Hebrews." PhD diss., Columbia International University, 2021.

Urga, Abeneazer G. "Possessions, Greed and the Christian Community: Interrogating the Prosperity Gospel in Africa in Light of Hebrews 13:1–6." Paper presented at the Evangelical Theological Society annual meeting. Fort Worth, Texas, November 16, 2021.

Chapter 7
Mission Hope in a Storm-Tossed World

Irwyn Ince

We live in a frustratingly broken world, and the common desire is to hope for things to become better. While this aspiration is regularly dashed, the remedy to the frustrations we experience in our broken world *is hope*—gospel hope. Gospel hope is not wishful thinking, but rather faith in the sure promises of God. A longing rooted in God's promises is a hope that cannot disappoint because *that* hope is validated by God himself. Moreover, hope is an ambition that is not predicated upon the decisions or circumstances of people. The author of Hebrews describes it as "the assurance of hope" (Heb 6:11). God will make all things new, and he empowers his people to missionally live in this age with a full assurance of hope. How do we endure with hope? What does a hopeful missional response to brokenness look like?

It is all rooted in a seeming paradox. The Son is heir over everything. The Son is the One through whom God created the world. He sustains all things by his powerful word. He does so as the radiance of God's glory and the exact representation of his being. Yet, he is the same One who made purification for sins by suffering unjustly, was crucified, then rose from the dead. From our vantage point, the world does not make sense because the worst things can happen to the best people and the best things can happen to the worst people. Try as we might, there does not appear to be an unassailable reason to be hopeful about justice, joy, and shalom in our world today. The author of Hebrews exhorts us to live by the paradox of the suffering, glorified, regal Savior. It is this missional endeavor that will demand endurance and is a sure and steadfast anchor for the soul (Heb 6:19).

The Storm-Tossed World

Before a hurricane there is a calm. Then there is a realization that the storm has hit, and you are no longer in control. After the storm passes, there is chaos. Devastation is all around. What we discover in the opening chapter of the book of Hebrews is a reversal of that order. There is a storm taking place in the pastor's congregation. Persecution and suffering are a reality in their lives. Their world has been turned upside-down. Precipitated by the chaos and upheaval, they are tempted to lose hope and drift away from their faith in Jesus Christ. Following Jesus is more costly than they had anticipated. When the pressure is most intense, when they want to quit, the pastor warns them not to abandon their confidence because there is a reward for those who patiently endure hardship (Heb 10:35–36).

What is interesting, though, is how the pastor[1] addresses their concerns. His desire is for them to endure, not to give up. However, he doesn't begin his letter by saying, "Hold on," "Don't be discouraged," or "Keep the faith." The pastor will offer that encouragement later in the letter. Instead, to commence his homily, he describes the unrivaled glory, majesty, and authority of the Son of God. The supremacy of Jesus Christ is their source of eternal hope in a topsy-turvy, upside-down world.

First, it is important to define hope. Theologian Marva Dawn writes:

> We use the English noun and verb *hope* in many ways—to signify what we anticipate or expect, what we would recommend if we could control things, what we most earnestly desire or wish for if we could have our own way, or what we truly believe in or in what or whom we have confidence.[2]

Key to the concept of hope are expectations, desires, and wishes—most particularly, desires that we hold earnestly. These characteristics are also true for the Greek noun and verb, ἐλπίς and ἐλπίζω, translated as "hope" in the English Bible. Moreover, it is commonly understood that what we desire is ἐλπίς ἀγαθή (good hope).[3] Indeed, in the New Testament the noun, verb, and their derivatives "never indicate a vague or a fearful anticipation, but always the expectation of something good."[4] Further, this chapter is primarily focused on Hebrews 1, and in Hebrews "hope" is intimately connected to covenant (διαθήκη). The pastor uses διαθήκη more than all the other writers of the New Testament combined. The word is directly used or implied twenty-five times.[5]

It is by means of covenant that God was pleased to express his desire for us to know him as our blessedness and reward.[6] As the pastor says in Hebrews 6:17 (ESV), "When God desired to show more convincingly to the heirs of the promise the unchangeable character of his purpose, he guaranteed it with an oath." This verse expresses God's voluntary condescension to establish and guarantee his covenant promise to his people. He was not forced or

---

1 Cockerill, *Epistle to the Hebrews*, rightly addresses the author of Hebrews as "pastor" throughout his commentary. In line with Cockerill, I refer to the author in this chapter as "pastor."
2 Dawn, *Unfettered Hope*, xii.
3 Bultmann, "Ἐλπίς, Ἐλπίζω, Ἀπ-, Προελπίζω," *TDNT* 2:518.
4 Hoffman, "Hope, Expectation," *NIDNT* 2:241.
5 Cara, "Covenant in Hebrews," 247–48.
6 Bower, *Confession of Faith*, 204: "The distance between God and the creature is so great, that although reasonable creatures do owe obedience unto Him as their Creator, yet they could never have any fruition of Him as their blessedness and reward, but by some voluntary condescension on God's part, which He hath been pleased to express by way of covenant."

hesitant to guarantee his promise. He desired to do so. The hope the pastor wants the Hebrews to possess is the covenant promises of God. He wants his hearers to live practically in this storm-tossed world as those who are expectantly waiting to receive the full and glorious inheritance that is theirs in Jesus Christ.

Living with this hope has missional implications. People who live with this hope demonstrate a calm during the storm that displays the trustworthiness of Jesus to their neighbors. The remainder of this chapter will focus on Hebrews 1, to examine a specific grounding for this hope—Jesus as the Glorious Prophet, the Glorious Priest, and the Glorious King.[7] Later, we will explore how the pattern of Chaos, Control, and Calm is reflected in the lives of His people.

The Glorious Prophet

The pastor begins this letter by reminding his readers that God has spoken. "Long ago, at many times and in many ways, God spoke to our fathers by the prophets, but in these last days he has spoken to us by his Son" (Heb 1:1–2a ESV). His audience consists of Christians—people who have put their hope and faith in Jesus Christ. Furthermore, the Old Testament was written to the nation of Israel. However, the pastor does not say that God spoke to their fathers. He says that God spoke to our fathers. In essence, he calls the Old Testament patriarchs their spiritual forefathers. These patriarchs are part of the history of their faith. Yes, a change took place when Jesus came on the scene, but God was not doing something completely new; he was doing something better for them through the mediation of his Son.[8] Thus,

> before allowing the Father to explain who the Son is through his own words, the author offers several summary statements of his own. To name a few, this Son is the means by which God speaks to "us" (1:2), is the radiance of God's glory (1:3a), and is seated at the right hand of God in heaven (1:3d). In his last statement, the author reveals the most striking characteristic about this Son. He has become as much superior to the angels as the name he has inherited is superior to theirs (1:4).[9]

The pastor points out that God has been speaking all along. And the word that he delivered through his prophets was for them. At various points and times in history, and in different ways, God raised up and anointed

---

[7] Bruce, *Epistle to the Hebrews*, 44–51.
[8] Jesus is the mediator of a better covenant (Heb 7:19, 22; 8:6; 9:23; 12:24). The angels were understood to have mediated the Law to Moses (Heb 2:2), and the superiority of the New Covenant is seen in the fact that the Son is superior to the angels (Heb 1:4).
[9] Pierce, *Divine Discourse*, 36.

prophets to declare his word with authority: Abraham, Moses, Samuel, Elijah, Elisha, Isaiah, Jeremiah, Ezekiel, Daniel, Hosea, Joel, Amos, and on and on for centuries.

God spoke to his people through the prophets, always to direct them to himself. It was always so that they would know what was necessary for them to honor and glorify him. God was not silent, but his people are often deaf (Isa 6:8–10; 42:18–19). Although the word spoken through the prophets was glorious, it was also varied, diverse, and fragmented because the prophets were many in number. But a change took place in the ministry of Jesus Christ.

"In these last days," the pastor says, "God has spoken to us by the Son, by the unique and only Son."[10] When God the Son took on human flesh, and was "born of woman, born under the law, to redeem those who were under the law" (Gal 4:4–5), Jesus's word became the final, complete, full word of God. "Therefore," the pastor says in Hebrews 2:1, "we must pay much closer attention to what we have heard, lest we drift away from it."

If the word of the various prophets was glorious and authoritative, how much more glorious is the unitary message given to us by Jesus Christ? God's word in Christ has been spoken fully and finally. The pastor wants his audience to grasp that what they have, the fathers of the faith did not have—i.e., the full, complete, and final word of God. That is the point of the pastor's phrase in Hebrews 1:2, "in these last days (ἐπ' ἐσχάτου τῶν ἡμερῶν τούτων)." The pastor means that, in Christ, God's revelation is complete.

In other words, God has upped the ante. The Son is far superior to the prophets. Hebrews 1:1–4 sets the tone and theme of the whole letter.[11] Jesus is supreme over everything that came before him: prophets, priests, and kings. They all pointed toward him, and he is the full and final word of God. He is not just one of the prophets; he is the heir of all things. He has an inheritance, which is the whole world. Not just people, but he came to lay claim to the entire creation. He came to lay claim to the entire creation as his own possession, because he is the One through whom the world was created. He is the glorious radiance and exact imprint of God's essence. *He is God!* And he makes the glory of God visible to us.

---

10 The pastor writes that God has spoken ἐν υἱῷ. The phrase lacks a definite article or personal pronoun. However, as Attridge (*Hebrews*, 39) attests, the phrase does not imply that there are many sons whom God could have chosen as agents of revelation. Rather the term emphasizes the exalted status of that final agent. … God, moreover, speaks through this Son not only in word, but in deed, in the entirety of the Christ-event, providing for humanity atonement for sin and an enduring covenant relationship. Therefore, it is fitting to refer to the Son as "God's unique and only Son."

11 Pierce, *Divine Discourse*, 36.

Thus, Jesus could say to his disciples in John 14:9, "Whoever has seen me has seen the Father." Who else can uphold "the universe by the word of his power" (Heb 1:3)? In other words, the pastor is assuring his congregation that their Savior is the One who sustains the universe and carries it along to its stated purpose and goal. Thus, when encouraging Christians to endure, the pastor begins with Jesus's glory. Furthermore, his glory extends to the priesthood.

The Glorious Priest

"After making purification for sins, he sat down at the right hand of the Majesty on high" (Heb 1:3c). In five words in the Greek text (καθαρισμὸν τῶν ἁμαρτιῶν ποιησάμενος ἐκάθισεν), and eight words in our English translation, the pastor says that Jesus is not only the glorious prophet, but he is also the glorious priest. "After making purification for sins, he sat down." In these eight words, the pastor describes the whole of Jesus's work.

Just like the comparison between God's word through the prophets and God's word through the Son, there is a comparison between the ongoing work of the Old Testament priests and the final work of the great High Priest, Jesus Christ the Anointed One. To be clear, this final work is the once-for-all offering up of himself for the sins of his people (Heb 7:27–28; 9:11–12). Thus, while the sacrificial work of Jesus Christ is complete, his ministerial work of intercession on behalf of his people is ongoing (Heb 7:23–25; 8:1–6).

In the Old Testament, God appointed Aaron as the first high priest, and all other priests came from his lineage (Exod 28–29). Their basic job description was to offer sacrifices, in the presence of God, on behalf of the people to cover their sins. What God did in the Old Testament was provide a line of priests whose daily ministry was to atone for the sins of the people by sacrificing lambs and bulls and goats (Lev 1:3–5; 4:1–12, 22–30). It was a gory and gruesome scene as blood flowed in the tabernacle every day. God takes sin seriously, which is why the pastor reminds his congregation, in Hebrews 9:22, that "without the shedding of blood there is no forgiveness of sins." Every day blood was shed so the people were not consumed. God's punishment for sin fell on lambs, bulls, and goats. However, as the pastor reminds us in Hebrews 10:4, it is impossible for the blood of bulls and goats to eradicate sins. The blood of bulls and goats could never finally, fully, and completely take care of the sin problem.

In Hebrews 10, the pastor contrasts the continual sacrifices of the Levitical priests and the singular sacrifice of Christ with the same Greek phrase, εἰς τὸ διηνεκὲς (continually/forever). The first use of this phrase occurs in Hebrews 7:3 in reference to Melchizedek, who, made like the

Son of God, remains a high priest continually (εἰς τὸ διηνεκὲς). The three other occurrences of the phrase are found in Hebrews 10:1, 12, and 14. In verse 1, the pastor confirms that the same sacrifices (ταῖς αὐταῖς θυσίαις) offered by the priest (εἰς τὸ διηνεκὲς) are never able (οὐδέποτε δύναται) to perfect those who draw near. Then, in verse 11 he confirms, after offering the same sacrifices (ταῖς αὐταῖς θυσίαις) these things are never able (οὐδέποτε δύναται) to carry away sins.

The only way to perfect those who draw near is to have their sins carried away. Hence, in verse 12, when Christ made one offering for sins εἰς τὸ διηνεκὲς (forever), he sat down at the right hand of God. Through Jesus's offering of himself for the sins of his people—sin was eradicated once and for all. Sins were carried away, which means the blood of bulls and goats were no longer necessary. The pastor reinforced his proclamation in Hebrews 10:14, by a single offering Christ has perfected (μιᾷ γὰρ προσφορᾷ τετελείωκεν) forever (εἰς τὸ διηνεκὲς) those who are consecrated and made holy.

Therefore, when the One who is the radiance of the glory of God stepped into time and space, he came as the unblemished, spotless Lamb of God who takes away the sin of the world. He came both as the sacrificial offering and as the offeror. He is the great high priest who offered himself as the only One who could crush sin. As he was being beaten and whipped, as the blood was flowing from his head, his hands, his feet, purification was being made for the sins of everyone who puts their trust in him. It is as the hymn writer, Isaac Watts, said in his hymn, "When I Survey the Wondrous Cross."

> See from His head, His hands, His feet,
> Sorrow and love flow mingled down!
> Did e'er such love and sorrow meet,
> Or thorns compose so rich a crown?

Jesus made purification for sins final and complete. How do we know that it is final and complete? Because Jesus sat down. In the tabernacle, the chair was missing—the priest stood to offer the blood atonement. As previously noted, this is precisely what the pastor said in Hebrews 10:11: the priests did not have a chair because they did not have rest. However, when Jesus made purification for sins, the pastor says that he sat down (Heb 1:3; 10:12). The work was finished; thus there was no longer a need for other sacrifices for sin. The pastor quoted Psalm 110:1 in Hebrews 1:13 to emphasize that God is the one who attests to the final and complete work of the Son. In Hebrews 5:6 and 7:1–28, he reengages with this same theme referring to Psalm 110:4. So,

God himself attests the sufficiency of his high priesthood by affirming his divine sonship (2 Sam 7:14; Ps 2:7) and sovereign deity (Pss 45:6–8; 102:25–27); by inviting him to be seated at his right hand (Ps 110:1); and finally, by affirming the high-priestly nature of that session (Ps 110:4).[12]

This begs a missional question. How do we deal with our mess in this upside-down world? It is not only people and systems outside of the church that are messed up; if we are honest, we must admit that we—as God's people—are also a mess. What are the ways that we attempt to clean ourselves up by our own means apart from dependence on the Spirit of God? What are the temptations that make us want to throw up our hands and not worry about how messed up we are? The only way to deal with our mess is to give ourselves over to God—mess and all. Any other approach is effectively spitting in God's face. The pastor is showing his congregation that Jesus is the Glorious Priest, because they are being tempted to take matters into their own hands. They are being tempted to make up their own way of salvation. The message is that Jesus is the only one who can make the impure pure. There is no other way than throwing yourself at his feet to bow down to Christ, who is the glorious King.

The Glorious King

That is the best place to find yourself. Not only because Jesus is the glorious prophet and the merciful high priest, but because he is also the great and glorious King. The fact that he sat down demonstrates that he had completed his work of purification for sins and that he is the supreme King and Judge. For "he sat down at the right hand of the Majesty on high" (Heb 1:3). Location matters! Jesus prayed to the Father in John 17:4–5: "I glorified you on earth, having accomplished the work that you gave me to do. And now, Father, glorify me in your own presence with the glory that I had with you before the world existed."

Jesus completed his work and was restored to his rightful position in heaven as the King of kings and the Lord of lords, as the One before whom every knee will bow and every tongue will confess. Because of where he sits, right now we are only able to know him as the Glorious King by faith. He reigns supreme over heaven and earth. Once again, the pastor's references to Psalm 110:1 (Heb 1:3, 13) are significant foundations for the Son's kingship. Whereas the heart of Hebrews 1:3 is the session of the Son at the right hand of the Majesty on high, the subordinate clauses in the verse (being [ὢν] the radiance of the glory of God, bearing [φέρων] all things by the word of his power, having made [ποιησάμενος] purification for sins), as well as

---

12 Cockerill, *Epistle to the Hebrews*, 45–46.

the clause in Hebrews 1:4 (having become [γενόμενος] as much superior to the angels), point to his exalted status and bring that regal exaltation into sharp focus.[13]

But as the pastor says in Hebrews 2:8, "At present, we do not yet see everything in subjection to him." Unbelief and fear blind people from understanding how everything is under subjection to Jesus. The declaration in Hebrews 1:2–3 that the Son is the heir of all things—through whom he created the world—the exact imprint of God's nature, and the sustainer of the universe is sweeping. There is truly no area of existence, material or immaterial, over which he does not have absolute authority. This is meant to be a comfort to those who believe and a warning to those who do not believe.

The pastor is talking to people who claim to know Jesus. He loves them and is pained that some are drifting away because things are getting rough. So, while all who come to God through faith in Jesus Christ are eternally secure in him (John 10:28), the pastor's warning is meant to exhort his people to faithfulness and self-examination.[14] Holding on to the assurance of hope and thriving in the Christian life begins with a clear view of the glory of Jesus Christ, the Glorious Prophet who declares God's final word to us, the Glorious Priest who purifies us, and the Glorious King who rules over us and protects us. This is necessary because the world will continue to be full of chaos until he returns.

Chaos

The pastor does not set forth the divine nature and glory of Jesus, the Son of God, as an idea that is disconnected from life. All this rich theology about Jesus Christ is not given in a vacuum simply as head knowledge. It is the epitome of theology applied to life. Jesus being God is important because the world is full of chaos. In Hebrews 1:10–12 (ESV), the pastor quotes from Psalm 102:25–27, in which God the Father is talking to God the Son:

> You, Lord, laid the foundation of the earth in the beginning,
> > and the heavens are the work of your hands;
> they will perish, but you remain;
> > they will all wear out like a garment,
> like a robe you will roll them up,
> > like a garment they will be changed.
> But you are the same,
> > and your years will have no end.

---

13 Guthrie, "Hebrews," 924.
14 Kruger, *Hebrews for You*, 28.

Why did the pastor quote Psalm 102? The heading from the Hebrew text—"A Prayer of one afflicted …"—provides the clue. The psalmist is in the middle of a storm. He is overwhelmed by the chaos of this world. The destruction of Jerusalem has turned his world upside-down. The temple is in ruins. The temple was supposed to be the place where God made his name dwell. It was the evidence that the Lord was with his people. Now, the thing that he thought was most secure and stable was gone. The Babylonians have crushed them and taken them into exile.

The following analogy falls short, but it will help illuminate this point. When I was a young boy, my father worked at the World Trade Center. Most days he took the train to and from work, but there were a few occasions when we drove into Manhattan to pick him up. As we sat parked outside the Twin Towers waiting for Dad to come out, I remember looking up at the Towers through the car's windows. No matter how much I strained my neck, I could not see the top of the Towers. I was amazed by those buildings, and in my mind they were permanent fixtures in the New York City (NYC) skyline. The photos that represented NYC always included the Twin Towers. Obviously, they were not the permanent fixtures I imagined them to be. The city was thrown into distress when the Towers fell on 9/11. The distress on the faces of New Yorkers when the Towers fell is akin to the distress of the psalmist:

> For my days pass away like smoke,
>   and my bones burn like a furnace.
> My heart is struck down like grass and has withered;
>   I forget to eat my bread.
> Because of my loud groaning
>   my bones cling to my flesh. (Ps 102:3–5, (ESV)

But there is a turning point in the psalm. In verse 12, the psalmist says,

> But you, O Lord, are enthroned forever;
>   you are remembered throughout all generations.

Amid the chaos that is around him, what the psalmist realizes is that the only stable, unchanging reality is that Yahweh, the Lord, is enthroned forever. That is the message the pastor is communicating in Hebrews 1. The distress you feel is real, but the One who walked the streets of Jerusalem and said, "Come to me all you who labor and are heavy laden, and I will give you rest" (Matt 11:28), is none other than Yahweh, the Lord your God. The pastor is communicating to his congregation that Jesus is the One who laid the earth's foundations in the beginning and the One who created the heavens. Those created things will wear out and be rolled up like an old garment and be replaced, but the Lord continues forever. He is the same and his years have no end (Ps 102:25–27; Heb 1:10–12).

Let's think about a hurricane again. They are so devastating because their impact is so real and tangible. The things around us, the things that we experience in life, grab our attention so strongly and captivate us so powerfully because they are so real. But as powerful as a hurricane is, it is created by God the Son. Created things seem to have permanence, but they are not permanent; they are temporal. Created things appear to have ultimate authority, but they do not have more authority than the Creator.

Moreover, the Son is the "actor" in Hebrews 1:10–12. This is noteworthy—he is the One performing the acts. The creation is passive; it is being acted upon. The Son *established* the earth. The heavens are the *work* of his hands. They will wear out. They will be changed. That is why the Lord says in Matthew 6:19, "Do not lay up for yourselves treasures on earth, where moth and rust destroy and where thieves break in and steal." Where is our treasure and hope? What do we value most? We spend our time pursuing the things that we think will bring us the most pleasure. The only unchanging reality is that Jesus Christ is the same, yesterday, today, and forever (Heb 13:8); every created thing we are tempted to trust will change, decay, and break down.

Jesus Is in Control

Therefore, the only way to endure the chaos is to know that Jesus is in control. As chaotic as life can get, the pastor wants his readers to remember that the reason things are being changed is because God is bringing the world to his purpose and goal. In other words, God is in control—not the storm. In the peak of a storm—when trees are being uprooted, cars are being tossed around, and siding is being torn off houses—at this moment, the storm has more control than people do. Yet God controls the storm. Everything that takes place in this entire universe is under the absolute control and authority of God. The pastor emphasizes this point in Hebrews 1:3: Jesus upholds (φέρων) the universe by the word of his power. The verb φέρω, translated *upholds* by the ESV, means "to carry."[15] Jesus is *carrying* the world along to his purpose and goal.

The seventh Old Testament quote in the chapter comes from Psalm 110:1:

> And to which of the angels has [God] ever said,
> "Sit at my right hand
> until I make your enemies a footstool for your feet"?

Psalm 110 is the most frequently quoted psalm in the New Testament. The pastor either cites it directly or echoes it thirteen times in the book of

---
15 BDAG, 1052.

Hebrews (1:3, 13; 5:6, 10; 6:20; 7:3, 11, 17, 21; 8:1; 10:12, 13; 12:2).[16] He echoes it in Hebrews 1:3, when he says, "After making purification for sins, he sat down at the right hand of the Majesty on high." He "sat down" in the position of absolute authority, control, and power. Sitting down also signifies that the Son faithfully and perfectly completed the work the Father gave him to do (John 4:34; 6:38–39), which was to defeat God's enemies (Heb 2:14–18; 10:13; 1 Cor 15:24–26). The crucifixion and resurrection of Jesus was the victory over his enemies. Now the Father says, I am going to "make your enemies a footstool for your feet" (Ps 110:1; Heb 1:13; 10:13). Therefore, creation is under the Son's authority, and the Son's completed work induces the calm.

The Calm

"The Son loves righteousness and hates wickedness; therefore, he is anointed by God with the oil of gladness" (Ps 45:6–7). The pastor quotes this psalm as an assurance that although there is great division and polarization—politically, socio-economically, racially, ethnically—Jesus's completed work brings a calm. Contrasting the unrighteousness and injustice experienced in our world with the righteousness and justice of the Son's dominion, Philip E. Hughes writes,

> The everlasting rule of the Son is marked by absolute justice and equity, whereas even in the best of human dominions there is some admixture of injustice and discrimination. It might well have been expected, in view of the frequency with which Psalm 110 is quoted or alluded to elsewhere in this epistle, that our author would have added verse 2 of that psalm, which states, "The Lord sends forth from Zion your mighty sceptre," to this chain of texts.[17]

Psalm 110:2 is so encouraging because Jesus is in control, and he brings the calm to every storm, which is the point the pastor so masterfully emphasizes. Arguably, the pastor encourages his congregation not just to correct their bad theology, but to encourage them with the truth. There is a *calm* that comes after the storm. There is a day coming when God "shall wipe away all tears from their eyes; and there shall be no more death ... for the former things are passed away (Rev 21:4).

There is not only a calm that comes after the storm, but there is a calm that exists *in* the storm for the people of God. The pastor lets them know that God sends out angels to minister on behalf of "those who are to inherit salvation" (Heb 1:14). The angels, these glorious creatures who worship

---

16 Hughes, *Commentary on Hebrews*, 69.
17 Hughes, 64.

Jesus, these powerful spiritual creatures who invoke terror in the hearts of people when they appear, are sent out by God to minister to the saints while they are in the storm. The angels cannot be compared to Jesus, but he sends them to help those who follow him.

The perfect example is found in 2 Kings 6:8–23. The prophet Elisha would warn the king of Israel where the Syrians were setting up their camp to attack him. The king of Syria decided Elisha's meddling was too much. When he discovered Elisha was staying in Dothan, he sent horses and chariots and a great army who came by night and surrounded the city.

When Elisha's servant arose early in the morning and saw the army surrounding the city, he was fearful, and said to Elisha, "What are we going to do?" The servant was petrified, but Elisha was calm. Elisha said, "Do not be afraid, for those who are with us are more than those who are with them." Elisha prayed, "O LORD, please open his eyes that he may see." So the LORD opened the eyes of the young man, and he saw, and behold, the mountain was full of horses and chariots of fire all around Elisha (2 Kgs 6:15–17). Because Elisha belonged to the Lord, he understood that nothing in this created world was more powerful than his God. Even the angels of God were at God's disposal to come and help him.

In Hebrews 1:14, the pastor asks a question, "Are they not all ministering spirits?" The answer is a resounding yes. In Hebrews 1:2, the pastor proclaims that the Son is the *heir* (κληρονόμος) of all things. In Hebrews 1:4, he has *inherited* (κληρονομέω) a name that is more excellent than that of the angels. The pastor continues his trajectory with these encouraging words: the angels are "sent out to serve for the sake of those who are to *inherit* (κληρονομέω) salvation" (Heb 1:14). The pastor uses the word *inherit* on purpose. He wants to link his congregation intimately with the Son and to emphasize God's intentions for them.

Conclusion

The strongest motive for missions in the letter to the Hebrews is laid out in this first chapter—the uniqueness of the Son of God. This uniqueness was not just as an unrivaled figure in history; rather, he also showed a unique ability and commitment to sustain the entire creation, carrying it and his people along to the fullness of redemption and glory. This is also the hope that answers the longings of those outside of the Christian faith. Regardless of race, nationality, geographical location, political affiliation, or life circumstance, human beings long for wrongs to be made right.

Jesus Christ—seated in glory—is the Savior who rights the wrongs in this world. He is reigning and ruling right now. God's mission to renew the entire creation under the Lordship of Jesus Christ is well under way. It is, after all, his inheritance. Although the storm is raging, God is in control. Just as the Father's plan was for the Son to complete his work of redemption and take his rightful place on the throne to claim his inheritance, it is the guaranteed plan of the Father and the Son to bring every Christian into the full inheritance of eternal life with them in glory. So, the Lord gives his children the strength to calmly endure through the storms, bearing witness to the unrivaled majesty and glory of Jesus in an upside-down world.

We end where we began. Although there does not appear to be any unassailable reason to be hopeful about justice, joy, and shalom in the world, the first chapter of Hebrews sets the stage for a robust missional endeavor. The pastor's call for his people is to live out the implications of the better paradox of the suffering, glorified, regal Savior. Living out this better paradox is not a private matter. While Christians are to encourage one another and help each other persevere in the faith firm to the end (Heb 6:11), their witness is public. In Hebrews 10:33, the pastor told them to remember the days when they were publicly exposed (θεατριζόμενοι) to reproach and affliction. Their faith was lived out in the open. New Testament scholar Larry Hurtado notes, "There must have been things about early Christianity that made it worthwhile to become an adherent in spite of social harassment and potential prosecution."[18]

This is the kind of open witness that Hebrews places before us. Christian hope bears witness to the world that Jesus is real and worthy of worship. Enduring by faith in a storm-tossed world demonstrates to the world that as unreasonable as Christian hope might appear, it is rooted in something far better than anything this world has to offer. Our mission hope in this storm-tossed world is grounded in the fact that Jesus Christ is seated at the right hand of the Father, and his work of salvation is complete.

Bibliography

Attridge, Harold W. *Hebrews.* Hermeneia. Minneapolis: Fortress Press, 1989.

Bower, John R. *The Confession of Faith: A Critical Text and Introduction.* Grand Rapids: Reformation Heritage Books, 2020.

Bruce, F. F. *The Epistle to the Hebrews*. Rev. ed. New International Commentary on the New Testament. Grand Rapids: Eerdmans, 1990.

Bultmann, Rudolf. "Ἐλπίς, Ἐλπίζω, Ἀπ-, Προελπίζω." *Theological Dictionary of the New Testament* 2:517–35. Grand Rapids: Zondervan, 1971.

---

18 Hurtado, *Destroyer of the Gods,* 35.

Cara, Robert J. "Covenant in Hebrews." In *Covenant Theology: Biblical, Theological, and Historical Perspectives*, edited by Guy Prentiss Waters, J. Nicholas Reid, and John R. Muether, 247–66. Wheaton: Crossway, 2020.

Cockerill, Gareth Lee. *The Epistle to the Hebrews.* New International Commentary on the New Testament. Grand Rapids: Eerdmans, 2012.

Danker, Frederick W., Walter Bauer, and William F. Arndt. *A Greek-English Lexicon of the New Testament and Other Early Christian Literature*. Chicago: University of Chicago Press, 2000.

Dawn, Marva J. *Unfettered Hope: A Call to Faithful Living in an Affluent Society.* Louisville: Westminster John Knox Press, 2003.

Guthrie, George H. "Hebrews." In *Commentary on the New Testament Use of the Old Testament*, edited by G. K. Beale and D. A. Carson, 919–95. Grand Rapids: Baker Academic, 2007.

Hoffman, Ernst. "Hope, Expectation." *New International Dictionary of New Testament Theology* 2:238–45. Grand Rapids: Zondervan, 1980.

Hughes, Philip E. *A Commentary on the Epistle to the Hebrews*. Grand Rapids: Eerdmans, 1977.

Hurtado, Larry W. *Destroyer of the Gods: Early Christian Distinctiveness in the Roman World.* Waco: Baylor University Press, 2016.

Kruger, Michael J. *Hebrews for You*. Surrey, UK: Good Book Company, 2021.

Pierce, Madison N. *Divine Discourse in the Epistle to the Hebrews: The Recontextualization of Spoken Quotations of Scripture*. Society for New Testament Studies Monograph Series 178. Cambridge: Cambridge University Press, 2020.

Part 3
The Missionary Methods of Hebrews

Chapter 8
Evangelism in the Epistle to the Hebrews
Abeneazer G. Urga

The motif of mission in the Epistle to the Hebrews is often either denied or is only given lip service. Such a stance is common when it comes to the Catholic Epistles, particularly to Hebrews, James, Jude, and 2 Peter. They are considered to "offer little material that bears directly on the issue of mission."[1] Therefore, reflections on New Testament theology of mission predominantly center on the Gospels, the Book of Acts, and the Pauline Epistles. The Epistle to the Hebrews—according to several scholars—says little or nothing about world mission or evangelism. Rather, they argue, the message of Hebrews is intended for believers; namely, as a message to Christians to persevere.[2] Scholars like John Howard Yoder lament that the author of Hebrews missed the opportunity to develop missionary theology in his composition of the epistle.[3]

Contrary to that position, in this chapter I will argue that the Epistle to the Hebrews is concerned about both the perseverance of the saints and evangelism. The believers are exhorted to hold onto their salvation—their reconciled status with God. They are also expected to proclaim that great salvation and their heavenly status to the outside world in the manner of the cloud of witnesses. I will give attention to Hebrews 2:1–4, 4:1–3, and 11:13–16 in order to demonstrate that evangelism/proclamation is expressed as a missionary method in reaching others.[4]

What Have Others Said about Hebrews and Mission?

Donald Senior and Carroll Stuhlmueller
Donald Senior and Carroll Stuhlmueller argue that in contrast to James, Jude, and 2 Peter, "Hebrews offers more potential for the question of mission."[5]

---

1 Senior and Stuhlmueller, *Biblical Foundations for Mission*, 309.
2 Hughes, *Hebrews and Hermeneutics*, 135; Senior and Stuhlmueller, *Biblical Foundations for Mission*, 309–10; York, *Missions in the Age of the Spirit*, 95; Ott and Strauss, *Encountering Theology of Mission*, 50–52, limit their discussion of mission in the General Epistles to 1 Peter; the lacuna of Hebrews' contribution to the missionary theology of the New Testament is also evident in Peters, *Biblical Theology of Missions*, 131–56; Barnett, ed., *Discovering the Mission of God*; Goheen, ed., *Reading the Bible Missionally*; Wright, *Mission of God*.
3 Yoder, *Theology of Mission*, 121; Yoder states: "The author of Hebrews did not develop missionary dimensions where he could have done so easily."
4 Unless otherwise noted, all Scripture quotations in this chapter come from the ESV.
5 Senior and Stuhlmueller, *Biblical Foundations for Mission*, 305.

Jesus's redemptive work and his superiority over the Aaronic cultus and priesthood, coupled with his divine ontology, are significant to the author's theology of mission. Senior and Stuhlmueller also detect "missionary preaching" (Heb 2:1–14) and the cost of "conversion" (Heb 10:32–34) in the epistle.

Nonetheless, instead of fleshing out these missionary elements, the authors assert that the letter tilts toward perseverance. They even claim further that "There is no real attention given to such issues as the fate of the Gentiles or the responsibility of Christians to the outside world."[6] This claim is unconvincing. If "the author is conscious of the missionary preaching of the community" and if conversion is taking place,[7] why do Senior and Stuhlmueller ignore the fact that the church is expected to persevere in order to proclaim "such a great salvation" to the outside world?

Richard W. Johnson

Richard W. Johnson, in his *Going Outside the Camp: The Sociological Function of the Levitical Critique in the Epistle to the Hebrews*, employs a sociological method in reading Hebrews to examine the letter writer's critique of the Levitical system and flesh out the social function of his critique. Doing so will enable us, Johnson posits, to identify the purpose for the composition of Hebrews.

Johnson argues that the ideal society the author of Hebrews envisioned, in contrast to the Hellenistic Jewish society, was "both more open to outsiders and more willing to assimilate fully new members."[8] The author of Hebrews desired his recipients to follow in the footsteps of the exemplars who confessed their status on earth as "foreigners and strangers" (Heb 11:13). The confession of the community allows the group to have a strong "group identity."[9] So the author exhorts his audience to be bold and remain steadfast in the face of suffering and persecution, because the message they received from the first-generation Christians was "first spoken by the Lord." Finally, Johnson concludes that Hebrews is composed to nudge the ideal community to be involved in "the world mission of the Church." He further states that, unlike "Paul [who] viewed the mission in terms of rescuing misplaced persons from peril, ... Hebrews conceived of the mission as welcoming and incorporating outsiders into the city of God."[10]

---

6   Senior and Stuhlmueller, 309–10.
7   Senior and Stuhlmueller, 309.
8   Johnson, *Going Outside the Camp*, 26, 145.
9   Johnson, 70.
10   Johnson, 151; cf. 174.

Johnson's observation of mission and confession in the Epistle to the Hebrews is helpful. He rightly acknowledges that Hebrews is not merely focused on internal matters but also on world mission. However, Johnson could have strengthened his argument of the letter writer's concern for world mission, for instance, based on the term ὁμολογέω ("to confess") in Hebrews 11:13, and the "hearing" (ἀκούω) and "speaking" (λαλέω, λέγω, ἐμφανίζω) terminologies in Hebrews 2:1–4 and 11:14. Johnson, rather, despite his contention that Hebrews says something about the church's mission to the world, appears to confine "confession" to worship and doctrinal assent as a group. Hence, he fails to highlight the evangelistic (proclaiming) aspects of ὁμολογέω.

Andreas J. Köstenberger

Andreas J. Köstenberger notes that Hebrews and 1 Peter have more to contribute to the theology of mission despite the scholarly skepticism toward these epistles. He states that these epistles "are more directly concerned with Christians' role in their world."[11] Köstenberger rightly observes that Hebrews has been the "unlikely candidate" in constructing biblical theology of mission in the New Testament since many consider the epistle to be all about "internal matters." Nonetheless, he identifies five themes in the epistle that contribute to a biblical theology of mission.

First, according to Hebrews, God is a speaking God, who in the past spoke through his prophets, "but in these last days he has spoken to us by his Son" (Heb 1:2). This implies that God "is active in mission 'today'."[12] Second, Jesus's relationship to his Father reveals that Jesus as the Son was completely dependent on his Father for his missionary task on earth. Thus, Köstenberger surmises that mission is theocentric. Third, the supremacy of Jesus, which Hebrews repeatedly asserts, indicates that Jesus definitively dealt with sin, Satan, and death. Fourth, "witness" and "race" terminologies betray the fact that Christians will face persecution and suffering. But they are to stay the course and persevere. Mission in Hebrews, Köstenberger contends, is presented as identifying with Christ and persevering in the midst of persecution rather than proclaiming the gospel. Köstenberger argues that the lexeme "witness" in Hebrews does not imply that Christians should bear witness to others. Instead, it is a call for Christians to "resist to the point of shedding blood." Finally, the expression "pilgrims" conveys the true identity of Christians on earth. Christians are on their way—because of their association with Christ—toward the heavenly city.

---

11 Köstenberger, "Mission in the General Epistles," 189–206, here 190. For a similar argument, see Köstenberger and Alexander, *Salvation to the Ends of the Earth*, 69–76.
12 Köstenberger, "Mission in the General Epistles," 194–95.

Köstenberger correctly counters the claim that Hebrews does not offer much to mission theology. The five themes he identifies in the epistle clearly point out the author's concern for mission. However, Köstenberger's assertion that Hebrews does not urge or call its audience to carry out verbal proclamation, but become passive witnesses in godliness, should be rejected.[13] Even his anecdote that Christians in a Communist context may not be involved in active evangelism is not convincing.[14] Contrary to his claim, in many contexts—whether Communist or Islamic—the number of Christians has grown because of verbal proclamation coupled with godly behavior, not just by witnessing silently. Rather, I contend that the author of Hebrews is concerned with world evangelization through verbal proclamation.

Nicolas Alexander Venditti

Nicolas Alexander Venditti wrote his doctoral dissertation comparing mission paradigms in Hebrews, Vatican II, and Liberation theologies in the context of Latin America.[15] In this study, Venditti aimed to "develop a missiological model for Latin America based on the Epistle to the Hebrews."[16] Venditti argued that the major theme of Hebrews is that "God ... speaks through his Son to his people for the world who are a pilgrim people."[17] The speaking God indicates that God is active in human affairs. This fact signals the reality that the author "has a concrete missiological paradigm relating to God's mission."[18] At the outset, the author of Hebrews declares that God through his prophets spoke in history and acted in human affairs in the past (Heb 1:1–4). But "in these last days," God's speaking has been done through his Son, Jesus Christ. Thus "God's missionary plan and purpose is being fulfilled in these 'last days'."[19]

Jesus's appointment to the office of priesthood is another sign of God's mission in Hebrews, because it is through Christ's priesthood that God speaks and reconciles humanity to himself.[20] Venditti posits: "The Priesthood of Christ was part of his mission."[21] God spoke (through the Old Covenant) and is speaking (through the New Covenant). The theme of covenant in Hebrews also indicates God's active involvement (deeds) in human history.

---

13 Köstenberger, 197.
14 Köstenberger, 199; Köstenberger and Alexander, *Salvation to the Ends of the Earth*, 72–74.
15 Venditti, "The God Who Speaks."
16 Venditti, 9.
17 Venditti, 43.
18 Venditti, 43.
19 Venditti, 45.
20 Venditti, 96.
21 Venditti, 95.

Venditti contends that "Hebrews portrays Jesus as God's missionary agent through his priesthood and sacrifice in a very unique way."[22] Hebrews also punctuates Jesus's missionary role by calling him an "apostle" who was sent by God, just like Moses was sent to carry out God's mission. He further claims that the New Covenant—which provides efficacy, atonement, and reconciliation—incorporates the Gentiles. He writes: "Non-Israel is no longer on the fringe. Now the door is open to the further fulfillment of God's missiological Covenant."[23]

Transitioning from Jesus as God's agent, Venditti argues that the mission of God's people (λαός) is to live a life characterized by "trusting-faith." Venditti intimates that the church's mission in Hebrews is centripetal.[24] He notes that the figures in Hebrews 11 are quintessential examples who demonstrated a lifestyle of "trusting-faith" through perseverance.

Venditti's work, although context-specific, is invaluable in highlighting the contribution of Hebrews to mission theology. Surprisingly, a number of works that deal with a biblical theology of mission have not consulted his study.[25] His work is vital on several points. First, he rightly contends that the mission is God's mission. Second, God's mission continues through his Son Jesus Christ, who is carrying out his priestly mission through believers' faithful lifestyle. Nonetheless, Venditti's limitation of the mission of God's people to lifestyle witnessing—as is true in Köstenberger's contention as well—is not convincing. My contention in this chapter is that the author of Hebrews expects his audience to engage both in lifestyle witnessing and verbal proclamation mission.

Hebrews' Missionary Theology

Hebrews, like any other New Testament writing, contains missionary theology. Perhaps it is pertinent to recall I. Howard Marshall's statement on the missionary nature of the New Testament: "The New Testament writings ... [are] the documents of a mission."[26] He goes on to say that

> the documents came into being as the result of a two–part mission, first, the mission of Jesus, sent by God to inaugurate his kingdom with the blessings that it brings to people and to call people to respond to it, and then the mission of his followers called to continue his work by proclaiming him as

---

22 Venditti, 53.
23 Venditti, 54.
24 Venditti, 139, 191.
25 I am thankful to Robert Gallagher, who brought Venditti's work to my attention.
26 Marshall, *New Testament Theology*, 34.

Lord and Savior, and calling people to faith and ongoing commitment to him, as a result of which his church grows.[27]

Marshall's contention is valid and applies not just to the Gospels and the Pauline Epistles; it also incorporates the General Epistles. In other words, the Epistle to the Hebrews is—as many other New Testament works are—a missional document that conveys God's redemptive mission through Jesus and his church. I am zeroing in on one particular aspect of Hebrews' theology of mission: proclamation, or evangelism.

Although detailed introductory matters on the Epistle to the Hebrews are not necessary, it is pertinent to highlight why this sermonic letter was composed and for whom it was composed. Hebrews was written to a predominantly Jewish Christian audience with a possible minority of Gentile Christians.[28]

Though in the past these Christians had stood their ground during severe persecution, they appear to be facing a serious and unprecedented danger now and fearing that it is beyond their ability to endure. The repeated warnings are evidence of the precarious position the recipients were in.[29] As such, the author calls on the audience to persevere and become mature so that they could finish the race in the manner of Jesus and following the example of the cloud of witnesses.[30] Doing so would enable them to execute their mission as God's regents on earth.

Hebrews 2:1–4: Successive Evangelism

> Therefore we must pay much closer attention to what we have heard, lest we drift away from it. For since the message declared by angels proved to be reliable, and every transgression or disobedience received a just retribution, how shall we escape if we neglect such a great salvation? It was declared at first by the Lord, and it was attested to us by those who heard, while God also bore witness by signs and wonders and various miracles and by gifts of the Holy Spirit distributed according to his will.

The warning in Hebrews 2:1–4 is couched in the author's explication of Christ's superior position in the previous chapter (Heb 1:1–14).[31] The exordium, in particular, betrays Jesus's unparalleled position. There Jesus

---

27 Marshall, 34–35.
28 Ellingworth, *Epistle to the Hebrews*, 27; Urga, "Background and Nature of Jesus' Intercession," 204. Scholars who argue for a predominantly Gentile audience include Whitlark, *Resisting Empire*, 12–16, 49–76; Schenck, *New Perspective on Hebrews*, 31–58.
29 Urga, "Background and Nature," 205.
30 Urga, "Possessions, Greed and the Christian Community," 4–5.
31 The author uses the prepositional phrase διὰ τοῦτο to make a link between the foregoing chapter (Heb 1:1–14) and the present pericope (Heb 2:1–4).

is painted as God's Son who is divine, the agent of God's creation, sustainer of creation, king-priest, and the one by whom God speaks to us in these last days. He is also superior to the angelic beings, who are God's creatures and servants.

The crux of the first warning is to alert the audience not to drift away (μήποτε παραρυῶμεν) from the gospel message they have heard. Their inattentiveness may lead them to severe theological slippage. As such, the author reminds his audience to be vigilant in holding on to the salvation message they heard.

By employing *argumentum a fortiori*, the author warns his audience that if those who transgressed the message delivered by the angels were punished, then those who disregard the message delivered by the Son would receive far worse punishment. There will be no escape for those who "neglect such a great salvation" (Heb 2:2). The warning unveils in what kind of spiritual reality the audience existed. As noted earlier, the recipients were about to go off their theological path like a ship that drifts away from its course because of a current.[32]

What is germane to this chapter from this first warning is the three key terms that convey the idea of verbal proclamation: to hear (ἀκούω), to speak (λαλέω), and to add further testimony (συνεπιμαρτυρέω). The motif of God speaking was already mentioned in the exordium. Several scholars have observed the parallel between Hebrews 1:1–4 and 2:1–4.[33] In Hebrews 1:1–4, God is depicted as the one speaking (λαλέω) both by the prophets and by his Son. Nonetheless, God's message conveyed by his Son is complete, superior, and final.

In the same vein, in Hebrews 2:1–4, God speaks through the angels, the Lord, and those who heard the Lord. The verb λαλέω, which occurs twice in the exordium, also appears twice in the current pericope:

| God spoke ... by the prophets (ὁ θεὸς λαλήσας τοῖς πατράσιν) 1:1 | declared through angels (δι' ἀγγέλων λαληθεὶς) 2:2 |
| he has spoken to us by his Son (ἐλάλησεν ἡμῖν ἐν υἱῷ,) 1:2 | declared ... through the Lord (λαλεῖσθαι διὰ τοῦ κυρίου) 2:3[34] |

Although the author here recalls God's speech through the angels for *a fortiori* argument, it is vital to note that God spoke through angels to convey his message to his people. Neglecting the message proclaimed by the angels brought about divine punishment. However, neglecting the superior message

---

32 Lane, *Hebrews 1–8*, 37; Attridge, *Epistle to the Hebrews*, 64.
33 Weiß, *Der Brief an die Hebräer*, 182; Lane, *Hebrews*, 1:37; Ellingworth, *Epistle to the Hebrews*, 134.
34 Weiß, 182.

"declared first by the Lord" would be far worse. As Kwame Bediako aptly argues, "Salvation in Christ is a serious matter; eternal issues are at stake and the subject requires the closest and most sustained attention and wholehearted response."[35] The great salvation (τηλικαύτης ... σωτηρίας) was proclaimed verbally and confirmed by four witnesses.[36]

The first proclaimer or evangelist of God who delivered the message of salvation was the Lord. The author has already pointed out that God has spoken by his Son (Heb 1:2), and here he reiterates that the gospel message that is salvific is first announced through the Lord (κύριος). The only difference between Hebrews 1:2 and 2:3 is that the title Son (υἱός) is replaced by the Lord (κύριος).[37] Scholars are divided as to when the first proclamation happened. Three primary options are proffered: his incarnation, his earthly preaching ministry, his exaltation. However, Harold W. Attridge asserts that the attempt to pinpoint the time of Jesus's declaration of the salvific message is unsustainable.[38] What makes the message of salvation great is because it was mediated and declared through the Lord. The title "Lord"—which echoes Psalm 110:1 (Heb 1:3, 13)—punctuates Jesus's divine status. The author has already asserted that Jesus is divine in the exordium (Heb 1:1–4). Again in 1:8, Jesus was addressed as "God" (θεός), and "Lord" (κύριος) in 1:10. The announcement of God's salvific message through God the Son has made the message unique and vital.

The second proclaimers of the gospel were those who directly heard the gospel message proclaimed through Jesus. These first-generation Christians were God's agents in evangelizing the recipients—the second-generation believers. Tesfaye Kassa contends, "Those who heard the message from the son were the apostles, whom he commissioned to proclaim his message. These apostles had *confirmed* the truth of the message to the Hebrews."[39] The first-generation Christians needed to proclaim to the audience in purview because they were "removed from the human ministry of Jesus and [were] dependent on the witness of others to that ministry."[40] The task of evangelism—according to Hebrews—is successive.[41] Note here that God is still the one carrying out the dissemination or attestation of the salvific gospel through human intermediaries. The content of the gospel message through the human

---

35 Bediako, "Christian Faith and African Culture," 49.
36 Kassa, "Hebrews," 1515–34, here 1518.
37 Attridge, *Hebrews*, 66.
38 See Attridge, *Hebrews*, 66–67; Ellingworth, *Epistle to the Hebrews*, 140–41.
39 Kassa, "Hebrews," 1518; emphasis in original.
40 Johnson, *Hebrews*, 88.
41 Hughes, *Epistle to the Hebrews*, 79.

witnesses is the same, for "those who heard" the message are agents who are being used by God to confirm what Jesus has already declared.

The third witness in the gospel proclamation is God the Father. He not only spoke through Jesus and through "those who heard," but he also witnessed alongside Jesus and the first-generation Christians "by signs and wonders and various miracles, and by gifts of the Holy Spirit distributed according to his will" (Heb 2:4). God the Father authenticated the gospel proclaimed both by Jesus and those who heard him preach. William L. Lane rightly posits, "The spoken word was complemented by the visible demonstration of the gospel, which foreshadowed the completion of salvation (cf. 6:5) and confirmed that the Lord continued to speak and act through the missionaries."[42]

Fourth, although God the Father gives testimony alongside his Son and the first Christians, we should also consider the Spirit as the fourth witness of the "great salvation" by gifting those who embrace the salvific message. Kassa is on the mark when he points out that "all three persons of the Godhead contributed to the preaching of this great salvation by their human agents, the apostles."[43]

In conclusion, Hebrews 2:1–4 demonstrates the successive nature of evangelism. The gospel message originated with the Lord, and "those who heard" the Lord proclaiming the "great salvation" in turn evangelized the subsequent generation. In all this, God was speaking both through his Son and his human witnesses and confirming the truthfulness of the gospel through divine manifestations and through the distribution of charismatic gifts.

Hebrews 4:1–3: Verbal Proclamation and Response to the Gospel

> Therefore, while the promise of entering his rest still stands, let us fear lest any of you should seem to have failed to reach for it. For good news came to us just as to them, but the message they heard did not benefit them, because they were not united by faith with those who listened. For we who have believed enter that rest, as he has said,
>
> > "As I swore in my wrath,
> >   'They shall never enter my rest,'"
>
> although his works were finished from the foundation of the world.

The author quotes Psalm 95:7–11 to give the recipients of his sermonic letter a second warning in Hebrews 3:7–19. In his second warning, the author uses the wilderness generation as the object lesson to alert them not to harden

---

42 Lane, *Hebrews*, 39–40.
43 Kassa, "Hebrews," 1518.

their heart and become inattentive to the voice of the Spirit.⁴⁴ The wilderness generation rebelled against the Spirit's voice, and therefore they were denied entrance into God's rest. The consequence of unbelief is severe. As such, the audience is exhorted to be watchful (βλέπετε) not to have "an evil, unbelieving heart, leading you to fall away from the living God" (Heb 3:12).

The author transitions from a severe warning against unbelief (Heb 3:7–19) to the promise of Sabbath rest (Heb 4:1–11). The inferential conjunction "therefore" (οὖν) invites the audience to apply lessons proffered in the second warning (Heb 3:12–19).⁴⁵ However, the "therefore" also signals a change in tone, as Hebrews 4:1–11 "looks at the positive side."⁴⁶ The shift in tone in Hebrews 4:1 is apparent because the author reminds his audience that there is still time to enter God's rest. This rest is given as a promise, hence the audience ought to believe it and act on it.⁴⁷ The exhortation to fear God and not to fall behind could indicate that some are struggling on the faith journey they have begun.⁴⁸

In Hebrews 4:2, the author exclaims, "For we also have been evangelized just as those ones, but the word (message) they heard did not benefit them, because they were not united in faith with those who heard."⁴⁹ This verse highlights several elements of the epistle's theology of proclamation.

First, the audience—including the author—has been evangelized by the disciples. Although the messengers are not mentioned here explicitly, we have noted above that the first-generation Christians—the apostles—proclaimed the gospel message to the audience after hearing the good news from the Lord (Heb 2:3). Alan C. Mitchell is on point to observe that the appearance of the perfect passive participle εὐηγγελισμένοι ("have been evangelized") signals that God carried out the evangelizing. Nonetheless, the divine passive does not exclude the involvement of human agency in evangelizing the audience (cf. Heb 2:2–4).⁵⁰ The author continues to use the wilderness generation heuristically. In Hebrews 4:2 he denotes that the audience has been evangelized in the same manner in which the wilderness generation was evangelized. Again, it is worthy to note here that both the wilderness generation and the audience were evangelized by witnesses or agents—whether divine or human.

---

44 Grässer, "Das Wandernde Grottesvolk: Zum Basismotiv des Hebräerbriefes," 160–79, here 167; Urga, "Background and Nature," 227.
45 Ellingworth, *Epistle to the Hebrews*, 237; Schreiner, *Commentary on Hebrews*, 133.
46 Osborne and Guthrie, *Hebrews*, 82.
47 Peterson, *Hebrews*, 119; Hughes, *Epistle to the Hebrews*, 155.
48 Peterson, *Hebrews*, 119.
49 My translation.
50 Mitchell, *Hebrews*, 96.

Second, the verb εὐαγγελίζω (*euangelizō*) and the phrase ὁ λόγος τῆς ἀκοῆς (*ho logos tēs akoēs*)—"the message they heard"—highlight the nature of the gospel message. The gospel has to go to people. The idea of the good news "going" or "coming" is captured in the ESV and NRSV rendering of Hebrews 4:2 as "good news came to us." Other translations render εὐηγγελισμένοι as "proclaimed" (LEB, NIV, NET), "preached" (ASV, AMP, CEB, KJV, NASB, NKJV), "told" (ISV), punctuating the fact that the gospel should be verbally communicated so that others could hear it. The need to convey the good news verbally in the epistle contradicts with the contention of certain scholars who claim that Hebrews promotes wordless witnessing.[51]

Third, the logical next step to verbal proclamation is the hearing of the message. Hebrews 4:2 denotes that evangelism entails not only speaking or proclaiming but also hearing. There are two separate expressions that convey the notion of hearing the good news. The first is ὁ λόγος τῆς ἀκοῆς ("the word they heard"). This phrase conveys the fact that "the message is intended for people to hear and so must be proclaimed."[52] The second expression, τοῖς ἀκούσασιν ("those who heard"), also betrays the idea of hearing the gospel. This substantival participle recalls the wilderness generation who heard the good news or the promise.

Fourth, the nature of the gospel, the evangel, not only mandates proclaimers, the message and hearing, but it also requires receiving the good news by faith. In other words, the word heard requisites one's obedience. The wilderness generation was evangelized; they heard the good news of God's promise as "God spoke ... by the prophets" (Heb 1:1). However, the message the wilderness generation heard did not benefit its hearers. Philip E. Hughes correctly argues that the goal of proclaiming the good news through proclaimers is to induce response to the gospel. He writes, "It follows that the message by itself, as an isolated concept, is of no avail; to be good news, it must be proclaimed so that there is a hearing of it; but, again, merely to hear it is in itself insufficient, for to hearing the response of faith must be added."[53]

The wilderness generation—with the exception of Caleb and Joshua—failed to benefit from the promise of rest and salvation. These two heard and responded in faith while the rest perished in the wilderness. Hence they were unable to join Caleb and Joshua. The lesson for the present audience is that

---

51 Köstenberger, "Mission in the General Epistles," 197, 199; Köstenberger and Alexander, *Salvation to the Ends of the Earth*, 72–74; Venditti, "The God Who Speaks," 139, 191.

52 Hughes, *Epistle to the Hebrews*, 157 n. 61.

53 Hughes, 157.

there is still hope for them to obtain rest and salvation, provided that they do not emulate the faithlessness of the wilderness generation.

The author reiterates the hope of entering God's rest in 4:3. He states, "For we who have believed enter [God's] rest." Unlike the wilderness generation who failed to enter, the present audience (including the author) has hope to experience God's rest. The wilderness generation did not enter since they lacked faith, but the present audience can enter because they "have believed."[54]

Hebrews 11:13–16: Godly Lifestyle and Public Declaration

> These all died in faith, not having received the things promised, but having seen them and greeted them from afar, and having acknowledged that they were strangers and exiles on the earth. For people who speak thus make it clear that they are seeking a homeland. If they had been thinking of that land from which they had gone out, they would have had opportunity to return. But as it is, they desire a better country, that is, a heavenly one. Therefore God is not ashamed to be called their God, for he has prepared for them a city.

One way the author of Hebrews encourages the recipients to persevere and carry out their missional task as a community is by listing a number of exemplars from the history of Israel. The key term in Hebrews 11 is *faith* (πίστις). At the outset of the chapter, the author provides a theoretical definition of what faith is (Heb 11:1). However, in the remaining sections of the chapter, the author concretizes what faith looks like in the lives of the patriarchs and matriarchs whom the audience ought to emulate, for these believers were commended for their faith-filled lives. The repeated use of the expression "by faith" (πίστει) throughout Hebrews 11 indicates that the exemplars lived and acted by means of faith.[55]

The expression "by faith" (πίστει) appears in the dative form throughout the chapter, beginning at Hebrews 11:3. However, our current pericope (Heb 11:13–16) uses the expression "according to faith" (κατὰ πίστιν) to emphasize that the patriarchs and matriarchs died in accordance to the faith. In other words, the phrase denotes that "these believers of the past did not allow the crisis of death to invalidate the principle of faith."[56]

---

54 Cf. Cockerill, *Epistle to the Hebrews*, 205.
55 Lane, *Hebrews 9–13*, 330.
56 Hughes, *Epistle to the Hebrews*, 477 n. 44; the change from πίστει to κατὰ πίστιν, some claim, is a mere stylistic variation. However, this argument does not hold water, as this is the only place the author utilizes κατὰ πίστιν, while he employs πίστει eighteen times throughout the chapter. See Lane, *Hebrews*, 2:345 n. *r*; Johnson, *Hebrews*, 292; Harris, *Hebrews*, 319; Bruce, *Epistle to the Hebrews*, 265.

The faithful believers demonstrated a life characterized by perseverance and a "forward-looking posture."[57] The author asserts that "according to faith these all died."[58] The immediate question which that audience or the contemporary reader might raise is "Who are 'these all'?" The most convincing answer is that "these all" refers to all those who lived, acted, and died according to faith, including "those whom the author could not mention" in his sermonic letter (cf. Heb 11:32).[59] Hebrews 11:13–16 entwines godliness and verbal proclamation. The believers' lives and actions reveal certain essential elements for the audience to mimic. The author indicates that the faithful believers *died* in accordance to the faith by carrying out the following:[60]

First, the believers died without receiving the promise. The promise was not realized during their lifetimes, but it was still a distant reality that would surely come to pass (cf. Heb 11:39).

Second, although they did not attain the promise, their hearts did not faint, nor did they despair. Instead, the faithful believers, "seeing" the promised things and "greeting" them, died. The patriarchs and the matriarchs were able to "see" because of their faith. "Their faith was not passive but active, for they 'greeted them.'"[61] Their faith in God enabled them to see the future. William Lane rightly comments: "Regulated by the principle of faith, the patriarchs were able to 'see' as certain to happen events that were 'as yet unseen.'"[62]

Third, the believers died "having declared that they were strangers and exiles on earth." These believers were not confined to godly, passive witnessing that was characterized by perseverance, gladness, and expectant (future-oriented) posture. They also engaged in declaring that "they did not belong here on earth as permanent residents because they had a glimpse of the promised Messiah and their future homeland, where they belonged as citizens."[63] The believers carried out verbal declaration (confession) among others. The reason we should render ὁμολογέω (*homologeo*) as public declaration (confession) rather than mere personal assent or acknowledgement is because the author is echoing Abraham's

---

57 Kruger, *Hebrews for You*, 175.
58 My literal translation.
59 Urga, *Reflection on Diaspora Cross-Cultural Evangelism*, 60; Allen, *Hebrews*, 553; contra Harris, *Hebrews*, 319.
60 The four participles, μὴ κομισάμενοι, ἰδόντες, ἀσπασάμενοι and ὁμολογήσαντες ("having not received," "having seen," "having greeted," and "having confessed," respectively), modify the final verb, ἀπέθανον ("died").
61 Urga, *Reflection on Diaspora*, 63.
62 Lane, *Hebrews*, 2:356.
63 Urga, *Reflection on Diaspora*, 63.

public declaration to the Hittites while he was seeking a plot of land to bury his dead wife Sarah (Gen 23:1–4; cf. Gen 47:9).

In Hebrews 11:14, the author uses two expressions that strengthen my contention that ὁμολογέω is a verbal proclamation. The phrase "those who speak" (οἱ λέγοντες) indicates that those believers used words in conveying their status as "strangers and exiles" (ξένοι καὶ παρεπίδημοί) to others. The expressions "strangers and exiles" and the reference to the city of God were the content of their verbal public declaration (cf. Heb 11:10, 14, 16). The second expression that conveys verbal proclamation is "make clear" (ἐμφανίζουσιν), or preferably, "explain." The believers not only identify themselves as citizens of another city, but they also actively seek to be in their future home. Johnson argues that, unlike the wilderness generation who desired to go back to Egypt instead of going forward to the Promised Land, these believers were future-oriented since they highlighted their status as "strangers and exiles" (Heb 11:13).[64]

The author, by mimicking the cloud of witnesses, reminds his audience that "here we have no lasting city, but we seek the city that is to come" (Heb 13:14). In other words, the author calls his audience to declare their alien status publicly, to declare that they have a city which God is preparing for them (cf. John 14:3) and to embrace death—instead of being spiritually callous, indifferent, and apathetic. Their ancestors were faithful in the face of persecutions, sufferings, and death. Their faith and hope transcended the power of death or the weapons of their persecutors; and they were able to proclaim their true status and what they were seeking, while fixing their eyes upon the promise to be realized.

Conclusion

The foregoing discussion of the three passages (Heb 2:1–4; 4:1–3; 11:13–16) demonstrates that Hebrews is on par with the Gospels and the Pauline Epistles in its contribution to theology of mission, and its concern for evangelism, or proclamation, is particularly evident.

The author has argued repeatedly that the gospel message requires intermediaries—both divine and human—in order to be communicated. The gospel communication continues from one generation to another through verbal proclamation. This successive evangelism enables every generation to have access to the good news and creates the opportunity either to reject or embrace the salvation message. The declaration of the message often happened in the context of sufferings and persecutions. However, the human

---

64 Johnson, *Hebrews*, 293.

witnesses persevered and declared their hope, their new home, and their alien status to those who needed to hear a message of hope themselves.

Our discussion has also highlighted that God is the source of the good news and the divine head is well-invested in the dissemination of the message. The author punctuates this fact by indicating that God is a speaking God who spoke in the past and who is speaking in the present. The author of Hebrews also points out that people need to listen and respond to the message proclaimed if they are to experience God's rest and salvation blessings. The author also stressed hearing the message and responding appropriately to it.

In conclusion, the theology of evangelism found in Hebrews stresses three essential facts: the salvific message requires verbal proclaimers; the notion that proclaimers are needed reveals, in turn the reality that there are people who need to hear the message; and finally, those who listen to the proclaimed message need to respond to it by faith.

Bibliography

Allen, David L. *Hebrews*. New American Commentary 35. Nashville: B&H, 2010.

Attridge, Harold W. *The Epistle to the Hebrews*. Hermeneia. Philadelphia: Fortress Press, 1989.

Barnett, Mike, ed. *Discovering the Mission of God: Best Missionary Practices for the 21st Century*. Downers Grove: IVP Academic, 2012.

Bediako, Kwame. "Christian Faith and African Culture: An Exposition of the Epistle to the Hebrews." *Journal of African Christian Thought* 13, no. 1 (June 2010): 46–57.

Bruce, F. F. *The Epistle to the Hebrews*. New International Commentary on the New Testament. Grand Rapids: Eerdmans, 1990.

Cockerill, Gareth L. *The Epistle to the Hebrews*. New International Commentary on the New Testament. Grand Rapids: Eerdmans, 2012.

Ellingworth, Paul. *The Epistle to the Hebrews: A Commentary on the Greek Text*. New International Greek Testament Commentary. Grand Rapids: Eerdmans, 1993.

Goheen, Michael W., ed. *Reading the Bible Missionally*. Grand Rapids: Eerdmans, 2016.

Grässer, Erich. "Das Wandernde Grottesvolk: Zum Basismotiv des Hebräerbriefes." *Zeitschrift für die Neutestamentliche Wissenschaft und die Kunde der älteren Kirche* 77, no. 3–4 (1986): 160–79.

Harris, Dana M. *Hebrews*. Exegetical Guide to the Greek New Testament. Nashville: B&H, 2019.

Hughes, Graham. *Hebrews and Hermeneutics: The Epistle to the Hebrews as a New Testament Example of Biblical Interpretation*. Society for New Testament Studies Monograph Series 36. Cambridge: Cambridge University Press, 2004.

Hughes, Philip E. *A Commentary on the Epistle to the Hebrews*. Grand Rapids: Eerdmans, 1977.

Johnson, Luke Timothy. *Hebrews: A Commentary*. New Testament Library. Louisville: Westminster John Knox Press, 2006.

Johnson, Richard W. *Going Outside the Camp: The Sociological Function of the Levitical Critique in the Epistle to the Hebrews*. Journal for the Study of the New Testament Supplement 209. New York: Sheffield Academic Press, 2001.

Kassa, Tesfaye. "Hebrews." In *Africa Bible Commentary: A One-Volume Commentary Written by 70 African Scholars*, edited by Tokunboh Adeyemo, 1515–34. Nairobi: WordAlive Publishers; Grand Rapids: Zondervan, 2006.

Köstenberger, Andreas J. "Mission in the General Epistles." In *Mission in the New Testament: An Evangelical Approach*, edited by William J. Larkin Jr. and Joel F. Williams, 189–206. New York: Maryknoll, 1998.

Köstenberger, Andreas J., and T. Desmond Alexander. *Salvation to the Ends of the Earth: A Biblical Theology of Mission*. 2nd ed. Downers Grove: IVP Academic, 2020.

Kruger, Michael J. *Hebrews for You*. Surrey, UK: Good Book Company, 2021.

Lane, William L. *Hebrews 1–8*. Word Biblical Commentary 47A. Dallas: Word Books, 1991.

Lane, William L. *Hebrews 9–13*. Word Biblical Commentary 47B. Dallas: Word Books, 1991.

Marshall, I. Howard. *New Testament Theology: Many Witnesses, One Gospel*. Downers Grove: IVP Academic, 2004.

Mitchell, Alan C. *Hebrews*. Sacra Pagina 13. Collegeville: Liturgical Press, 2009.

Osborne, Grant R., and George H. Guthrie. *Hebrews: Verse by Verse*. Bellingham: Lexham Press, 2021.

Ott, Craig, and Stephen Strauss. *Encountering Theology of Mission: Biblical Foundations, and Contemporary Issues*. Grand Rapids: Baker Academic, 2010.

Peters, George W. *A Biblical Theology of Missions*. Chicago: Moody Press, 1972.

Peterson, David G. *Hebrews*. Tyndale New Testament Commentaries. Downers Grove: IVP Academic, 2020.

Schenck, Kenneth. *A New Perspective on Hebrews: Rethinking the Parting of the Ways*. Lanham: Lexington Books; London: Fortress Academic, 2019.

Schreiner, Thomas R. *A Commentary on Hebrews*. Biblical Theology for Christian Proclamation. Nashville: B&H, 2015.

Senior, Donald, and Carroll Stuhlmueller. *The Biblical Foundations for Mission*. Maryknoll: Orbis Books, 1983.

Urga, Abeneazer G. "The Background and Nature of Jesus' Intercession in Heaven as a High Priest for Believers in the Epistle to the Hebrews." PhD diss., Columbia International University, 2021.

Urga, Abeneazer G. "Possessions, Greed and the Christian Community: Interrogating the Prosperity Gospel in Africa in Light of Hebrews 13:1–6." Paper presented at the Evangelical Theological Society Annual Meeting, Fort Worth, Texas, November 16, 2021.

Urga, Abeneazer G. *A Reflection on Diaspora Cross-Cultural Evangelism: An African Perspective*. Clemson: East Park Printing, 2015.

Venditti, Nicholas Alexander. "The God Who Speaks: A Comparative Study of Mission Paradigms in Hebrews, Vatican II and Liberation Theologies." PhD diss., Fuller Theological Seminary, 1998.

Weiß, Hans-Friedrich. *Der Brief an die Hebräer*. Kritisch-Exegetischer Kommentar über das Neue Testament. Göttingen: Vandenhoeck und Ruprecht, 1991.

Whitlark, Jason A. *Resisting Empire: Rethinking the Purpose of the Letter to the Hebrews*. Library of New Testament Studies 484. New York: T&T Clark, 2014.

Wright, Christopher J. H. *The Mission of God: Unlocking the Bible's Grand Narrative*. Downers Grove: IVP Academic, 2006.

Yoder, John Howard. *Theology of Mission: A Believers Church Perspective*. Edited by Gayle Gerber Koontz and Andy Alexis-Baker. Downers Grove: IVP Academic, 2014.

York, John V. *Missions in the Age of the Spirit*. Springfield: Logion Press, 2000.

Chapter 9
Superior Communication Skills
Modes of Divine Communication in Hebrews and the Implications for Christian Mission

Sigurd Grindheim

The Epistle to the Hebrews may be read as a treatise on God's manner of communication. Throughout the epistle, the author compares and contrasts God's revelation by his Son to his revelation in the old covenant. The old covenant is characterized by an impressive display of power, but it is ultimately proven to be impotent in comparison with God's revelation in Jesus, a revelation that appears in the guise of shame and weakness.

In this chapter, I will unpack the epistle's understanding of divine communication and apply the findings to the church's mission. It can be argued that the church is most effective as a witness of the Lord when that witness is borne out through suffering and humility, rather than when it comes from a position of power. The chapter is divided into two parts, with the first part developing the theology of Hebrews and the second part discussing the epistle's implications for missiology.

The Superiority of the New Covenant

Right from the outset, the author of Hebrews draws a contrast between God's communication by the prophets and his communication by his Son:

> Whereas God in the olden days had spoken to the ancestors in extensive and multifaceted fashion by the prophets, in the last of these days, he has spoken to us by a Son, the one he appointed heir of all, as the one through whom he also made the created order. (Heb 1:1–2)[1]

Some commentators note that the Greek word that is translated "extensive" (*polymerōs*) is derogative, implying a criticism of the former revelation.[2] The point should not be pressed, as the author consistently appeals to the

---
[1] All translations from the Epistle to the Hebrews are my own. Translations from other books of the Bible are taken from the NIV.
[2] Attridge, *Epistle to the Hebrews*, 37. Calvin maintained that the initial revelation's "variety was an evidence of imperfection" (*Commentaries on the Epistle of Paul the Apostle to the Hebrews*, 32). The term *polymerōs* may be used for something that is complicated and inaccessible, such as discourse that is difficult to understand (Plutarch, *Obsolescence of Oracles* 32 (427B); 33 (427F); *On Envy and Hate* 5 (537E); Strabo, *Geography* 2.4.8). It contrasts with that which is characterized by simplicity (Plutarch, *Against the Stoics on Common Conceptions* 14).

prophetic witness in order to substantiate his argument. Nevertheless, his opening words signal a priority: the new revelation takes precedence. The reason is not that the former revelation was unreliable, but that the new revelation is characterized by a different level of intimacy. Whereas God previously spoke through middlemen, he has now spoken by his Son.[3] With a modern analogy, the old and the new revelation relate to each other like a video conference to a live encounter.

It soon becomes clear that this contrast is a contrast between the old covenant, communicated through Moses, and the new covenant, revealed in Jesus.[4] The author proceeds to declare Jesus's superiority to the angels (1:4), as angels were known as the mediators of the old covenant (2:2).[5] Before he goes on to explain that Jesus is also greater than Moses (3:1–6), he warns his audience that disobedience of the gospel message is a more serious offense than disobedience of the Mosaic law (2:1–3).[6]

Jesus is superior because he is the eternal Son (1:5, 8), enthroned in heaven (1:13), but also because he is the eternal high priest. The author's most important Old Testament text is Psalm 110:4, which promises to the messianic king: "You are high priest forever according to the pattern of Melchizedek" (quoted or alluded to in Heb 5:6, 10; 6:20; 7:17). According to the author of Hebrews, to be a high priest according to the pattern of Melchizedek entails being greater than Abraham, and, therefore, by implication, greater than the Levitical priests (7:4–10). It also means to be eternal (7:3) and immortal, to be a priest "according to the power of an imperishable life" (7:16). Consequently, the author announces that God "has

---

3 This kind of distinction between the different kinds of divine revelation is also in evidence in the writings of Philo, who finds a contrast between the ten commandments that God has spoken directly and those he has spoken through Moses as his middleman. Speaking of the Mosaic law, he maintains:

> On the one hand there are the ten heads or summaries which we are told were not delivered through a spokesman but were shaped high above in the air into the form of articulate speech: on the other the specific ordinances of the oracles given through the lips of a prophet (*Rewards* 2; cf. *Decalogue* 18–19, 175; *Moses* 2.188–91).

The idea that we find in Hebrews, however, that a new revelation is deemed to be superior even to the law of Moses, would probably be unthinkable to Philo.

4 Moses was the preeminent prophet (Deut 34:10–12).

5 Similarly, Meier, "Symmetry and Theology in the Old Testament Citations of Heb 1:5–14," 522; Barrett, "Christology of Hebrews," 116. In a study on Zion traditions in Hebrews, Kiwoong Son notes that the Scriptural quotations regarding the Son in Heb 1:5–14 (from Ps 2:7; 2 Sam. 7:14; Pss 110:1; 45:6–7; 102:25–27) may be considered as Zion texts, whereas the two regarding the angels (Deut 32:43; Ps 104:4) are associated with Sinai, providing further evidence that the angels are associated with the old covenant (*Zion Symbolism in Hebrews*, 105–24).

6 "covenant" (*diathēke*) and "law" (*nomos*) are closely related terms, the former referring to the system regulating the relationship, the latter to the specific regulations.

made the first [covenant] obsolete, and what is obsolete and old is nearly extinct" (8:13).

Jesus's eternal nature is the reason why his ministry is superior to that of the old covenant. The old covenant and its institutions are ineffective. Its sacrifices and cleansing rituals were not able to provide forgiveness of sins (10:4), and they were not able to cleanse people internally (9:9). Above all, the ineffectiveness of the old covenant is seen in the fact that the job was never done. The sacrifices had to be repeated over and over, *ad infinitum*. If they had been truly effective, it would not have been necessary to repeat them.

> The law ... can never, by the same sacrifices that they are offering in perpetuity year after year, make those approaching complete. Otherwise, would they not have ceased to be offered, as the worshipers would no longer have a conscience burdened by sins after having been cleansed once for all? (Heb 10:1–2)

The impotence of the law is seen most clearly when it is compared to the ministry of Jesus. He offered himself once, and it was sufficient for all eternity. "Once, at the completion of the ages, he has appeared in order to abolish sin by the sacrifice of himself" (9:26). With his sacrifice, he secured the inward cleansing of his people. He cleanses "our conscience from dead works so that we may serve the living God" (9:14). "For with one offering he has forever made complete those who are sanctified" (10:14).

In the author's evaluation, the law failed to help the people come near to God. In fact, it brought separation instead. Its central institution, the tabernacle, was a constant testimony to the people's alienation from their God. By the very existence of two chambers, known as the Holy Place and the Most Holy Place, "the Holy Spirit is making clear that the way into the Most Holy Place was not yet disclosed while the first tent was still decreed" (9:8). In contrast, Jesus is the one who enables the people to "boldly step up to the throne of grace, so that we may receive mercy and find grace, so that we may be helped at the right time" (4:16; cf. 10:22).

Whereas Jesus brought intimacy between God and the people, the legislation at Sinai did quite the opposite. In the author's recounting, the Sinai event represented

> something tangible and a blazing fire and darkness and gloom and storm and a sound of a trumpet and words of a voice whose hearers pleaded that not another word was spoken to them, for they could not bear the order that was given: If even an animal touches the mountain it shall be stoned. And so terrifying was the manifestation that Moses said: I am terrified and trembling. (Heb 12:18–21)

The author's retelling portrays the event as a terrifying encounter. While his language is based on the account in Deuteronomy 4:11–12 LXX (cf. also Exod 19:16), he has phrased it in such a way that he also alludes to the ninth Egyptian plague. The unusual term that is translated "tangible" (*psēlaphōmenō*) echoes Exodus 10:21 LXX and its reference to "darkness over the land of Egypt, palpable (*psēlaphēton*) darkness" (Exod 10:21 LXX).[7] His selective list of details also recalls the "darkness, gloom, hurricane, on all the land of Egypt for three days" (Exod 10:22 LXX).

Unlike the evaluation of Deuteronomy 5:29, where the people are commended for their response, the author describes the people's reaction negatively. They are said to have "pleaded that not another word was spoken to them." The term that is translated "pleaded" (*paretēsanto*) has negative overtones and is used for rejection in Hebrews 12:25.[8] This apparent discrepancy between Hebrews and Deuteronomy probably owes to the fact that the author reads the Sinai and wilderness stories together and interprets the Sinai event in light of the people's disobedience.[9] His account of Moses being terrified (v. 21) is taken from the golden-calf narrative (Deut 9:19).

Once again, the negative effect of the old covenant stands out even more sharply in comparison with the new. In contrast with the terrifying Mount Sinai, the author offers a picture of Mount Zion, the scene of a euphoric celebration:

---

7 Some scholars object to this negative picture of the Sinai covenant, insisting the point is that the mountain was accessible and "touchable" (Kibbe, *Godly Fear or Ungodly Failure?*, 200). Such negative language is not unprecedented in Hebrews, however. The earthly tabernacle is called "handmade" (9:11, 24), a term with associations to idolatry. In the Septuagint, this adjective is used exclusively with idols, which are not really gods, just the work of human hands (Lev 26:1, 30; Isa 2:18; 10:11; 16:12; 19:1; 21:9; 31:7; 46:6; Dan 5:4, 23; 6:28; Judith 8:18; Wisdom of Solomon 14:8 LXX; Bel and the Dragon 5 Θ; cf. also *Sibylline Oracles* 3.606, 618, 722; 14.62; *Sibylline Fragments* 3:26; *Lives of the Prophets* 2:7; *2 Enoch* 10:6; Philo, *On the Life of Moses* 1.303; 2.165, 168).

8 Cf. also *4 Maccabees* 11:2; Luke 14:18, 19; Acts 25:11, and especially 1 Tim 4:7; 5:11; 2 Tim 2:23; Titus 3:10. Similarly, Attridge, *Hebrews*, 373; Koester, *Hebrews*, 543; Guthrie, "Hebrews," 988.

9 Kibbe notes that the author's portrayal of the law-giving at Sinai is unprecedented both in the Pentateuch and in the literature of Second Temple Judaism, although he finds a hint of it in Deuteronomy's narrative, in which the giving of the law leads to the golden-calf incident. He argues that the author's negative view of the Sinai-event stems from his reading of the wilderness generation's story as a whole, understanding Sinai in light of subsequent events. In Heb 12:21, Kibbe finds convincing evidence for this hypothesis, as the author apparently conflates the Sinai-event and the golden-calf incident. Without similarly convincing direct evidence, Kibbe also suggests that the reason for the disapproval of the Israelites was their request for a mediator, as they would eventually withdraw from this mediator just as they had withdrawn from God (*Godly Fear*, especially 201–7).

> But you have come to Mount Zion and a city of the living God, heavenly Jerusalem, and myriads of angels, a festal gathering, and a congregation of firstborn inscribed in heaven, and to a judge, God of all, and to spirits of the righteous that have been made complete, and to a mediator of a new covenant, Jesus, and to sprinkled blood that is speaking better than that of Abel. (Heb 12:22–24)

Unlike the desolate and uninhabitable Mount Sinai, God's salvation is enjoyed in a city, in the joyful fellowship of God and his people, including not only his people throughout the ages, but the angels as well.[10]

This fellowship is made possible by the mediator of a new covenant, Jesus, whose sprinkled blood is speaking better than that of Abel. Jesus's superior communication is now compared to the blood of Abel, the blood which spoke of fratricide and cried out for God to react in judgment (Gen 4:11–12). Jesus's blood, on the other hand, advocates for God to be gracious and to show favor. His blood communicates with God even more effectively, because he did not only cry from the ground; he addressed God from inside the heavenly sanctuary (Heb 9:11–12).[11]

If the law compares so poorly to the new covenant, one might be led to conclude that the old covenant had been a failure. On a variant reading of 8:8, the implication seems to be precisely that. The variant may be translated: "For because he is finding fault, he says to them" (rather than: "For because he is faulting them, he says").[12] On this reading, the object of God's "finding fault" is left unstated, but the flow of the argument might indicate that the object is the old covenant itself. This reading is unlikely to be original, however, as it is inconsistent with the author's style.[13]

A blanket dismissal of the old covenant would also come into conflict with the author's logic. Even if the old covenant is unable to bring salvation, it

---

10 Similarly, Chrysostom, *Homilies on Hebrews* 32.2.
11 Similarly, Grässer, *An die Hebräer*, 324.
12 The variant, reading the dative pronoun *autois* ("to them"), is found in the Chester Beatty Papyrus (*46) from ca. 200 CE, as well as the most reliable of the early codices, the Codex Vaticanus from the fourth century, and the third correctors of Codex Sinaiticus and Codex Claromontanus. On the other hand, the accusative *autous* ("them"), which is preferred by NA28, is attested by the original hand of Sinaiticus, Alexandrinus, and Claromontanus, as well as in Latin and Coptic translations.
13 The author frequently introduces OT quotations with the verb "says" (*legei*), but he does not include an indirect object (2:6, 12; 3:7, 15; 4:3, 7; 6:14; 9:20; 10:5, 15; 12:5, 26). It is unlikely, therefore, that the pronoun belongs with the finite verb, as it would do on the variant reading. Most probably, the pronoun is the direct object of the participle, which means that the accusative form is original (Koester, *Hebrews*, 385). However, there is also a strong argument to be made in favor of the dative *autois*. Wolmarans plausibly suggests that a scribe would have changed an original *autois* to *autous* in order to avoid the challenging idea that God found fault with his own covenant ("Text and Translation of Hebrews 8.8," 139–44).

has an essential function to serve.[14] According to Hebrews 10:3, the sacrifices prescribed by the law ensure that "there is a reminder of sins year after year." The author's argument also presupposes the revelatory function of the law, providing the necessary framework for understanding what God is doing in his Son Jesus. The institutions of the old covenant, especially the Day of Atonement (7:27; 9:6–14, 23–28: 13:11–12), but also other rituals such as the daily sacrifices (7:27; 10:11), the water of cleansing after contact with a corpse (9:13), and the covenant sacrifice (9:18–20; 12:24), are given a typological interpretation. They are understood both as the negative counterpart and as a positive prefiguration of the sacrifice offered by Jesus. As a negative counterpart, their inefficiency points to the superior quality of Jesus's sacrifice. As a positive prefiguration, they illustrate the accomplishments of his ministry: to secure forgiveness and genuine cleansing. Without the old covenant, the new covenant would be incomprehensible.

The deficiencies of the old covenant illustrate the superiority of the new covenant most clearly. In contrast to the inefficient sacrifices of the old covenant, Jesus's sacrifice is eternally effective. "For with one offering he has forever made complete those who are sanctified" (10:14). He has given his people genuine cleansing from sin (1:3; 9:14), broken down the barrier that prevented their access to God (10:20), and enabled them to approach him with boldness (4:16; 10:22).

Despite the complete superiority of Jesus's high priesthood, however, it appears that the audience of Hebrews was struggling to appreciate it. This struggle was probably the reason why they were in danger of losing heart (12:3) and abandoning the church (10:25). Their challenge is easily understood. They had been Christians for a considerable amount of time (cf. 5:12), but their experience of Christian life was characterized by shame, not glory. In the past, they had gladly accepted their suffering. The author reminds them:

> At times you were made to be a public spectacle of vitriol and oppression, at other times you stood in solidarity with those who were subjected to such treatment. For you had empathy with the prisoners and welcomed the seizure of your possessions with joy, because you knew that you had a better and lasting property. (Heb 10:33–34)

But now, all the hardship had begun to wear on them. That is apparently why the author felt compelled to encourage them with the examples of the ancestors (11:1–40). The example of Moses in particular would probably

---

14 It should also be noted that the author presupposes that the believers under the old covenant belong to the people of God and have a share in the eternal inheritance (11:1–40). However, this understanding is not predicated on their law-observance, but on their faith.

have felt directly relevant to the audience. "He chose to be abused together with the people of God rather than to have a temporary enjoyment of sin. He regarded the vitriol suffered by Christ to be a greater wealth than the treasures of Egypt because he was focusing on the reward" (11:25–26).

Preferring shame to glory, Moses served as a foreshadowing of Jesus, whose life was the ultimate paradigm of such priorities. Toward the conclusion to his epistle, the author draws the application: "Therefore, Jesus also, in order that he might make the people holy through his own blood, suffered outside the gate. Therefore, let us go to him outside the camp while we are bearing the vitriol he bore" (13:12–13).

In addition to being an excruciatingly painful form of capital punishment, crucifixion was also designed to be an extremely shameful and degrading way to die. The victims were tortured, made to carry their own cross to the place of execution, nailed naked to the cross, left to die a slow and agonizing death while any passersby could watch them writhe in pain, hear their wailing, see their despair, and observe the manner in which they faced death. All their dignity was stripped away.[15]

For all its glory, God's revelation by his Son does not appear very attractive. It does not manifest itself in a way that seems impressive and powerful in this world. To the contrary, Jesus's life was marked by weakness and shame. He appeared utterly powerless, even taking the role of a beggar, as he "offered prayers and pleas with loud cries and tears to the one who was able to save him out of death" (5:7).

However, his appearance in weakness was a carefully crafted element of the divine plan. In this way, he could fulfill his role as the ultimate high priest, and the author of Hebrews could confess: "We do not have a high priest who is unable to empathize with our weaknesses; he has been tested in all things in the same way as we, but without sin" (4:15). As the audience is going through a test of their commitment to the Lord, they are reminded that Jesus was also tested. It is likely that the author specifically has in view the traditions regarding Jesus being tempted by the devil, when his commitment to go the way of suffering and the cross was being put to the test.[16]

Precisely because Jesus has gone through the same kind of challenges that the audience is facing, he is able to facilitate their bold approach "to the throne of grace, so that [they] may receive mercy and find grace, so that

---

15 See further Chapman, *Ancient Jewish and Christian Perceptions of Crucifixion*; Hengel, *Crucifixion*; Bøe, *Cross-Bearing in Luke*, 50–78; Chapman and Schnabel, *Trial and Crucifixion of Jesus*, 299–754.

16 Similarly, Bruce, *Epistle to the Hebrews*, 116.

[they] may be helped at the right time" (4:16).[17] The term that is translated "helped" (*boētheia*) is typically used for God's deliverance in a time of distress.[18] Jesus's own experience of weakness and trials is the motivation for such deliverance to be given.

Jesus's ability to empathize and identify with the audience serves as a presupposition for the author's exhortations. As he urges them to persevere in the race set before them, he appeals to the example of

> Jesus, the originator and finisher of faith, the one who, for the joy that lay before him, endured a cross, regarding the shame as nothing, and is seated at the right hand of God's throne. Consider him, who has endured such opposition from sinners against himself, so that you do not become fatigued and lose heart. (Heb 12:2–3)

The concluding exhortation in the Epistle to the Hebrews also draws the motivation from Jesus's characteristic pattern of ministry. Observing that "Jesus also, in order that he might make the people holy through his own blood, suffered outside the gate," the author calls the audience to imitate him: "Therefore, let us go to him outside the camp while we are bearing the vitriol he bore" (13:12–13).

As Jesus suffered shame and humiliation, so is the audience encouraged to embrace the lot that is befalling them, being the object of contempt and disgrace in this world. As in the case of Jesus, so will their suffering also be crowned with victory: "For here we do not have a remaining city, but we are desiring the coming one" (13:14). They may take comfort in the fact that glory in the heavenly world corresponds to shame in this world. Like Moses before them, they may have to "be abused together with the people of God." At the same time, they may take courage from his example, as he "regarded the vitriol suffered by Christ to be a greater wealth than the treasures of Egypt because he was focusing on the reward" (11:25–26).

---

17 The author does not specify whether the throne of grace is God's throne or Jesus's throne. (NIV translates "Let us then approach God's throne of grace with confidence" [cf. NEB; NLT], but the word *God's* is not found in the Greek text.) Elsewhere in Hebrews, both Jesus (1:3, 8, 13; 10:12) and God are enthroned (8:1; 12:2). Chrysostom identifies the throne of grace as the throne of Jesus, seated at God's right hand. Assuming this interpretation, he observes that "a Priest doth not sit, but stands. Seest thou that [for Him] to be made High Priest, is not of nature, but of grace and condescension, and humiliation?" (*Homilies on Hebrews* 7.6). However, the concept of Jesus as high priest, his people's representative, lends itself better to the idea that God is seated on the throne and that Jesus ensures his people's access to it.

18 Cf. 2 Kgs 18:3; 1 Chr 12:17; Esth 4:14; Pss 19:3 (ET 20:2); 21:20 (ET 22:19); 34:2 (ET 35:2); 37:23 (ET 38:23); 59:13 (ET 60:11); 61:8 (ET 62:7); 69:2 (ET 70:1); 70:12 (ET 71:12); 107:13 (ET 108:12); 120:1–2 (ET 121:1–2); 123:8 (ET 124:8); Jer 16:19; Lam 3:57 LXX; Judith 6:21; 7:31; 8:11, 17; Sirach 34:16; 40:24; 1 Maccabees 12:15; 16:3; 2 Maccabees 8:20, 23, 35; 12:11; 13:13; 15:35; 3 Maccabees 5:35; Psalms of Solomon 5:5; 15:1.

Throughout his argument, the author of Hebrews presupposes that God's most powerful revelation appears shameful and pitiful in the eyes of the world. Ironically, the divine revelation that excelled in an outward display of power has proved to be impotent by comparison with the outwardly unimpressive communication by the Son. The audience should not be fooled, however; only those who persevere on the way of suffering with Jesus will see his glory in the end.

Mission and Power

The author of Hebrews does not specifically apply his arguments regarding Jesus's superiority to mission strategy, but his understanding of divine communication establishes a pattern that is readily applicable to the church's mission. The church is most effective as a witness of the Lord when that witness is borne out through suffering and humility, rather than when it comes from a position of power. With a rather free translation, Tertullian is often quoted as saying, "The blood of the martyrs is the seed of the church." A more literal translation reads: "The oftener we are mown down by you, the more in number we grow; the blood of Christians is seed."[19]

Although the persecution of Christians has often resulted in a near eradication of Christian believers, as in the Middle East, it is not difficult to find examples that confirm Tertullian's assessment. In recent years, Protestant churches in China and Ethiopia have experienced exponential growth during periods of violent persecution.

In many cases, however, modern missionary endeavors invite comparisons with the impressive display of power characteristic of the old covenant. The successes of Western mission have often been chronicled, bringing significant advances in education, health care, and economic development to many countries around the world. Recent studies have also drawn attention to the shortcomings of this kind of ministry.[20] In short, Western mission has brought a power imbalance between rich donors and poor recipients. Structures that originated in relatively wealthy societies were exported to less affluent economies where they could never be sustained by means of indigenous resources. The result was a power structure that prevented the young churches from reaching maturity as it created its own dynamic of perpetual dependence upon wealthy donors far removed from the actual ministry. Even when formal decisions were made locally, they would be based on the availability of funds from abroad, not on local priorities.

---

19 Tertullian, *Apologetics* 50 (*ANF* 3:55).
20 For example, Sørensen, "Polycentric Christian Mission in a Post-Colonial World," 26–39; Biehl, "Mission at Risk," 240–58.

Some of the most scathing critique of traditional Western mission has been delivered by the American missionary and scholar Jonathan Bonk. In his book *Missions and Money*, first published in 1991 and later in an expanded edition in 2006, he describes the inadvertent, negative effects of the huge economic differences between missionaries and the people they intend to serve.[21] Even if they may live in close proximity to them, the missionaries are unable to relate naturally to their neighbors due to their radically different standards of living. Bonk finds in their ministry "an inversion of the Incarnation depicted in Hebrews 4:15, effectively functioning as comfortable high priests who cannot sympathize with the vulnerabilities of the poor."[22]

Their witness is compromised, as their lifestyle inevitably testifies to the values of consumption, wealth, and social status. As Bonk puts it,

> Verbalization of "the real gospel" by missionaries who make a comfortable living from their religion is potentially obscured, subverted, or contradicted by the *good news of plenty*, of which they themselves constitute "exhibit A."[23]

One wonders if such ministry inadvertently has left the impression that to be Christian is a means of becoming rich. In response, Bonk calls for a "missiology of weakness," built on the belief in the incarnation, the cross, and weakness as power.[24] Mission should aim at imitating Jesus, whose ministry was unimpressive and insignificant by worldly standards, focused as he was on being present with ordinary people in their everyday struggles. In Bonk's assessment, Jesus "spent his adult life as a laughably parochial figure, never venturing beyond the borders of his own foreign-occupied country." Jesus's method, as Bonk describes it, was "mission by interruptions."

> Almost everything written in the Gospel accounts of his life relates directly or indirectly to the wrenching, but strategically petty, personal agendas of the ordinary men and women who pressed in on him on all sides during the few short years of his ministry. The Creator God incarnate, bent on saving the whole world, allowed himself to be interrupted by the sick, the lame, the blind, the withered, the bereaved, the outcast, the deaf, the demon possessed, the grieving.[25]

Bonk calls for a missionary strategy that imitates the methods of Jesus, and he argues that missionaries are at their most effective when they adopt a

---

21 Bonk, *Missions and Money*.
22 Bonk, 71.
23 Bonk, xxv, emphasis his.
24 Bonk, 182–88.
25 Bonk, 171–72.

lifestyle that does not differ fundamentally from that of the people they intend to serve.[26] In this way, their ministry is not hindered by economic disparities.

This kind of ministry requires sacrifice. Indeed, some missiologists have called for a renewed consideration of the Apostle Paul's advice to the unmarried in Corinth. His recommendation not to marry (1 Cor 7:27) was based on an awareness of "the present crisis" (1 Cor 7:26). Scholars are divided over whether this crisis was specific to Corinth at the time of writing, such as a famine, or whether it referred to the eschatological tribulations that take place in the time leading up to Christ's return.[27] In any case, Paul proceeds to explain that "those who marry will face many troubles in this life, and I want to spare you this" (1 Cor 7:28). At the same time, he makes it clear that to marry is a good thing and that the one who gets married does well (1 Cor 7:38).

The Protestant ethos has traditionally focused on Paul's positive stance toward marriage and devoted less attention to his words of warning. Whatever Paul meant by "the present crisis," however, it is worth asking whether his logic is applicable to certain forms of mission activity today. Missionary families from wealthy countries that are sent to some of the poorer places on earth face impossible dilemmas. The responsibility they feel to provide for their children's health care and education requires that they maintain a lifestyle that makes them incomparably wealthier than the people they are intended to serve. They have to choose between caring adequately for their children or committing themselves to the ministry by accepting a standard of living that brings them closer to the people.

In their case, the apostle's words are immediately applicable: "An unmarried man is concerned about the Lord's affairs—how he can please the Lord. But a married man is concerned about the affairs of this world—how he can please his wife—and his interests are divided" (1 Cor 7:32–34). There is every reason to ask, therefore, if certain forms of cross-cultural ministry are best served by missionaries that have committed themselves to celibacy or childlessness.[28]

---

26 The trend to pursue so-called "incarnational ministry" embraces many important biblical principles, such as loving and identifying with one's neighbor; but it is fundamentally flawed, as it fails to account for the unique nature of the incarnation as God's decisive, once-for-all intervention to save the world through his Son. It is not an event to be repeated or imitated. See Billings, "Incarnational Ministry and Christology," 187–201.

27 For the former, see Winter, *After Paul Left Corinth*, 216–22; for the latter, see Fitzmyer, *First Corinthians*, 315; for a mediating position, see Thiselton, *First Epistle to the Corinthians*, 573; Ciampa and Rosner, *First Letter to the Corinthians*, 337.

28 William Isley calls for a specific spirituality for the missionary vocation. Based on Paul's exhortations in 1 Cor 7, he suggests that this spirituality may include celibacy ("A Spirituality for Missionaries," 306–7). With a more modest proposal, Larry Poston recommends to "give serious consideration to the ideas of celibacy of limited family

Bonk's call for conformity with Christ's method of ministry represents an important corrective to the priorities of traditional Christian mission, but a balanced evaluation will conclude that he has overstated his case. A biblical scholar may question the exclusive focus on the earthly ministry of Jesus as it is recorded in the Gospels. Certainly, his continued ministry through the Holy Spirit, recorded in the Book of Acts (cf. Acts 1:1), should not be ignored. While this mission continued Jesus's focus on underprivileged people, it does demonstrate some of the exact characteristics that Bonk insists are absent in Jesus's ministry. Primary attention is given to major cities, until the gospel reaches Rome, the world capital of the time.

Conclusion

Perhaps a model inspired by God's different modes of communication according to Hebrews may offer a more balanced perspective. Such a model might suggest that there is room for substantial outlays of money and material resources in the church's mission, just as there was a necessary place for the impressive display of power provided in the old covenant. Wise stewardship of money may be necessary in order to proclaim the gospel in areas in which it is poorly known or not known at all.

But, just as the old covenant did not bring God's forgiveness, so can the church's use of such resources never be a means of salvation. The success of mission can never be measured by the size of its budget, the splendor of its buildings, the number of employees, the distinction of educational degrees, or the political and societal influence of its members. In order to accomplish its true purpose, to proclaim the kingly rule of God, the church's mission has no other means of communication than what was demonstrated by its Lord Jesus: a witness that is borne out through suffering and identification with the poor and marginalized. The role of an effective missionary is not to be a king, but a servant, not an object of admiration, but, in many cases, an object of scorn. Such a missionary conforms to the paradigm that is set by God's own communication, in his suffering Son, Jesus.

The concluding exhortation in the Epistle to the Hebrews will always represent a clarion call to everyone involved in mission: "Therefore, Jesus also, in order that he might make the people holy through his own blood, suffered outside the gate. Therefore, let us go to him outside the camp while we are bearing the vitriol he bore" (Heb 13:12–13).

---

size" ("Role of Higher Education in the Christian World Mission," 172). For the view that Paul's advice to remain unmarried primarily aims at childlessness, see Gundry, "Affliction for Procreators in the Eschatological Crisis," 141–68.

Bibliography

The Ante-Nicene Fathers. Edited by Alexander Roberts and James Donaldson. 10 vols. 1885–87. Repr. Peabody: Hendrickson, 1994.

Attridge, Harold W. *The Epistle to the Hebrews*. Hermeneia. Minneapolis: Fortress, 1989.

Barrett, C. K. "The Christology of Hebrews." In *Who Do You Say That I Am? Essays on Christology in Honor of Jack Dean Kingsbury*, edited by Mark Allan Powell and David R. Bauer,110–27. Louisville: Westminster John Knox, 1999.

Biehl, Michael. "Mission at Risk: Structures of Co-Operation in the Perspective of 'Mission and Power.'" In *Mission and Power: History, Relevance, and Perils*, edited by Atola Longkumer, Jørgen Skov Sørensen, and Michael Biehl, 240–58. Regnum Edinburgh Centenary Series 33. Oxford: Regnum, 2016.

Billings, J. Todd. "Incarnational Ministry and Christology: A Reappropriation of the Way of Lowliness." *Missiology* 32 (2004): 187–201.

Bøe, Sverre. *Cross-Bearing in Luke*. Wissenschaftliche Untersuchungen zum Neuen Testament II, 50–78. Tübingen: Mohr Siebeck, 2010.

Bonk, Jonathan J. *Missions and Money: Affluence as a Missionary Problem—Revisited*. Revised and expanded ed. American Society of Missiology Monograph Series 15. Maryknoll: Orbis, 2006.

Bruce, F. F. *The Epistle to the Hebrews*. Rev. ed. New International Commentary on the New Testament. Grand Rapids: Eerdmans, 1990.

Calvin, John. *Commentaries on the Epistle of Paul the Apostle to the Hebrews*. Calvin's Commentaries. Translated by John Owen. Grand Rapids: Baker, 1979.

Chapman, David W. *Ancient Jewish and Christian Perceptions of Crucifixion*. Wissenschaftliche Untersuchungen zum Neuen Testament II/244. Tübingen: Mohr Siebeck, 2008.

Chapman, David W., and Eckhard J. Schnabel. *The Trial and Crucifixion of Jesus: Texts and Commentary*. Wissenschaftliche Untersuchungen zum Neuen Testament 344. Tübingen: Mohr Siebeck, 2015.

Ciampa, Roy E., and Brian S. Rosner. *The First Letter to the Corinthians*. Pillar New Testament Commentary. Grand Rapids: Eerdmans, 2010.

Fitzmyer, Joseph A. *First Corinthians: A New Translation with Introduction and Commentary*. Anchor Bible 32. New Haven: Yale University Press, 2008.

Grässer, Erich. *An die Hebräer (Hebr 10,19–13,25)*. EKK XVII/3. Zürich: Benziger/Neukirchener, 1997.

Gundry, Judith M. "Affliction for Procreators in the Eschatological Crisis: Paul's Marital Counsel in 1 Corinthians 7.28 and Contraception in Greco-Roman Antiquity." *Journal for the Study of the New Testament* 39 (2016): 141–68.

Guthrie, George H. "Hebrews." In *Commentary on the New Testament Use of the Old Testament*, edited by G. K. Beale and D. A. Carson, 919–95. Grand Rapids: Baker, 2007.

Hengel, Martin. *Crucifixion: In the Ancient World and the Folly of the Message of the Cross*. Translated by John Bowden. Philadelphia: Fortress, 1977.

Isley, William L. "A Spirituality for Missionaries." *Missiology* 27 (1999): 299–309.

Kibbe, Michael H. *Godly Fear or Ungodly Failure? Hebrews 12 and the Sinai Theophanies*. Beihefte zur Zeitschrift für die neutestamentliche Wissenschaft 216. Berlin: De Gruyter, 2016.

Koester, Craig R. *Hebrews: A New Translation with Introduction and Commentary*. Anchor Bible 36. New York: Doubleday, 2001.

Meier, John P. "Symmetry and Theology in the Old Testament Citations of Heb 1:5–14." *Biblica* 66 (1985): 504–33.

Poston, Larry. "The Role of Higher Education in the Christian World Mission: Past, Present and Future." In *Teaching Them Obedience in All Things: Equipping for the 21st Century*, edited by Edgar J. Elliston. Evangelical Missiological Society Series 7, 144–84. Pasadena: William Carey Library, 1999.

Son, Kiwoong. *Zion Symbolism in Hebrews: Hebrews 12:18–24 as a Hermencutical Key to the Epistle*. Paternoster Biblical Monographs. Milton Keynes, UK: Paternoster, 2005.

Sørensen, Jørgen Skov. "Polycentric Christian Mission in a Post-Colonial World: A Lutheran Perspective." In *Mission and Power: History, Relevance, and Perils*, edited by Atola Longkumer, Jørgen Skov Sørensen, and Michael Biehl, 26–39. Regnum Edinburgh Centenary Series 33. Oxford: Regnum, 2016.

Thiselton, Anthony C. *The First Epistle to the Corinthians*. New International Greek Testament Commentary. Grand Rapids: Eerdmans, 2000.

Winter, Bruce W. *After Paul Left Corinth*. Grand Rapids: Eerdmans, 2001.

Wolmarans, Johannes L. P. "The Text and Translation of Hebrews 8.8." *Zeitschrift für die Neutestamentliche Wissenschaft und die Kunde der älteren Kirche* 75 (1984): 139–44.

Chapter 10
African American Missiological Use of Hebrews
From the Antebellum Period to the Twentieth Century

Jessica N. Janvier

> The sacred history of God's liberation of his people would be reenacted in the American South. In times of despair, they repeated the story of Exodus and took hope. As a slave named Polly eloquently explained to her mistress: "We poor creatures have need to believe in God, for if God Almighty will not be good to us some day, why were we born? When I heard of his delivering his people from bondage, I know it means the poor Africans."[1] —Albert J. Raboteau

Religious historians and theologians have well recognized the central role of the black church in racial uplift efforts in the years following the Civil War. In his classic work, *Slave Religion: The "Invisible Institution" in the Antebellum South*, Albert J. Raboteau notes that

> black religious institutions have been the foundation of Afro-American culture. An agency of social control, a source of education, and a refuge in a hostile white world, the black [c]hurch has been historically the social center of Afro-American life.[2]

While this is true, African American Christianity cannot be reduced *in toto* to the ethical dimensions of its lived theology. What is much less explored are the quotidian concerns of pastoral theology present within African American Christianity—namely, the means of edifying one's congregation in the faith and being missional while in the midst of racial hostility. Exploring the use of the Epistle to the Hebrews by post-Civil-War black evangelicals provides a window to view the way in which the black church in this period simultaneously worked to uplift the race—benefiting the broader community—worked to theologically edify its members, and to be missional.

The Epistle, Jewish Christians, and African American Christianity

African American Christianity, birthed in the antebellum period, produced a unique missiology that intertwined seeking to convert the lost sinner *and* the

---

1 Raboteau, *Fire in the Bones*, 12.
2 Raboteau, *Slave Religion*, ix.

lost Christian in the United States. African American missiologists, wrestling with the theodicean dilemma of how fellow Christians could condone their enslavement, led them to the conclusion that a part of their missiology needed to address unChristlike Christianity in an effort to see authentic Christianity flourish in America. Stressing the crucicentric characteristic of the evangelical theology of the era, inflections of Christus Victor, and necessitating liberation as a part of the gospel and outwork of Christian faith, also found expression in their Christianity. The Epistle to the Hebrews became a useful tool in their missiological efforts.

The title, ΠΡΟΣ ΕΒΡΑΙΟΥΣ or "To the Hebrews," reflects the mind of the early church's belief that the text which most modern English Protestant Bibles simply refer to as "The Epistle to the Hebrews," had as its original audience a group of Jewish Christians.[3] As Christianity spread outside its primal Jewish environment, evolving beyond simply being an ethnic Jewish movement to include Gentile converts and God-fearers, the focus of the nascent group quickly shifted from a narrative concerning Jewish people to one that primarily concerned Gentiles.[4] Christianity began as a movement that initially enabled shared space between Jewish and Gentile believers in the Messiahship of Jesus, along with shared temple and synagogue space between Jewish-Christians and non-Jewish-Christians. Quickly socially fracturing, historian Shaye Cohen notes that "before long the Jesus movement was no longer Jewish; it became something different, a social phenomenon of its own."[5] He argues that this division, "sometimes called 'the separation of Christianity from Judaism,' usually called 'the parting of the ways,'" occurred by the early second century.[6]

Jewish-Christians represented a short-lived midpoint between Judaism and Christianity, in which their socioreligious location attracted persecution from within their faith communities and by outside detractors. Likewise, African American Christianity, particularly in its early antebellum setting and into the twentieth century, shared a similar socioreligious location that

---

[3] Papyri 46 in the early part of the third century is the first to designate this title for the text. There has been long standing argument whether Hebrews is a letter or a sermon. Contemporary English Bibles in Protestant milieus sidestep this debate over the title, whether it should be designated as an epistle or a sermon by reflecting the papyri 46 title.

[4] Gentiles who converted to Christianity from a purely pagan background, as opposed to Gentiles who were already associated with and attracted to Judaism, referred to as "God-fearers," were often differentiated within the Second Temple period, as reflected in the New Testament. An example of this is Cornelius, who is described in Acts 10 as εὐσεβὴς καὶ φοβούμενος τὸν θεόν [devout and God-fearing].

[5] Cohen, "In Between: Jewish-Christians and the Curse of the Heretics," 207–8.

[6] Cohen, 207–36.

also incurred ethnic and religious persecution, reflecting much of the spirit and timbre of Jewish-Christianity's woes.

Both groups experienced the world as disordered, not only in a metaphysical spiritual sense but in their lived political realities as oppressed people. For early Jewish-Christians, salvation carried within it the notion of freedom from communal and personal sin, along with the notion of God's justice accompanying the birth of a new world to come. This is reflected in the summarizing nomenclature of their message as εὐαγγέλιον, a word that carried both religious and political connotations in their context to announce the reign of a new king and the benefits of his kingdom.[7] For African Americans, their Christianity, as Howard Thurman succulently expressed, was oriented toward "what the teachings and the life of Jesus have to say to those who stand, at a moment in human history, with their backs against the wall."[8] For both groups, pressed by the world around them, their *pistis* reflected an expectation of God's δικαιοσύνη, which does not separate his giving of righteousness and justice.[9]

African American Christians saw their lives in the stories of the New Testament and perhaps even more so in the Scriptures of the Hebrew Bible. The socioreligious environment of Jewish-Christians and the Israelites of the Old Testament, which intertwined the need for physical and spiritual deliverance, resonated with enslaved Africans in America and their descendants. As early Jewish-Christians understood a sign of the messianic age to be the coming in of the Gentiles, bringing to fullness their scriptural

---

[7] Contra the common definition of εὐαγγέλιον by evangelical historians to simply mean "good news." For a representation of this view, see Noll, *Rise of Evangelicalism*, 16. There he says,

> The English word *evangelical* comes from a transliteration of the Greek noun *euangelion*, which was regularly employed by the authors of the New Testament to signify the glad tidings—the good news, the gospel—of Jesus who appeared on earth as the Son of God to accomplish God's plan of salvation for needy humans.

Noll, like others, draws from the etymology but neglects the word's contextual meaning. However, cultural and linguistic scholarship has refuted this notion and brought back into the forefront of New Testament studies the social, religious, and political connotations of εὐαγγέλιον in the period of the New Testament. See the work of Deissmann, *Light from the Ancient East*; and Koester, *Ancient Christian Gospels*. See also Evans, "Mark's Incipit and the Priene Calendar Inscription," 67–81; Dechow, "The 'Gospel' and the Emperor Cult," 63–88. Additionally, for a New Testament primer that brings out εὐαγγέλιον in its context and is integrated with New Testament studies, see Wright and Bird, *New Testament in Its World*.

[8] Thurman, *Jesus and the Disinherited*, 1.

[9] For the "righteous/justice" definition, see Liddell and Scott, *Greek-English Lexicon*, 429. See also Keener, *Romans*, 56–57. He notes in the opening of his excursus on *dikaiosunē* that "In common Greek, *dikaiosunē* normally meant 'justice.'"

narrative,[10] African Americans imbibed the stories of the Hebrews as their own, not in a supersessionist articulation of the faith but to understand the character of God and his dealings with the marginalized in the world. It allowed them to view their enslavement as temporary, encouraging one another with spirituals such as "Didn't My Lord Deliver Daniel?" which declared, "Didn't my Lord deliver Daniel? Then why not every man?"

Gleaning hope from God's deliverance of his people—both through physical and spiritual liberation—antebellum African American Christianity into the black church of the twentieth century expressed a Christianity that understood salvation as God's work to free his people from enslavement to *sin* and *Sin*'s bewitching prompting of humans to enslave.[11] Utilizing Scripture this way shaped their self-understanding, faith outlook, Scripture interpretation, and missionary endeavors; thus, African American Christianity carried a distinct social flare and theological orientation within American Christian traditions, reminiscent of early biblical faith and deeply molded by stories of the Hebrew people, from Old to New Testament. With their unique place in American Christianity in view, the focus of this essay, in line with this compendium's quandaries, is to explore a specific phenomenon in the life of African American Christianity—namely, how this body utilized the auspicious text of the Epistle to the Hebrews in their missiological endeavors from the antebellum period up until the twentieth century.

The African American Matrix of Scripture Interpretation

Before one can adequately understand how early African American Christianity into the twentieth century utilized the Epistle to the Hebrews in their missiological endeavors, it is necessary to grasp the context of African American Scripture interpretation within this time period. As noted above, African American Christianity from its inception had to deal with the theodicean problem of believing in the goodness of a God who was also the God of their enslavers, whose holy writ was used to justify their

---

10 To see this perspective from an Eastern Orthodox point of view, see De Young, *Religion of the Apostles*. For a Protestant perspective, see Wright and Bird, *New Testament in Its World*.

11 *Sin* with a capital S follows the understanding of many contemporary New Testament theologians who see Paul's use of *sins* and *Sin* differentiated: *sins* pertaining to trespasses, while *Sin* pertaining to "an active agent that manipulates"—as seen in McKnight, *Reading Romans Backwards*, 151. In other words, *Sin* is a power active in the world, not merely something we do that misses the mark of God's righteousness. *Sin* produces *sins* through humanity in the world.

enslavement.[12] For this task, the musings of twentieth-century theologian Howard Thurman, who grappled with theodicy in the black church by looking back on the experience of enslaved black Christians, is instructive. Thurman's opening question in *Jesus and the Disinherited* has served as a representative of the everyday angst many black Christians wrestled with early on.

> This is the question which individuals and groups who live in our lands always under the threat of profound social and psychological displacement face: Why is it that Christianity seems impotent to deal radically, and therefore effectively, with the issues of discrimination and injustice on the basis of race, religion and national origin? Is this impotence due to a betrayal of the genius of the religion, or is it due to a basic weakness in the religion itself?[13]

Thurman's grandmother was born a slave and was a fervent Christian, and yet she was scarred by slaveholding Christianity.[14] She greatly influenced her grandson as he wrestled with the paradoxical relationship between the racist Christianity within his milieu and the Christianity of his grandmother and

---

12 My intention here is not to ignore Kongolese and Angolan Christianity, which some of the enslaved Africans brought with them already as Christians before the encounter with the Transatlantic Slave Trade. Crucial to my understanding of this stream of early African American Christianity has been Daniels, "Kongolese Christianity in the Americas of the 17th and 18th Centuries," 215–26. Additionally, the work of Vince Bantu on early African Christianity with its possible influence and stretching into Western Africa also comes to mind when thinking about early African American Christianity. See Bantu, *Multitude of All Peoples*. With this, I am not discounting the Christianity that accompanied some enslaved Africans but including these Christians in the theodicean wrestle of African Americans, as they found themselves enslaved by their brothers and sisters in Christ. This dilemma was not theirs alone, as some early Anglo-American slave owners militated against evangelizing slaves because of the connection in their context between conversion and manumission. This problem was eliminated by first demanding that slaves who were becoming a part of the early American Christian community had to vow that they did not seek manumission as a means for conversion and subsequently, eliminating through legal adjudication the connection between conversion and manumission—a connection that early Catholic Kongolese and Angolan Christians maintained and argued for. See further, "Kongolese Christianity in the Americas," 215–26.

13 Thurman, *Jesus and the Disinherited*, xix.

14 Thurman, 20. Thurman's grandmother's Christian faith was in tension with her relationship with slaveholding Christianity. Thurman recounts in *Jesus and the Disinherited* his grandmother's faith and the love she had for Scripture. He recalls that he frequently read to her from the Bible but noticed that she would not allow him to read the letters of Paul to her. "During the days of slavery," she said, "the master's minister would occasionally hold services for the slaves. Old man McGhee was so mean that he would not let a Negro minister preach to his slaves. Always the White minister used the text: 'Slaves, be obedient to them that are your masters ... as unto Christ.' Then he would go on to show how it was God's will that we were slaves and how, if we were good and happy slaves, God would bless us. I promised my Maker that if I ever learned to read and if freedom ever came, I would not read that part of the Bible."

other slaves. His diagnosis of the problem is characteristic of how African American Christianity came to deal with this issue. He maintained that the inability of Christianity within the dominant culture to deal effectively with discrimination and racism in its various forms was due to a separation of Jesus and his message from his first-century Jewish context as an oppressed person, within an oppressed people group living under the Roman Empire.

> We begin with the simple historical fact that Jesus was a Jew. The miracle of the Jewish people is almost as breathtaking as the miracle of Jesus. Is there something unique, some special increment of vitality in the womb of people out of whose loins he came, that made of him a logical flowering of a long development of racial experience, ethical in quality and Godlike in tone? It is impossible for Jesus to be understood outside of the sense of community which Israel held with God. ... How different, might have been the story of the last two thousand years on this planet grown old from suffering if the link between Jesus and Israel had never been severed![15]

This broken link produced a Christianity estranged from its original social context, arranging social hierarchies and visions for Christian flourishing and missional praxis antithetical to Jesus's social teachings. Thurman argued,

> It reveals to what extent a religion that was born of a people acquainted with persecution and suffering has become the cornerstone of a civilization and of nations whose very position in modern life has too often been secured by a ruthless use of power applied to weak and defenseless peoples.[16]

Thurman was responding to the history of Western European Christianity's legacy, in Catholic and Protestant iterations, of expansion associated with violence, usurping of lands, and oppression justified through religious dogmas. These means of living out Christian faith in ecclesiology, evangelism, and missional practices were considered within the bounds of orthopraxy during eras of Western colonization and imperialism. Thurman, who was a fervent advocate of integration, pastoring the integrated Church for the Fellowship of All during his lifetime, was not discounting the voices of protest against this presentation of Christian imagination present in this history. However, it was an acknowledgment of the prevailing vision of Christendom and missiology draped in Gomes Eannes de Zurara's prayers in

---

15 Thurman, 5–6.
16 Thurman, 2.

the West.[17] This vision would become a part of Western national mythologies and Christian identity, especially in the United States. Advocates of slavery and abolitionists alike shared a vision of the rightness of Christianity's augmentation through this legacy of expansion.[18] The result was a profound distinction between African American Christianity—which had been birthed through the crucible of Western expansionism—and the dominant culture's expression of the faith. From early on, Black Christians during the antebellum period sensed this difference and would go on to articulate their faith through the paradigm of, as David Walker so eloquently summarized, the "God of the Blacks."

African American Christianity was largely birthed through the Awakening Revivals of the seventeenth and eighteenth centuries. Before these evangelical revival surges, few widespread conversions of enslaved Africans were recorded. Organizations such as the Society for the Propagation of the Gospel (SPG) among Anglicans, mainly in the South, were created with the purpose of convincing reluctant slave owners to allow for their slaves to be evangelized and receive Christian catechetical learning. Puritanical and Reformed congregations in the North fared with little success as well.

The first large-scale conversions of Blacks in America occurred during the revival period alongside many White converts. Early evangelicalism provided a brief lowering of the social barriers between Black and White Christians, and others. In its early years, evangelicalism had various contributors that helped spread the revival-birthed movement because of its simple message and openness to untrained laypeople proselytizing.

Among early White leading voices in the Northern colonies was a Northampton preacher, Jonathan Edwards, who witnessed a diverse acceptance to the message centered around spiritual rebirth, spiritual equality, and repentance. For the Southern colonies, George Whitefield's ministry in the 1740s proved to be electric, as diverse crowds of thousands responded to

---

17 A brief overview of Gomes Eannes de Zurara's diary recalling his experience as a theologian who saw the early era of what would become the Transatlantic Slave Trade is captured in Raboteau's *A Fire in the Bones*, 8. He records,

Zurara, who witnessed the brutal separation and sale of a group of captive Africans and was moved to tears by the event, later repented that his emotions had gotten the better of his Christian conscience, because the slaves would receive the benefits of civilization and Christianity. Zurara's rationalization was repeated for more than four centuries by successive generations of Christian apologists for slavery.

For a fuller look into Zurara's world, see Gomes Eannes de Zurara, *Chronicle of the Discovery and Conquest of Guinea*.

18 Edwards, "Latter-Day Glory Is Probably to Begin in America," 56–57; also Beecher, "A Plea for West," 130.

his preaching. When Whitefield and Edwards brought their characteristically evangelical preaching to their colonial milieus, they entered plural Christian contexts, which before evangelicalism struggled to view each other as authentically Christian. The ability of evangelicalism to bridge theological and ecclesiological divisions became a hallmark of the movement.

However, for detractors, primarily those from established churches, it represented a danger because of the possibility of upsetting existing social hierarchies, which were undergirded by church doctrines. Paul Harvey conveys this sentiment well in noting the alarm of an upper-class Virginia man processing the revivals: "Evangelical persuasions, said one Virginia legal authority, would be the means by which, 'Wives are drawn from their Husbands, Children from their Parents, and Slaves from Obedience of their Masters.'"[19]

This concern over social boundaries was not purely imagined by detractors, as the early evangelical revivals provided greater opportunity for women exhorters, along with, and more importantly for our purposes, strands of open antislavery sentiment to be heard.[20] Early Baptists and Methodists, for example, pressed for slavery to be abolished and for slaveholders to be purged from their membership. Nevertheless, experiencing much resistance judicially and from slaveholding members, antislavery rhetoric and the possibility of spiritual equality pouring out into temporal equality died down with the calming of revival fires in the South and post-Revolutionary-War zeal in the North. In 1785, Thomas Coke led the Methodists in jettisoning their antislavery position, and Baptists followed suit.[21]

The spiritual equality and hierarchy-upsetting ability present within early evangelical Christianity was the hope that African American Christians initially relied on to overcome a form of Christianity that maintained discriminatory racial ideals. It was in this period that the self-theologizing Black church was born, which produced the first independent "African" churches in America, Black denominations, and hush-harbor services that provided a means for enslaved African Americans to worship and theologize according to their own convictions. Black evangelicals, like Richard Allen, George Liele, Jarena Lee, and many unnamed enslaved and free Black preachers, helped to lead and spread the tradition of evangelical

---

19 Harvey, *Christianity and Race in the American South*, 35.
20 For concerns over social boundaries and antislavery sentiment beyond Harvey's *Christianity and Race*, see Kidd and Hankins, *Baptists in America*, 1–148; Wesley, *Thoughts Upon Slavery*. For concerns specifically over gender boundaries, see Brekus, *Strangers & Pilgrims*, 1740–1845.
21 Gewehr, "Great Awakening in Virginia, 1740–1790," 190–92.

Christianity, giving them a "common grammar of belief"[22] with White Christians within this tradition, nevertheless they went on to establish a form of evangelicalism distinct among themselves.[23] In response, Raboteau, in "The Black Experience in American Evangelicalism," says,

> Black Evangelicals, no less than whites, sought conversion, attended revivals, and viewed their lives in biblical terms. There was a fundamental difference between the two, however. American slavery and the doctrine of white supremacy, which rationalized and outlived it, not only segregated evangelical congregations along racial lines, but also differentiated the black experience of evangelical Christianity from that of whites. The existence of chattel slavery in a nation that claimed to be Christian, and the use of Christianity to justify enslavement, confronted black Evangelicals with a basic dilemma, which may be most clearly formulated in two questions: What meaning did Christianity, if it were a white man's religion, as it seemed, have for blacks; and, why did the Christian God, if he were just as claimed, permit blacks to suffer so?[24]

As Raboteau displays in his description of black evangelicalism, it had much in common with traditional White evangelicalism and its characteristic markers, which David Bebbington has defined in his classic quadrilateral. Bebbington contends,

> There are four qualities that have been the special marks of Evangelical religion: *conversionism*, the belief that lives need to be changed; *activism*, the expression of the gospel in effort; *biblicism*, a particular regard for the Bible; and what may be termed *crucicentrism*, a stress on the sacrifice of Christ on the cross. Together they form a quadrilateral of priorities that is Evangelicalism.[25]

For Black evangelicals, these characteristics remained true, but added to Bebbington's quadrilateral within the African American experience of evangelicalism would be the core theological tenet of liberation. Whereas White evangelicalism utilized crucicentrism, stressing the sacrifice of Christ, which pertains to their theology of atonement, Black evangelical atonement theology could be said to have inflections of Christus Victor, as this atonement model more frequently incorporated the Exodus paradigm, which centers

---

22 Albert J. Raboteau quotes his former graduate student, Glaude, *Slave Religion*, 331.
23 I am echoing Raboteau's language in "Black Experience in American Evangelicalism," 98–116. In this essay he notes that black evangelicals created a "distinctive evangelical tradition."
24 Raboteau, 101.
25 Bebbington, *Evangelicalism in Modern Britain*, 2.

God's work of liberation.[26] In other words, while Black evangelicals did not shy away from traditional evangelical crucicentric atonement theology, there was also an understanding that there is no complete work of God's salvation without liberation affecting the spiritual and temporal realities. *God Struck Me Dead: Voices of Ex-Slaves* recounts the conversion stories of manifold former slaves, in which there are many accounts telling the story of how they understood themselves as being freed from sin by the cross of Christ.[27] Yet there are also numerous accounts that depict former slaves understanding their salvation through the Exodus paradigm as well.[28] On this, Raboteau notes:

> A white Union Army chaplain working among freedman in Decatur, Alabama, commented disapprovingly on the slaves' fascination with Exodus: "There is no part of the Bible with which they are so familiar as the story of the deliverance of Israel. Moses is their *ideal* of all that is high, and noble, and perfect, in man. I think they have been accustomed to regard Christ not so much in the light of a *spiritual* Deliverer, as that of a second Moses who would eventually lead *them* out of their prison-house of bondage."[29]

Whereas sectors of White evangelicalism could make peace with and provide rationalizations for Black enslavement and other inequalities following the antebellum period, in articulating the meaning of Christianity, Black evangelicalism necessitated liberation and crucicentrism in their soteriology, missiological praxis, and scriptural interpretation. The Black evangelical experience remained within the root system of African American Christianity into the twentieth century.[30]

---

26 For more on the Christus Victor model of atonement, see Aulén, *Christus Victor*. Additionally, see Boyd, "Christus Victor View," 23–66. There he argues for Christus Victor as the organizing atonement model rather than Penal Substitution. He argues that Christus Victor holds within it the paradigm of substitutionary atonement, while centering the victory of Christ in a way that atonement models do not. Boyd also notes in this essay the preference of contemporary black liberation theologians for Christus Victor. Whereas black liberation theologians would seek to do away with substitutionary atonement altogether, I would argue that early black evangelicals married the categories of Penal Substitution and Christus Victor.

27 Clifton Johnson, ed., *God Struck Me Dead*.

28 For more on slaves and their Exodus paradigm, see Raboteau, *Fire in the Bones*, 17–36. Also, see Noll, "Image of the United States as a Biblical Nation, 1776–1865," 43–45.

29 Raboteau, *Fire in the Bones*, 33.

30 This is not to say that the influence of Black evangelicalism ended in the twentieth century. I am in agreement with theologian Jonathan Walton who argues that the Black church is "principally evangelical in its Great Awakening origins and contemporary orientation." See Walton, "Response: What Black Prophetic Politics?" However, I do want to acknowledge the presence of Black liberation theology, womanism, and Pentecostal theology that are now influentially a part of African American Christianity in a way they were not in the twentieth century.

With this in mind, we are now on good ground to understand how African American Christianity employed the Epistle to the Hebrews missionally in their tradition.

The Missiological Use of the Epistle in African American Christianity

African American scriptural interpretation within our time period frequently tied together the sacrificial work of Christ for the forgiveness of sins and the liberating work of God's power to deliver his people. Seeing themselves in and as God's people, they blurred the lines between the stories of Scripture concerning the Hebrew people and themselves. Therefore, what resulted in the main thrust of their missional ethic, living in a country they understood to be out of sync with the God they had come to know in worship, in suffering, and through his Word and Spirit was a primarily homeward bound missional focus that saw as its most imperative task both an outward and inward focus. The outward was concerned with Christianizing Christians—converting those around them practicing a malformed version of Christianity that allowed for racial discrimination and oppression to abide within its midst. They believed, as the Reverend Francis Grimke expressed:

> God has promised to give to his Son the heathen for his inheritance, and the uttermost parts of the earth for his possession and in that promise this land is included. Christianity shall one day have sway even in Negro-hating America ... Jesus Christ is yet to reign in this land. I will not see it, you will not see it, but it is coming all the same. In the growth of Christianity, true, real, genuine Christianity in this land, I see the promise of better things for us as a race.[31]

The inward focus was more conventional, in that it focused on converting the lost.[32] This inward and outward, homeward focus reflected a missiology that put its emphasis on seeing genuine Christian discipleship flourish, mirroring the first command of the Great Commission.[33] During the antebellum period, the Epistle to the Hebrews was no exception to this

---

31 Grimké, *Works of Francis J. Grimké*, vol. 2, 269.
32 Emphasizing the homeward bound focus isn't to ignore those within the Black Church of this time period that left America to carry the gospel elsewhere. It is only to acknowledge that the majority, for a variety of reasons, were not able to participate in missions outside of the US. It is also important to acknowledge that it was not due to lack of zeal for global missions, either. A glimpse into this zeal can be seen in Raboteau, *Fire in the Bones*.
33 The Greek of Matthew 28:19—πορευθέντες οὖν μαθητεύσατε πάντα τὰ ἔθνη, βαπτίζοντες αὐτοὺς εἰς τὸ ὄνομα τοῦ Πατρὸς καὶ τοῦ Υἱοῦ καὶ τοῦ Ἁγίου Πνεύματος—has as its first command to make disciples, suggesting this as the emphasis and "going" being a perceived given.

tradition and was employed in the African American scriptural matrix to accomplish its goal.

Outward and Inward

The outward focus appears in petitions of the Revolutionary period, a time in which the first wave of Great Awakening revivals had provided a surge in African American conversions. The language undergirding revolutionary zeal mixed ideologies of natural rights and Christian idealism. Within this context, African American Christians petitioned for freedom on the basis that authentic Christianity, which they hoped to see in America, demanded it. In the Petition of 1779, by Slaves of Fairfield County for the Abolition of Slavery in Connecticut, they argued "[O]ur Right (by the Laws of Nature and by the whole Tenor of the Christian Religion, so far as we have been taught) [is] to be free."[34] Looking at the nature of the Christian religion and utilizing the Epistle to the Hebrews, they argued in the petition Slaves' Appeal to Thomas Gage, Royal Governor of Massachusetts, that slavery subverted the faith and prevented the command given in Hebrews 13:1, not allowing brotherly love to flourish. In an interconnected use of Scripture, characteristic of evangelicals in this period, one can observe how the epistle was included in their missiological focus to call for true Christianity to arise.

> By our deplorable situation we are rendered incapable of shewing our obedience to Almighty God how can a slave perform the duties of a husband to a wife or parent to his child How can a husband leave master and work and cleave to his wife How can the wife submit themselves to there husbands in all things. How can the child obey thear parents in all things. There is a grat number of us sencear ... members of the Church of Christ *how can the master and the slave be said to fulfil that command Live in love let Brotherly Love contuner* and abound Beare yea onenothers Bordenes How can the master be said to Beare my Borden when he Beares me down whith the Have chanes of slavery and operson against my will and how can we fulfill our parte of duty to him whilst in this condition and as we cannot searve our God as we ought whilst in this situation ...[35]

---

34 "Petition of 1779 by Slaves of Fairfield County," Petition of 1779 for the abolition of slavery in Connecticut. Accessed February 28, 2022. http://www.hartford-hwp.com/archives/45a/021.html. I am greatly indebted to the work of Bowens, *African American Readings of Paul* for this section in directing me to this text and others that display the masterful index she provides of African American use of the Apostle Paul.

35 "Slaves' Appeal to Thomas Gage, Royal Governor of Massachusetts, May 25, 1774." Internet Modern History Sourcebook. Accessed February 28, 2022. https://sourcebooks.fordham.edu/mod/1774slavesappeal.asp.

As seen in these early petitions, slavery was considered untenable and not able to be reconciled with the faith. As a result, chattel slavery would appear in evangelistic efforts—in situations when the speaker was able to speak freely, as an abject expression of evil. John Jea, a formerly enslaved preacher and, once freed, a missionary who traveled within the United States and beyond, used slavery in this way. In his 1811 biographical text *The Life, History, and Unparalleled Sufferings of John Jea, the African Preacher: Compiled and Written by Himself* Jea intended to tell the story of his life and use it as a means of converting the lost, and he used the Epistle to the Hebrews in this way. In speaking about unsaved people's fear of death in an effort to get them to turn to life, he said

> Thus desperate sinners, that know there is a sentence of eternal death proclaimed against them in the court of the king of kings, and that from this sentence there is no appeal nor escape, must needs be in continual fears, such foresee the fearful image of death that disturbs their quiet, and St. Paul expresses himself, *"Through fear of death were all their lifetime subject to bondage." Heb. ii. 15. That is, they are like so many wretched slaves, that tremble under the inhuman power of a merciless tyrant.*[36]

Jea, who was a frequent evangelist to the enslaved, like many preachers used vivid examples of life to bring home meaning for his listeners. Death as a slave master, as portrayed in Hebrews 2:15, as cruel as merciless human slave masters, was an illustration that would have connected deeply with his audience, serving well his missional purposes.

Jea represented the more conventional, inward missional focus but also maintained the outward African American missional thrust that sought to work for authentic Christianity in America. This intermingled missiology comes across in his writing, sermonizing, and especially in arguments with White Christians who tried to convince him that enslavement was supported biblically. This intermingled missiology seen in Jea also found expression in the lives of other Black Christians, such as Maria Stewart, who combined politics, exhortation, and activism in their Christian witness. Stewart, an educated black woman, born free in Connecticut in 1803, was a maverick in her time. She was, as Lisa Bowens in *African American Readings of Paul: Reception, Resistance, and Transformation* acknowledges, the "first American-born woman of any race to lecture to men and women on political themes" and a fervent preacher, following in the legacy of Julia Foote and Jarena Lee.[37] Venturing out to educate and strengthen Christians through

---
36 Jea, *Life, History, and Unparalleled Sufferings of John Jea*.
37 Bowens, *African American Readings of Paul*, 227–28.

the ministry of the word and in efforts to win converts, her outstanding life made her a frequent target, as her life was often threatened because of her Christian witness. Her troubled life occasioned her writing "Mrs. Stewart's Farewell Address to Her Friends in the City of Boston." Preparing to leave Boston to avert death, her farewell address was a recollection of her work and ministry, as well as an encouragement to her listeners to continue their sojourning in faith. She encouraged them by saying "To my brethren and sisters in the church I would say, be ye clothed with the breast-plate of righteousness, having your loins girt about you with truth, prepared to meet the bridegroom at his coming."[38] Echoing the Apostle Paul, she invited her audience to see themselves in her life, not shying away from the sacrifices they would have to make if they were to continue as Christians reflecting her example of Christian witness. She admonished her listeners with Hebrews 11:25, along with other immersed Scripture and allusions.

> Well was I aware that if I contended boldly for his cause I must suffer. *Yet I chose rather to suffer affliction with his people than to enjoy the pleasures of sin for a season.* And I believe that the glorious declaration was about to be made applicable to me that was made to God's ancient covenant people by the prophet: "Comfort ye, comfort ye, my people; say unto her that her warfare is accomplished, and that her iniquities are pardoned. I believe that a rich reward awaits me, if not in this world, in the world to come." O, blessed reflection. The bitterness of my soul has departed from those who endeavored to discourage and hinder me in my Christian progress: and I can now forgive my enemies, bless those who have hated me, and cheerfully pray for those who have despitefully used and persecuted me.[39]

As seen above in the petitioners, through John Jea and Maria Stewart, African American use of the Epistle to the Hebrews in the antebellum period in their missiology did not consist of systematic expositions but fit more within the realm of narrative theology. Their frequent use of scriptures nestled together reflected their tendency to view their faith through the "whole Tenor" of their religion. For the Epistle to the Hebrews, it was another means to not only understand the grand schematic of Christianity but as a way of understanding their lives in God. African American theologian Reverend Dr. James Earl Massey, sees this in his commentary on the Epistle to the Hebrews,

> The beneficial precedents set by faith heroes and heroines have encouraged and sustained Christian believers of subsequent generations during hard

---

38 Stewart, "Mrs. Stewart's Farewell Address to Her Friends."
39 Stewart.

times. The patterned accounts in Hebrews 11 meant much to believing African Americans during the slavery era as they endured the condition Miles J. Jones aptly described in one of his homilies as "historic denigration and dehumanization"... Bound together with those enumerated in the biblical account, and bound with Jesus, by the core of faith and experienced struggle, African American slaves knew what it meant to feel like "strangers and foreigners" (11:3) and to "desire a better country" (11:16), one in which God would be rightly honored and in which they could live in freedom. They "saw" the desired freedom from a distance, and greeted it, their view always ahead to the realization yet to be.[40]

Moving beyond the era of slavery, the epistle does encounter systematic expression in the writing of Charles Octavius Boothe in *Plain Theology for Plain People*. The Baptist minister, known as "the apostle of uplift" was a former slave living in the first decades after the Civil War.[41] Stating his endeavor for the text, he noted "The writer would therefore remind the reader that this little book's only mission is to help *plain* people in the study of the *first* principles of divine truth."[42] For his sharecropper audience, the twenty-seven references to the Epistle to the Hebrews followed the outline of systematic theology textbooks. Outside of his writing, Boothe's life exhibited his commitment to missional endeavors and to the church as a means for racial uplift. His legacy as a church planter, one of which was Dexter Avenue Baptist Church in Montgomery, Alabama, bore the fruit of being a catalyst for the Civil Rights Movements under the church's pastoral leadership of Martin Luther King, Jr.

The tradition within African American Christianity of seeing the Epistle to the Hebrews through the lens of narrative theology, a means of understanding black Christian life, and the intertwined inward and outward, homeward focused missiology provided the context for black Christian participants in the Civil Rights Movement for seeing it as a Christian effort. Because of this tradition within the African American scriptural matrix of interpretation, Fannie Lou Hamer could bind together the idea of personal, sanctifying faith and missional faith that empowered her as a believer to participate in the work she was doing in the Civil Rights Movement. Demonstrating this, she said in a 1966 interview,

> Because of what Christ has said has been said and until all of the scriptures have been fulfilled, because when the time comes he will make the war

---

40 Massey, "Hebrews," 457.
41 Boothe, *Plain Theology for Plain People*, vii.
42 Boothe, 3.

cease, even to the end of the earth because God knows I believe in that Holy life. That's stupid to some people, but I believe it. I believe it with enough faith that made me what I am today because through prayer—prayer is the substance, *faith is the substance of things hoped for and the evidence of things not* [seen] … Some of the work we're doing today, we prayed for this a long time and today its becoming a reality, an actual reality … (emphasis mine).[43]

Hamer's usage of the Epistle to the Hebrews aligns with her community's tradition, reflecting the ways African American Christianity utilized the text in their missional thinking, which long embodied a Christianity that could confront inauthentic expressions of the faith that upheld oppression, in the hopes that an authentic Christian faith would flourish, because they believed it was the answer to the ills they saw around them.

Bibliography

Beecher, Lyman. "A Plea for West." In *God's New Israel: Religious Interpretations of American Destiny*, edited by Conrad Cherry, 122–30. Chapel Hill: UNC Press, 1998.

Boothe, Charles Octavius. *Plain Theology for Plain People*. Bellingham: Lexham Press, 2017.

Bowens, Lisa. *African American Readings of Paul: Reception, Resistance, and Transformation*. Grand Rapids: Eerdmans, 2020.

Boyd, Gregory. "Christus Victor View." In *The Nature of the Atonement: Four Views*, edited by James Beilby and Paul R. Eddy, 23–66. Downers Grove: InterVarsity Press, 2009.

Brekus, Catherine A. *Strangers & Pilgrims: Female Preaching in America, 1740–1845*. Chapel Hill: University of North Carolina Press, 1998.

Cohen, Shaye J. D. "In Between: Jewish-Christians and the Curse of the Heretics." In *Partings: How Judaism and Christianity Became Two*, edited by Hershel Shanks, 207–36. Washington, DC: Biblical Archaeology Society, 2013.

Daniels, David D. "Kongolese Christianity in the Americas of the 17th and 18th centuries." In *Polycentric Structures in the History of World Christianity*, edited by Klaus Koschorke and Adrian Hermann, 215–26. Harrassowitz: Wiesbaden, 2014.

Dechow, Jon F. "The 'Gospel' and the Emperor Cult: From Bultmann to Crossan." *Forum Third Series* 3, no. 2 (2014): 63–88.

Deissmann, Adolf. *Light from the Ancient East: The New Testament Illustrated by Recently Discovered Texts of the Graeco-Roman World*. Eugene: Wipf & Stock, 2004.

---

43 Wisconsin Historical Society, "Romaine—Anne Romaine Interviews, 1966–1967."

De Young, Stephen. *The Religion of the Apostles: Orthodox Christianity in the First Century.* Chesterton: Ancient Faith Publishing, 2021.

de Zurara, Gomes Eannes, and Charles Raymond Beazley. *The Chronicle of the Discovery and Conquest of Guinea.* London: Hakluyt Society, 1899.

Edwards, Jonathan. "The Latter-Day Glory Is Probably to Begin in America." In *God's New Israel: Religious Interpretations of American Destiny*, edited by Conrad Cherry, 54–60. Chapel Hill: University of North Carolina Press, 1998.

Evans, Craig A. "Mark's Incipit and the Priene Calendar Inscription: From Jewish Gospel to Greco-Roman Gospel." *Journal of Greco-Roman Christianity and Judaism* 1 (2000): 67–81.

Gewehr, Wesley M. "The Great Awakening in Virginia, 1740–1790." *Baptist Quarterly* 5, no. 4 (1930): 190–92.

Grimké, Francis. *The Works of Francis J. Grimké.* Vol. 2. Washington, DC: Associated Publishers, 1942.

Harvey, Paul. *Christianity and Race in the American South: A History.* Chicago: University of Chicago Press, 2016.

Jea, John. *The Life, History, and Unparalleled Sufferings of John Jea, the African Preacher: Compiled and Written Himself.* https://docsouth.unc.edu/neh/jeajohn/jeajohn.html.

Johnson, Clifton H., ed. *God Struck Me Dead: Voices of Ex-Slaves.* Eugene: Wipf and Stock, 2011.

Keener, Craig S. *Romans.* New Covenant Commentary Series. Cambridge: The Lutterworth Press, 2009.

Kidd, Thomas S., and Barry Hankins. *Baptists in America: A History.* Oxford: Oxford University Press, 2015.

Koester, Helmut. *Ancient Christian Gospels: Their History and Development.* Harrisburg: Trinity Press, 1990.

Liddell, Henry George, and Robert Scott. *A Greek-English Lexicon.* Oxford: Clarendon Press, 1996.

Massey, James E. "Hebrews." In *True to Our Native Land: An African American New Testament Commentary*, edited by Brian K. Blount et. al., 444–60. Fortress Press: Minneapolis, 2007.

McKnight, Scot. *Reading Romans Backwards: A Gospel of Peace in the Midst of Empire.* Waco: Baylor University Press, 2019.

Noll, Mark. "The Image of the United States as a Biblical Nation, 1776–1865." In *The Bible in America: Essays in Cultural History*, edited by Mark Noll and Nathan O. Hatch, 39–58. New York: Oxford University Press, 1982.

Noll, Mark A. *The Rise of Evangelicalism: The Age of Edwards, Whitefield and the Wesleys.* Downers Grove: InterVarsity Press, 2010.

"Petition of 1779 by Slaves of Fairfield County." Petition of 1779 for the abolition of slavery in Connecticut. http://www.hartford-hwp.com/archives/45a/021.html.

Raboteau, Albert J. "The Black Experience in American Evangelicalism: The Meaning of Slavery." In *African-American Religion: Interpretive Essays in History and Culture*, edited by Timothy E. Fulop and Albert Raboteau, 98–116. New York: Routledge, 1997.

Raboteau, Albert J. *A Fire in the Bones: Reflections on African-American Religious History*. Boston: Beacon Press, 1996.

Raboteau, Albert J. *Slave Religion: The "Invisible Institution" in the Antebellum South*. Oxford: Oxford University Press, 1978.

"Slaves' Appeal to Thomas Gage, Royal Governor of Massachusetts, May 25, 1774." Internet Modern History Sourcebook. Accessed March 2, 2022. https://sourcebooks.fordham.edu/mod/1774slavesappeal.asp.

Stewart, Maria. "Mrs. Stewart's Farewell Address to Her Friends in the City of Boston." Iowa State University: Archives of Women's Political Communication. Accessed March 2, 2022. https://awpc.cattcenter.iastate.edu/2020/11/20/mrs-stewarts-farewell-address-to-her-friends-in-the-city-of-boston-sept-21-1833/.

Thurman, Howard. *Jesus and the Disinherited*. Boston: Beacon Press, 1996.

Walton, Jonathan L. "Response: What Black Prophetic Politics?" *Religion Dispatches*, 30 Sept. 2009, religiondispatches.org/iresponsei-what-black-prophetic-politics/.

Wesley, John. *Thoughts Upon Slavery*. London: R. Hawes, 1774.

Wisconsin Historical Society. "Romaine—Anne Romaine Interviews, 1966–67 (Archives Main Stacks, SC 1069, Folder 1)." Freedom Summer Digital Collection. Accessed March 2, 2022. https://content.wisconsinhistory.org/digital/collection/p15932coll2/id/14003/.

Wright, N. T., and Michael F. Bird. *The New Testament in Its World: An Introduction to the History, Literature, and Theology of the First Christians*. Grand Rapids: Zondervan Academic, 2019.

Chapter 11
From Milk to Meat
Implications in Hebrews for Missiological Developments in Discipleship Methods

Sarah Lunsford

The central command within the Great Commission is to "make disciples." The question of how to do so, therefore, is a chief concern for missiology. Discipleship methods today are radically different than they were one hundred years ago. We are seeing a fruitful harvest among the nations like never before in Christian history.[1] There is much to be applauded in recent discipleship developments, but they are not without controversy and critique. A missiological reading of Hebrews 5:11–6:3 offers abundant insight into the process of spiritual growth and discipleship methods to use among believers. The teachings and examples presented in Scripture speak both affirmation and admonition to modern discipleship methods.

Overview of Missiological Developments in Discipleship Methods

Roland Allen: Unhindered Indigenous Methods
In 1927, Roland Allen initiated a revolution in missionary methods when he wrote *The Spontaneous Expansion of the Church*.[2] He critiqued the missionary discipleship methods of his time as being excessively controlling and urged missionaries to avoid hindering the work of the Spirit, particularly through their heavy teaching requirements. Instead, they should equip indigenous churches to rely on the Word and the Spirit for their spiritual growth. Allen suggested that the Bible is descriptive rather than prescriptive regarding the methods we use in spreading the gospel and that missiological methods depend on the various details of each context.[3]

Donald McGavran: Homogenous Church-Growth Methods
Building on these concepts, from the 1960s to the 1980s Donald McGavran and a few of his colleagues at Fuller Theological Seminary initiated the

---
[1] Pocock, Van Rheenen, and McConnell, *Changing Face of World Missions*, 9.
[2] Allen, *Spontaneous Expansion of the Church*.
[3] Allen, *Missionary Methods*, 6, 119, 197. See also Dayton and Fraser, *Planning Strategies for World Evangelization*, 195. Allen's argument can be seen as the voice behind such oft-repeated comments such as "The Bible is not a handbook for methodology" (Crawley, *Biblical Light for the Global Task*, 10–13).

church growth movement, which urged missionaries to utilize scientific methodologies, including testing, refining, and replicating whichever methods produce fruit.[4] The church growth school put a top priority on evangelism and worked to overcome hindrances to church growth. They taught the importance of cultural adaptation of the message, along with easily reproducible methods, planting indigenous churches that are encouraged to multiply.[5]

Perhaps McGavran's most important insight focused on the homogenous unit principle (HUP). HUP postulates that because people prefer not to cross cultural barriers to accept the gospel—church growth and reproduction will occur (indeed, *should* occur)[6]—most rapidly in homogenous units, such as people groups and family units, rather than amid cultural diversity.[7] Inspired by the HUP, an emphasis on *oikos* evangelism and discipleship developed, which encourages the spread of house churches following natural family and affinity group lines.[8] The HUP also led to a people-group emphasis in missiological strategy. However, "the nations" (*ethne*) did not refer to modern political and geographical boundaries separating countries but to cultural/ethnic groups.[9] At this point, missiological strategies and methods subtly shifted in emphasis from the mandate to "make disciples" to a focus on reaching "all peoples."[10] Zeal to reach every unreached people group within a generation motivated missionaries to prioritize methods that resulted in rapid multiplication.[11] Contrary to the limitations of knowledge-based discipleship methods, a new

---

4 McGavran advocated using strategies and methods that would intentionally encourage church growth. Fuller Theological Seminary soon became the spearhead institution for this way of thinking, as missiologists such as Alan Tippett, Peter Wagner, Arthur Glasser, Charles Kraft, and Ralph Winter joined McGavran and worked together to form the school of thought which came to be known as the "Church Growth Movement" (McGavran and Hunter, *Strategies that Work*, 16–18). See also Terry and Gallagher's chapter on "Church Growth Movement" in *Encountering the History of Missions*, 304–20.

5 Crawley, *Global Mission*, 271–74.

6 "The normal clannishness of the new group being discipled must be cheerfully accepted and, indeed, encouraged" (McGavran, *Bridges of God*, 130). See also McGavran and Hunter, *Church Growth Strategies That Work*.

7 McGavran, *Understanding Church Growth*, 223, and McGavran, *Bridges*, 130.

8 Wolf, "Oikos Evangelism: The Biblical Pattern," 110–17 and Simpson, *Houses that Change the World*. *Oikos* is the Greek word for "household."

9 The Great Commission says to make disciples of all *ethnē*. McGavran, *Understanding*, 40; McGavran, *Ethnic Realities and the Church*, 21; Winter and Koch, "Finishing the Task," 15–25.

10 Mulholland, "Donald McGavran's Legacy to Evangelical Missions," 64–70. The church growth movement received heavy criticism for its emphasis on numerical growth without adequate theological foundations. See Peters, *Theology of Church Growth*, 255; Terry and Gallagher, *Encountering the History*, 304–320; and Engel and Dyrness, *Changing the Mind of Missions*, 67–80.

11 Mott, *Evangelization of the World*.

emphasis on obedience-based discipleship developed. Thus, measurement for spiritual growth shifted from head-knowledge of doctrinal categories to outward evidence of obedient application of scriptural principles.[12]

David Garrison: CPM-Driven Methods

In the 1990s, missionaries who followed principles initiated by Allen and influenced by McGavran's church growth school began to see astounding numbers of conversions and church multiplication as the gospel ignited and spread throughout previously unreached people groups. David Garrison launched a study of these church planting movements (CPMs) to uncover their key traits and characteristics for the purpose of recreating this phenomenon. Garrison noted, based upon all the CPMs studied, that the gospel is spread widely but planted in small house churches along natural affinity groups that are programmed from the start to reproduce rapidly. These house churches rely on inductive Bible study and the Holy Spirit as their teachers, and they operate under local lay leadership.[13] Garrison also noted that most CPMs occurred in an atmosphere of suffering, persecution, and social instability.[14]

Within a short time, most North American mission agencies set their objectives on sparking CPMs among unreached people groups (UPG). In China, Ying Kai developed a CPM-driven discipleship method, Training for Trainers (T4T),[15] which was employed by East Asia missionaries with the International Mission Board (IMB), under the direction of Steve Smith. The T4T method was so effective as a CPM strategy that it was quickly exported to other mission regions. Similarly, David Watson created the extremely popular Disciple Making Movement (DMM) method, also incorporating CPM strategies and principles.[16] These and other CPM-driven discipleship methods minimize direct missionary involvement as much as possible to encourage indigenous ownership, using simple and easily reproducible methods. The key shared concepts to these current discipleship methods include obedience-based discipleship—with skepticism toward theological teaching—rapid reproducibility, small *oikos* groups, and reliance on the Spirit.[17]

---

12 Patterson, "Spontaneous Multiplication of the Church," 610; Payne, *Discovering Church Planting*, 103–20.

13 Garrison, *Church Planting Movements*, 171–98.

14 Garrison, 121–38. Social instability refers to a people group feeling displaced in the world, a people without a secure place and identity in the current geographical and political landscape.

15 See Smith and Kai, *T4T*.

16 Watson and Watson, *Contagious Disciple Making*. See also Trousdale, *Miraculous Movements*.

17 Rhodes, *No Shortcut to Success*, 79–95.

Analysis of Discipleship Making

There is no doubt missionary methods are more productive now than ever before in the history of the church. However, the missiological outcry against many of these methods is growing louder. Common objections to these methodologies suggest numerical growth does not necessarily reflect spiritual growth and these discipleship methods are overly managerial, reductionistic, and pragmatic.[18]

Today's missiological methods for discipleship lack theological reflection.[19] However, this may not be a surprising consequence for accepting the notion that "the Bible is not a handbook for methodology."[20] Robert Gallagher offers a profound critique of Roland Allen's original hermeneutic. Gallagher contends that Scripture *does* speak to missiological methods when the author emphasizes a normative principle through repeated patterns and direct commentary.[21] In that light, Hebrews 5:11–6:3 can be explored for its author's intended implications for discipleship methods, particularly regarding the topics of obedience-based discipleship, rapid reproducibility, *oikos* churches, and reliance on the Spirit.

Lessons from Hebrews 5:11–6:3

> We have much to say about this, but it is hard to make it clear to you because you no longer try to understand. In fact, though by this time you ought to be teachers, you need someone to teach you the elementary truths of God's word all over again. You need milk, not solid food! Anyone who lives on milk, being still an infant, is not acquainted with the teaching about righteousness. But solid food is for the mature, who by constant use have trained themselves to distinguish good from evil.
>
> Therefore, let us move beyond the elementary teachings about Christ and be taken forward to maturity, not laying again the foundation of repentance from acts that lead to death, and of faith in God, instruction about cleansing rites, the laying on of hands, the resurrection of the dead, and eternal judgment. And God permitting, we will do so.[22]

---

18 Engel and Dyrness, *Changing the Mind*, 67–80; Pocock, Van Rheenen, and McConnell, *Changing Face of World Missions*, 11. For a very thorough description and analysis of CPM-focused discipleship methods, see Rhodes, *No Shortcut to Success*.

19 For a robust and thorough critique, see Rhodes, *No Shortcut*. See also Ashford and Bridger, "Missiological Method," 31; Ashford, ed., *Theology and Practice of Mission*, 294; Verkuyl, *Contemporary Missiology*, 205.

20 Allen, *Missionary Methods*, 6, 119, 197; Crawley, *Biblical Light*, 10–13.

21 Gallagher, "Missionary Methods," 8.

22 Unless otherwise noted, all Scripture quotations come from NIV.

Milk or Meat: Teachings about Righteousness

This passage highlights a contrast between spiritual infants who rely on milk and the spiritually mature who can eat solid food or "meat" (cf. 1 Cor 3:1–2; Eph 4:14). The milk refers to elementary teachings, while the meat refers to the deeper teachings about righteousness. The author of Hebrews interrupted his theological teachings about Jesus as high priest to confront his audience about their unwillingness to understand his teaching. Thus, this passage emphasizes the ability to process deeper theological teachings as a significant part of spiritual maturity.

The author continues to describe the content of the elementary "milk" teachings. The "foundation of repentance from acts that lead to death, and of faith in God" is the core description, while matters related to outward religious practices and the final judgment fill out some included topics.[23] The "meat" teachings build upon the elementary teachings by going deeper.[24] The author wants to move beyond the gospel basics to flesh out the fundamental concept of righteousness; it is not by works that lead to death, but by faith in Christ.[25]

Lazy or Trained: Holding Fast the Faith

The spiritually immature are "no longer trying to understand," which is also translated as "sluggish" and "lazy." They are not simply babies who are incapable of understanding, but they are babies by choice—a choice the author reprimands.[26] On the other hand, the spiritually mature "by constant use have trained themselves." This concept of training does not refer to external practice in doing good works, as if acting like a Christian eventually increases their understanding of theological teachings.[27] The author describes the spiritually mature as those who persistently hold fast to the elementary teachings of righteousness until they truly know them.[28] It is important to understand that the Hebraic concept of "knowing" is far more than mere cognitive assent (Jas 2:19). Rather, it is both relational and experiential, as a man "knows" his wife.[29] This relationship between endurance and spiritual

---

23 Guthrie, *Hebrews*, 205.
24 Schreiner, *Commentary on Hebrews*, 175.
25 Schreiner, 172.
26 Schreiner, 169.
27 Cf. 2 Timothy 3:5. All believers have the potential for godliness, but the mature are in a state of realized potential, similar to how a student has the potential to play an instrument which is realized when the lesson has been acquired (Kiley, "Note on Hebrews 5:14," 501–3).
28 Köstenberger, *Handbook on Hebrews through Revelation*, 1–67; Schreiner, *Hebrews*, 174.
29 Ortlund, *Deeper: Real Change for Real Sinners*, 71–72. See also Ferris, "Leadership Development in Missions Settings," 460.

maturity is repeated often in Hebrews and other Scriptures (Heb 3:6; 3:14; Rom 5:2–6; 1 Tim 1:19; 3:9; 2 Tim 1:14; 1 Thess 5:21).

William Lane demonstrates how this passage perhaps emphasizes the cost of discipleship, particularly in the context of suffering and persecution. The inability to endure suffering and persecution is judged a moral failing, a failing that results from not absorbing theological instruction.[30] In contrast, the spiritually mature are actively holding fast to the theological teachings of righteousness and are trained through the process. The author of Hebrews refers to this training through perseverance again in 12:11 (NKJV), "Now no chastening seems to be joyful for the present, but painful; nevertheless, afterward it yields the peaceable fruit of righteousness to those who have been trained by it."[31]

There is no inertia described in the spiritual pilgrimage. We are either holding fast, overcoming, enduring, and persevering or we are growing weary, falling away, and becoming sluggish.[32] The object of our steadfast endurance is our hope in Christ. "We might have strong consolation, who have fled for refuge to lay hold of the hope set before us. This hope we have as an anchor of the soul, both sure and steadfast" (Heb 6:18–19 NKJV). One might picture the spiritual process like a man in the ocean. He can hold fast to the anchor because if he loses his grip, the waves will pull him away. Holding fast to the anchor of hope is an active growing and strengthening process. As waves of trial and temptation pull at new believers, they look to the anchor of their souls, to Jesus the pioneer and perfecter of their faith. They come to "know" the depth of meaning to the elementary theological teachings and feed on ever stronger meat. Their discernment about righteousness is trained as they actively hold fast to theological teachings. In other words, their doctrinal knowledge sustains them in their obedient pursuit of the kingdom of righteousness.

Throughout Hebrews the author addresses several trials that his audience was probably facing, including persecution and suffering (Heb 2:14–15; 10:32–35), weariness from the long obedience of living as spiritual pilgrims (Heb 10:36–39; 11:13–16; 12:3), and the unpleasantness of discipline (Heb

---

30 Lane, *Hebrews 1–8*, 137–38. See also Guthrie, *Hebrews*, 204.

31 Again in 1 Timothy 4:7 the same idea is presented: "… train yourself to be godly." There is a great deal of overlap with the teachings in James 1:2–4 and 12. "Consider it pure joy, my brothers and sisters, whenever you face trials of many kinds, because you know that the testing of your faith produces perseverance. Let perseverance finish its work so that you may be mature and complete, not lacking anything. … Blessed is the one who perseveres under trial because, having stood the test, that person will receive the crown of life that the Lord has promised to those who love him."

32 Schreiner, *Hebrews*, 171.

12:4–13).[33] The author addresses each situational temptation to their faith by feeding them with deeper theological teachings and urges them to hold unswervingly to their hope in Christ (Heb 3:6; 6:11–12, 18–20; 7:18–19; 10:23). In this passage, we can see the author's deepest concern for his audience, that their laziness in clinging to even the basic doctrinal teachings could lead to apostasy.[34]

Student or Teacher: Exhorting One Another

As the author stated in Hebrews 5:12, "… by this time you ought to be teachers." This is not the same teaching role as that of the pastor or elder.[35] The pastoral role requires spiritual gifting to teach, as well as spiritual maturity, and bears serious dangers if undertaken by a new believer (Rom 12:8; Jas 3:1; 1 Tim 3:6). However, the author does expect all spiritually mature believers to teach the foundational lessons of righteousness to others, to exhort and encourage one another, just as he himself teaches, admonishes, and encourages them. The disciple in Christ is not alone in a sea, clinging to the anchor of his hope. He is part of a larger body of faith, and he is just as invested in helping a brother or sister to hold fast as he is in saving himself.

In Hebrews 10, the author makes direct application to his teachings in relation to perseverance in the faith as he reaches a "therefore" point in his letter.

> And having a High Priest over the house of God, let us draw near with a true heart in full assurance of faith, having our hearts sprinkled from an evil conscience and our bodies washed with pure water. Let us hold fast the confession of our hope without wavering, for He who promised is faithful. And *let us consider one another* in order to stir up love and good works, not forsaking the assembling of ourselves together, as is the manner of some, but *exhorting one another*, and so much the more as you see the Day approaching. (Heb 10:21–25 NKJV, emphasis mine)

Here, the author asserts that because of these doctrinal teachings, we can hold fast to the faith *and* consider one another. Believers are told both to cling to the anchor of their soul *and* to motivate each other toward love and good works.[36]

---

33 See Lane, *Hebrews 1–8*, 298, wherein Lane follows the argument from Polycarp that the author of Hebrews exhorts endurance in the face of suffering and persecution.
34 Schreiner, *Hebrews*, 171.
35 Schreiner, 170.
36 "It is the revelation of Christ's high priesthood as the means by which the pastor's hearers will be able to follow the 'righteous' (10:38; 11:4, 7) of ch. 11 and thus persevere in faithfulness" (Cockerill, *Epistle to the Hebrews*, 258).

In fact, the author describes the community of faith as a *new household*. "But Christ is faithful as the Son over God's house. And we are his house, if indeed we hold firmly to our confidence and the hope in which we glory" (Heb 3:6). Believers enter a new creation that connects them across all cultural/ethnic/economic barriers in a family *koinonia* whose bonds are so much like an ethnic group that they can be described as a new people group.[37] Their new identity as a people-group united in the household of faith is further characterized in Hebrews 10:39 as those who do not fall away but who hold to their faith. "But we do not belong to those who shrink back and are destroyed, but to those who have faith and are saved."

Not only does the author of Hebrews urge believers to assemble with fellow local believers, but he also challenges them by reminding them about the saints who have gone before. In the Hall of Faith in chapter 11, the author offers encouragement, perspective, and even chastisement[38] through the lives of the faithful who have held fast through all manner of trial and temptation. He concludes with Hebrews 11:39–12:3:

> These were all commended for their faith, yet none of them received what had been promised, since God had planned something better for us so that only together with us would they be made perfect.
>
> Therefore, since we are surrounded by such a great cloud of witnesses, let us throw off everything that hinders and the sin that so easily entangles. And let us run with perseverance the race marked out for us, fixing our eyes on Jesus, the pioneer and perfecter of faith … so that you will not grow weary and lose heart.

The idea the author presents here is that those who have already died are still waiting to receive their promised hope until each and every one of us has finished the race. The faithful endurance of the absent saints reaches out and grabs the hand of a weary fellow pilgrim and guides them back to the anchor of their hope. Likewise, the believer holds fast by looking to Jesus with an eye on his fellow believers, both present and absent, both by teaching others and by receiving teaching, both encouraging and being encouraged.

Passive or Engaged: Cooperating with the Spirit

Several lessons on spiritual maturity have been drawn from Hebrews 5:11–6:3, but there remains one final phrase to explore—"God permitting."

---

37 John H. Yoder, "Social Shape of the Gospel" in *Exploring Church Growth*, ed. Wilbert R. Shenk, 282–83. See also Robert Ramseyer, "Christian Mission and Christian Anthropology," in *Exploring Church Growth*, 112. *Koinonia* is the Greek word for community, often used in reference to a church.

38 The saints in Hebrews 11 condemn the unbelieving world through their ability to endure in faith.

While this phrase was a common rhetorical device in Judaism, considering the following verses, they seem to indicate a more significant and deeper theological principle—that spiritual growth ultimately relies on the Lord.[39] In fact, Hebrews 6:13–20 goes on to describe how secure we are in our hope, not because we can or must persevere, but because God, who cannot lie, made a promise. Again, at the conclusion of his letter to the Hebrews, the author reaffirms this security we have in Christ with the idea that the anchor of hope to which we cling is actually holding onto us.[40]

> Now may the God of peace who brought again from the dead our Lord Jesus, the great shepherd of the sheep, by the blood of the eternal covenant, equip you with everything good that you may do his will, working in us that which is pleasing in his sight, through Jesus Christ, to whom be glory forever and ever. Amen. (Heb 13:20–21 ESV)

The teachings of righteousness begin and end with the work of Christ, the pioneer and perfecter of our faith (Heb 12:2).

Indeed, the Spirit is the seal of promise (Eph 1:14; 2 Cor 1:21–22), our guarantee that the Lord grows each member of his household (Phil 1:6; Col 1:9–10; Rom 5:2–6; John 16:13; 2 Cor 1:21–22) and ultimately will present us as blameless (1 Cor 1:8). The role of the Holy Spirit in the discipleship process cannot be minimized. The author of Hebrews emphasizes the Spirit's direct involvement in his readers' discipleship by relaying that the Spirit speaks directly to the household of faith (Heb 3:7–11; 10:15–17) in warning against hardness of heart (Heb 3:12–19), in promise of rest (Heb 4:1–11), and in forgiveness (Heb 10:15–18).[41]

While all spiritual growth is the work of the Spirit, the Spirit also exhorts believers to take responsibility for their spiritual growth and to persevere in hope. We must be actively engaged in the process by holding fast and encouraging the household of faith. The mature can actively chew on and digest more challenging theological teachings, while infants sit back and receive the easily digestible "milk" teachings. Likewise, it is immature to rely on the Spirit for growth apart from our own active participation. As our eyes are habitually trained on Jesus, clinging to ever-deeper teachings, we gain perspective on the challenges to our faith and we take loving responsibility for our fellow believers, encouraging them also to hold fast.

---

39 Ellingworth, *Epistle to the Hebrews*, 317. Lane, *Hebrews 1–8*, 140–41.
40 See Whitlark, *Enabling Fidelity to God*, 166–67.
41 Pierce, *Divine Discourse*, 135.

Implications for Missiological Developments in Discipleship Methods

Obedience Reflects Faith in the Teachings about Righteousness
Disciples are accountable for their spiritual growth, and sluggishness should be admonished. Obedience is a key indication of inner transformation, but any outward behaviors that are not reflecting inner faith are empty.[42] "For CPM-style advocates, obedience *initiates* the process of spiritual growth. Faith and knowledge of God are the result."[43] Some CPM methods encourage even unbelievers to lead discipleship groups if they seem obedient.[44] However, if we encourage disciples to "act like" believers apart from a transforming inner faith, we are preaching another gospel (esp. Gal 1:6–8).[45] Our faith rests on a repentance from dead works and a steadfast hope in righteousness that comes by faith. Disciples mature as their faith transforms their behavior from the inside out, but outward obedience cannot transform their inner faith.

Disobedience reflects a faith problem and should be corrected with sound teaching. Teaching is the key method for growing a faith that yields good works. Current discipleship methods that treat theological teachings with profound skepticism and remove theological teachings as a hindrance to the spread of the gospel are cutting out a key principle of discipleship. Faithful discipleship includes both knowledge and obedience, transforming behaviors through a transformed mind (Rom 12:2).

Discipleship methods need to move believers beyond the foundational "milk" lessons toward the "meat" teachings that are harder to process. If discipleship methods emphasize multiplication to the extent that a believer is caught in a perpetual repetition of foundational lessons, then they could be stuck in spiritual infancy. This can become a new form of dependency if they are only equipped to live on the milk lessons of a basic discipleship curriculum and are never given stronger doctrinal food.[46]

Oikos Identifies with the Household of Faith
All believers are expected to teach others about the elementary principles of the gospel, but biblical obedience is about more than reproducing the faith. More often, Scripture describes good works in terms of love for the

---

42 Sinclair, *Vision of the Possible*, 143.
43 Rhodes, *No Shortcut*, 96; emphasis in original.
44 Rhodes, 101.
45 See Yoder, "Social Shape of the Gospel," 280–83.
46 "… when church growth outstrips trained leadership troubles multiply quickly … results in carnal leadership, strife and division" (Pratt, Sills, and Waters, *Introduction to Global Missions*, 193.

household of faith. Discipleship methods that measure spiritual growth solely in terms of obedience in evangelism and church multiplication are insufficient.

Small discipleship groups built on natural *oikos* affinity-group lines often have strong bonds and can easily demonstrate the vital aspects of mutual encouragement, warning, exhortation, and admonishment. However, the believers have also joined into the much larger household of faith. In Christ's *oikos*, the missionary is no longer a foreigner or outsider but a brother or sister who bears body-life responsibilities toward new disciples.[47] Discipleship methods that treat the missionary as an outsider whose teachings are invasive and damaging do not reflect biblical perspectives of *koinonia*. Many CPM methods go so far as to forbid the "outsider" missionaries to teach.[48] The missionary bears responsibility—as a brother or sister in the faith—to encourage, admonish, comfort, and correct converts, just as the missionary also humbly receives edification from them.

The *oikos* transforms from a natural ethnic/cultural/affinity group to one that identifies more broadly with the global household of faith (Heb 3:6; 11:39–12:1). Not only does unity in Christ overcome cultural barriers, but unity also connects believers with saints who are physically separated by time and distance. Discipleship methods today ought to connect disciples with the full riches available to them in the global body of Christ, especially the rich theological writings of those who have gone before. Likewise, the theological lessons gained by each local congregation as they persevere through their unique trials can offer rich encouragement to the kingdom as it expands its global theology.

Spiritual growth relates to perseverance. As disciples look to Jesus and draw upon the community of faith for encouragement, discipleship connects deep teachings with the specific trials and temptations believers are experiencing. This kind of discipleship requires a personal relationship. Discipleship curriculum that is abstractly disconnected from the contextual needs of the believing community will not be as helpful as those that are taught organically from within the *oikos* context. Discipleship must provide empathetic teaching that helps each group hold fast to their faith through their unique challenges. For example, weeping with those who weep

---

[47] "CPM-style methods overstate the importance of cultural differences. They see missionaries as *cultural outsiders*, inherently unable to enter fully into or understand another culture, and not *cultural immigrants*, who are on a journey into another culture and who will over time learn to understand and interact with it in largely seamless ways" (Rhodes, *No Shortcut*, 89; emphasis in original).

[48] Rhodes, *No Shortcut*, 79.

(Rom 12:15), which happens when the missionary is relationally connected to the *oikos* body.[49]

The author of Hebrews demonstrates reproducible methods for distance discipleship, as he communicates through a letter and as he connects them to the wealth of encouragement and teachings they can find in a living connection to the Old Testament saints. Missionaries likewise can employ a variety of distance methods that maintain the personal family-bond in Christ, connect teachings to context, and supply believers with examples and teachings from our rich theological heritage.[50]

Rapid Reproduction Initiates Further Training to Maturity

As Roland Allen argued a hundred years ago, discipleship methods should not be hindered or restrained by a missionary's excessive control or interference.[51] The disciple grows when his/her eyes are habitually turned to Jesus—the pioneer and perfecter of our faith—not when the disciple's eyes are trained to focus on the missionary's teachings and expectations. Disciples need teaching to encourage them to hold fast to the anchor of their faith, but cognitive knowledge of doctrinal principles is not always an accurate measure of spiritual growth. Discipleship methods must be simple enough for disciples to easily reproduce, but simplicity in methods and depth of teaching are not mutually exclusive.[52]

Spiritual maturity takes time.[53] The faith in Christ that declares us righteous is the same faith that transforms us into full godliness over time as we persevere. The author of Hebrews expected that believers, after a given time, ought to reach enough spiritual maturity that they will teach the fundamental principles of righteousness to others. This level of fundamental teaching is expected of all believers within a reasonably short time of their conversion. At the same time, we cannot rush multiplication to the extent that we place an infant believer in the role of church pastor or elder.

---

49 "Furthermore, we must not let the desire for efficiency short-circuit our responsibility to teach effectively. Discipleship requires personal interaction. We must be present to ask and answer questions until we know that people understand" (Rhodes, *No Shortcut*, 181–82).

50 Books like Reeves, *Theologians You Should Know*, which present major theological teachings from within the given historical contexts that demanded answers in the face of various contextual challenges to the faith, are a terrific example of how theology relates to endurance, and the storied presentation of events helps disciples find connection with those theologians as fellow pilgrims.

51 Allen, *Spontaneous Expansion*, 6–17.

52 Payne, *Discovering Church Planting*, 112–13.

53 Rhodes, *No Shortcut*, 99.

Reliance on the Spirit Includes Human Responsibility

Ultimately, spiritual maturity is a gift of God that comes by his grace. However, this does not negate the disciple's responsibility to hold fast, look to Jesus, and love the body by helping one another to run this race with endurance. Likewise, the Spirit equips and empowers the missionary in their efforts to reach the nations, but the missionary has the responsibility to teach the word of righteousness by faith. Missiological discipleship methods must go beyond rudimentary lessons of inductive Bible study and offer ongoing theological teachings to help disciples habitually and consistently endure through a variety of trials. Discipleship methods that emphasize the Spirit's role to the extent that they minimize the missionary's responsibility are confronted by the author of Hebrews.[54]

The author of Hebrews explores several aspects pertaining to spiritual maturity, although teaching—in the context of discipleship—is his chief focus. The author addresses his audience's faith trials regarding theological teachings. In this key passage, Hebrews 5:11–6:3, he confronts their immaturity for relying on "milk" teachings and urges them to progress toward understanding deeper and richer "meat" teachings. The author desires to illuminate the idea that teaching is central to discipleship (cf. 1 Cor 2:6; 14:20; Eph 4:13; Phil 3:15).[55] Disciples around the world are crying out, begging for theological training, as they grieve the loss of tens of thousands of converts to cults.[56] Men like Roland Allen, Donald McGavran, and David Garrison highlighted significant correctives to former missiological methods in discipleship, ones that hindered the movement of the Spirit, but today's developing CPM-driven discipleship methods must take warning lest their reactive trajectory continues to swing far past the biblical plumbline.

The Lord instructs us to spread the gospel to all nations, and he left his Spirit to guide and equip us in that mission. The emphasis of the Great

---

[54] Rhodes, 28–34.

[55] "Put simply, discipleship is focused primarily on changing people's mindsets—on leading them to greater faith in Jesus—and only secondarily on changing their actions. It is through the renewing of our minds that we are transformed (Rom 12:2), and it's as we teach 'everyone with all wisdom' that people grow 'mature in Christ' (Col. 1:28). Indeed, the New Testament almost always speaks of maturity in relation to our thinking" (Rhodes, *No Shortcut*, 184).

[56] "One IMB field leader responsible for developing a training program for pastors in East Asia surveyed twenty-one pastors of large churches and networks of churches regarding their greatest need. They all said without hesitation, 'Our pastors need training!' They also commented, 'Our churches are under attack by cults and false teaching. Our pastors don't have a good understanding of how to apply theology.' '… We are losing 10,000 churches a year to the cults'" (Massey, *Theological Education*, 6).

Commission is *making disciples*. The missionary makes disciples and strengthens the faith of the convert by teaching them the Word, taking them deeper into a transformative *knowing* that our righteousness comes not by works but by faith in Jesus, and exploring new facets of theological insight as each new trial of faith reveals fresh riches in the love of Christ.

Let us not be so obsessed with reaching *all nations* that we neglect our role of *making disciples*. Let us *make disciples* of all nations. Let us initiate rapidly reproducing small groups who are encouraged to be actively obedient as a reflection of a living faith. Let us not fail to continue teaching them to digest the deeper theological teachings and to connect them with their identity in the global household of faith. Let us take responsibility in cooperation with the Spirit to disciple the nations in the teachings of righteousness—from milk to meat.

Bibliography

Allen, Roland. *Missionary Methods: St. Paul's or Ours?* London: World Dominion Press, 1930.

Allen, Roland. *The Spontaneous Expansion of the Church.* Eugene, OR: Wipf & Stock, 1962.

Arn, Win, ed. *The Pastor's Church Growth Handbook.* Pasadena: Church Growth Press, 1979.

Ashford, Bruce, ed. *Theology and Practice of Mission: God, the Church, and the Nations.* Nashville: B&H Academic, 2011.

Ashford, Bruce, and Scott Bridger. "Missiological Method." In *Missiology: An Introduction to the Foundations, History, and Strategies of World Missions*, 2nd ed., edited by John Mark Terry, 31–40. Nashville: B&H Academic, 2015.

Cockerill, Gareth L. *The Epistle to the Hebrews.* Grand Rapids: Eerdmans, 2012.

Crawley, Winston. *Biblical Light for the Global Task: The Bible and Mission Strategy.* Nashville: Convention Press, 1989.

Crawley, Winston. *Global Mission: A Story to Tell.* Nashville: B&H, 1985.

Dayton, Edward, and David Fraser. *Planning Strategies for World Evangelization.* Grand Rapids: Eerdmans, 1990.

Ellingworth, Paul. *The Epistle to the Hebrews: A Commentary on the Greek Text.* New International Greek Testament Commentary. Grand Rapids: Eerdmans, 1993.

Engel, James F., and William A. Dyrness. *Changing the Mind of Missions: Where Have We Gone Wrong?* Downers Grove: InterVarsity Press, 2000.

Ferris, Robert. "Leadership Development in Missions Settings." In *Missiology: An Introduction to the Foundations, History, and Strategies of World Missions*, edited by John Mark Terry, 457–69. Nashville: B&H, 2015.

Gallagher, Robert L. "Missionary Methods: St. Paul's, St. Roland's, or Ours?" In *Missionary Methods: Research, Reflections and Realities*, edited by Craig Ott and J. D. Payne, 3–22. Pasadena: William Carey Library, 2013.

Garrison, David. *Church Planting Movements: How God is Redeeming a Lost World*. Arkadelphia: WIGTake Resources, 2004.

Guthrie, George H. *Hebrews*. Grand Rapids: Zondervan Academic, 1998.

Kiley, Mark. "A Note on Hebrews 5:14." *Catholic Biblical Quarterly* 48 (1980): 501–3.

Köstenberger, Andreas J. *Handbook on Hebrews through Revelation*. Grand Rapids: Baker Academic, 2020.

Lane, William. *Hebrews 1–8*. Word Biblical Commentary 47A. Dallas: Word, 1991.

Massey, John David. "Theological Education and Southern Baptist Missions Strategy in the Twenty-First Century." *Southwestern Journal of Theology* 57, no. 1 (Fall 2014): 5–16.

McGavran, Donald A. *The Bridges of God*. Rev. ed. New York: Friendship Press, 1981.

McGavran, Donald A. *Ethnic Realities and the Church: Lessons from India*. Pasadena: William Carey Library, 1979.

McGavran, Donald A. *Understanding Church Growth*. Rev. ed. Grand Rapids: Eerdmans, 1980.

McGavran, Donald, and George Hunter. *Church Growth Strategies That Work*. Nashville: Abingdon Press, 1980.

Mott, John K. *The Evangelization of the World in This Generation*. New York: Student Volunteer Movement for Foreign Missions, 1900.

Mulholland, Kenneth. "Donald McGavran's Legacy to Evangelical Missions." *Evangelical Missions Quarterly* 27, no. 1 (January 1991): 64–70.

Ortlund, Dane. *Deeper: Real Change for Real Sinners*. Wheaton: Crossway, 2021.

Ott, Craig, and J. D. Payne, eds. *Missionary Methods: Research, Reflections and Realities*. Pasadena: William Carey Publishing, 2013.

Patterson, George. "The Spontaneous Multiplication of the Church." In *Perspectives on the World Christian Movement: A Reader*, edited by Ralph D. Winter and Steven C. Hawthorne, 633–42. Pasadena: William Carey Library, 1981.

Payne, J. D. *Discovering Church Planting: An Introduction to the Whats, Whys, and Hows of Global Church Planting*. Colorado Springs: Paternoster, 2009.

Peters, George. *A Theology of Church Growth*. Grand Rapids: Zondervan, 1981.

Pierce, Madison N. *Divine Discourse in the Epistle to the Hebrews: The Recontextualization of Spoken Quotations of Scripture*. Society for New Testament Studies Monograph Series 178. Cambridge: Cambridge University Press, 2020.

Pocock, Michael, Gailyn Van Rheenen, and Douglas McConnell. *The Changing Face of World Missions*. Grand Rapids: Baker Academic, 2005.

Pratt, Zane, M. David Sills, and Jeff K. Waters. *Introduction to Global Missions.* Nashville: B&H, 2014.

Reeves, Michael. *Theologians You Should Know: An Introduction from the Apostolic Fathers to the 21st Century.* Wheaton: Crossway, 2016.

Rhodes, Mark. *No Shortcut to Success: A Manifesto for Modern Missions.* Wheaton: Crossway, 2022.

Schreiner, Thomas R. *Commentary on Hebrews.* Nashville: B&H, 2015.

Shenk, Wilbert, ed. *Exploring Church Growth.* Grand Rapids: Eerdmans, 1983.

Simpson, Wolfgang. *Houses that Change the World.* Waynesboro: Authentic Lifestyle, 2003.

Sinclair, Daniel. *A Vision of the Possible: Pioneer Church Planting in Teams.* Colorado Springs: Authentic, 2006.

Smith, Steve, and Ying Kai. *T4T: A Discipleship ReRevolution.* Monument: WIGTake Resources, 2011.

Terry, John Mark, ed. *Missiology: An Introduction to the Foundations, History, and Strategies of World Missions.* Nashville: B&H, 2015.

Terry, John Mark, and Robert L. Gallagher. "The Church Growth Movement." In *Encountering the History of Missions*, 304–20. Grand Rapids: Baker Academic, 2017.

Trousdale, Jerry. *Miraculous Movements: How Hundreds of Thousands of Muslims Are Falling in Love with Jesus.* Nashville: Thomas Nelson, 2012.

Verkuyl, J. *Contemporary Missiology.* Grand Rapids: Eerdmans, 1978.

Watson, David, and Paul Watson. *Contagious Disciple Making: Leading Others on a Journey of Discovery.* Nashville: Thomas Nelson, 2014.

Whitlark, Jason. *Enabling Fidelity to God: Perseverance in Hebrews in Light of the Reciprocity Systems of the Ancient Mediterranean World.* Eugene: Wipf & Stock, 2009.

Winter, Ralph, and Bruce Koch. "Finishing the Task: The Unreached Peoples Challenge." *International Journal of Frontier Missions* 19, no. 4 (2002): 15–25.

Wolf, Thomas A. "Oikos Evangelism: The Biblical Pattern." In *The Pastor's Church Growth Handbook*, edited by Win Arn, 110–17. Pasadena: Church Growth Press, 1979.

Part 4
Review and Response

Chapter 12
Looking through Three Hermeneutical Lenses
A Review of *Reading Hebrews Missiologically*

Robert L. Gallagher

As I begin my quest to examine *Reading Hebrews Missiologically*, I need to ask a number of questions that I believe are crucial to any hermeneutical process. Will I find a consideration of the importance of proper biblical hermeneutics by considering the metanarrative of the scriptural text and an awareness of our biases? Will I find an appreciation of the intentionality of the writer as shown in the epistle's structure and purpose in relation to the original audience? Will there be a comprehension of the construct of "mission" that searches for the original interpretation rather than automatically defaulting to a historic or contemporary definition? Do the chapters take into consideration the primary focus of the first-century work in its sustained exhortation to Jewish believers to persevere in enduring faith no matter what is happening around them that belies the fact that God cares and appears to have deserted them?

You can quickly see that the volume is carefully constructed by viewing the table of contents. My first impression of the project was that it is so much more than I had expected in terms of author diversity and depth, breadth, and richness of scholarship and topics. Overall, the writing is well expressed and easy to read, with helpful headings, expositions, and summaries to guide the reader in following the flow of each contributor's thought.

Diversity of Authorship

There are eleven authors: four women and seven men. There is a diversity of both gender and ethnicity. For instance, there are representatives from the African American, Asian American, Caucasian American, Ethiopian, and Norwegian Christian communities, with cross-cultural experience in China, East Africa, Latin America, the Middle East, North Africa, Scandinavia, and Southeast Asia. Primarily they are history, intercultural studies, or theology educators in northern America, yet they also teach in Africa, Asia, Europe, and Latin America. They are well-accomplished and productive writers, with tertiary education qualifications that range from institutions such as the universities of Edinburgh, Oxford, Pretoria, and Wales, in addition to theological seminaries like Columbia International, Covenant, Gordon-Conwell, Princeton, Southeastern Baptist, Trinity Evangelical, and Yale.

Scholarly Observations

Let me list a few structural observations of the book. There are three major parts: the missionary motivation, missionary message, and missionary methods of Hebrews. Part 1 has four chapters, part 2 has three chapters, part 3 has four. Each chapter has its own introduction, conclusion, and bibliography. Of key importance are these questions: What is the thesis of this chapter, and do the parts and sections of Hebrews support this argument or claim?

Breadth and Depth
Every chapter in the book offers extensive research, evinced in the space devoted to the footnotes. From the referencing in part 1 (four chapters), we witness an indication of the breadth and depth of the Catholic and Protestant (charismatic, evangelical, conciliar, and/or Pentecostal) contemporary scholars (primarily Western males), who are historians,[1] missiologists,[2] specialists in Hebrews,[3] or theologians.[4] The scholarship referenced is predominantly northern-American based, which is not surprising since the majority of the authors were trained in the United States and since the affluent West dominates publications in biblical, historical, missional, and theological studies.

Perspectives and Case Studies
Within the edition, a number of academics—such as Roland Allen, Orlando E. Costas, David Garrison, Richard J. Johnson, Andreas J. Köstenberger, Donald A. McGavran, Donald Senior, Carroll Stuhlmueller, and Nicholas Alexander Venditti—have their specific contribution to the topic at hand scrutinized. Moreover, case studies are presented to support the contention being addressed, such as early antebellum African American Christianity, the homogenous-unit principle of the church growth movement, Latin American liberation theology, and the theology of the Muslim world.

Missionary Tapestries in Three Parts

The review now turns to inspect the missionary tapestries of Hebrews declared in each of the three parts of the book.

---

[1] Historians: Philip Jenkins, Mark A. Noll, Ruth A. Tucker, and Andrew F. Walls.

[2] Missiologists: Roland Allen, David J. Bosch, Orlando E. Costas, Arthur F. Glasser, Paul G. Hiebert, Donald A. McGavran, and Ralph D. Winter.

[3] Specialists in Hebrews: F. F. Bruce, David A. deSilva, Paul Ellingworth, Craig R. Koester, William L. Lane, James A. Moffatt, and David Peterson.

[4] Theologians: Lesslie Allen, Richard Bauckham, Kwame Bediako, Walter Brueggemann, James D. G. Dunn, Joseph Fitzmyer, John Goldingay, Tremper Longman III, Scot McKnight, John R. W. Stott, Anthony C. Thiselton, Christopher J. H. Wright, N. T. Wright, and Amos Yong.

Missionary Motivation

In part 1, which assesses the missionary motivation of Hebrews, the motifs addressed are the renarrating of the world according to the biblical story and worldview of Christ's coming, the grand narrative of the *missio Dei*, ministry to the marginalized who are outside the gate, and the incarnation of Jesus as the mission of God. In other words, the catalysts for the motivation of mission are the telling of the big-picture story of God's salvation through the redeeming work of Christ on the cross by taking upon himself the humble body of a human being to bring the kingdom of God to the powerless on the fringe of society.

Missionary Message

The issues, in the second part, that speak to the missionary message of Hebrews are missional hospitality, the pilgrim people of God, and hope in a chaotic world. That is, the missionary message is hospitality, immigration, and hope. Is this true? There are certainly biblical texts that come to mind which would indicate that these themes are evident. But do they represent the primary message of Hebrews? In my reading of Hebrews, this is not the prevailing message. Christ in his highest splendor as the Son of God is superior and better than anyone and everything that the old covenant offers. That is why Hebrews puts so much emphasis on the messianic coronation in Psalms 2 and 110, which highlights the glorious and victorious ascension into God's presence of the Son, who then is crowned with glory and honor, majesty and power.[5]

Missionary Methods

The third and final part is the missionary methods of Hebrews, which focuses on the proclamation of evangelism, God's communication in the suffering Servant, use of Hebrews in the early antebellum African American church context, and the essential need of maturity and development of discipleship in mission. In simpler terms, the missionary methods of Hebrews are evangelism, communication, and discipleship. What appears to be missing is the method of witness in Hebrews that the Lord God propagates through disciplining his beloved children to rely on their hardships and conflicts to accomplish his missional purposes (Heb 12:14–17).

---

5 In Psalm 2:6–8 (NIV), we read, "I [Father God] have installed my king on Zion, my holy mountain." I [Jesus] will proclaim the LORD's decree: He said to me, "You are my son; today I have become your father. Ask me, and I will make the nations your inheritance, the ends of the earth your possession" (see Heb 1:2, 5; 5:5–6). And again, in Psalm 110:1, 4, 6a, "The LORD [God the Father] says to my lord [Jesus the Son]: "Sit at my right hand until I make your enemies a footstool for your feet." ... The LORD has sworn and will not change his mind: "You [Lord Jesus] are a priest forever, in the order of Melchizedek." ... He [Lord Jesus] will judge the nations" (see Heb 1:1–3, 13; 4:16–7:28, esp. 5:5–6).

Looking through the Lens of Interpreting the Metanarrative

In part 1: Matthew Aaron Bennett paints the biblical worldview with a sweeping brush, as Hebrews provides an explanation of the Old Testament—a commentary on the first covenant. Linda P. Saunders sets the stage by referring to the first three verses of Hebrews 1 to establish Jesus as God's supreme sacrifice. She sees the entire text as a cohesive communication of the *missio Dei*, the chief object of the grand narrative of Scripture (Abraham, covenantal promises and fulfillment, and the Law). The exposé features the supreme work of Christ as Redeemer, High Priest, and Savior, and completes God's mission of reconciliation with fallen humanity. All the while, Saunders is conscious of the original audience and their ministry context. Finally, Allen Yeh sees Hebrews as the interpretative guide to the Old Testament bringing a Judaistic worldview that recenters mission by considering those who are powerless, sitting outside the gate.

In part 2: Edward L. Smither explores the biblical meaning of missional hospitality by tracing—through Abraham, Israel's call, and the ministry of Christ—the reoccurring theme of welcoming the stranger, and thus welcoming God. He then suggests that the audience of Hebrews connected the practical admonition of hospitality to Israel's ancient texts.

Looking through the Lens of Understanding Hebrews

In part 1: Michael P. Naylor displays an awareness of the importance of structure and purpose in Hebrews. He reveals the role of Jesus Christ through the letter's Old Testament Scriptures as the promised Davidic messianic heir, the victorious King of Psalm 110, and the high priestly ministry after the order of Melchizedek. All these roles were dependent on Jesus's incarnation to demonstrate the divine purpose of redemptive history.

In part 2: Jessica A. Udall reminds us of the plight of eighty-nine million people in our world today who have been forcibly displaced from their homes. She relates this tragic statistic to the message of Hebrews that emphasizes the pilgrimage of Abraham and the journeys of the faithful in Hebrews 11. Looking to Jesus as our example and standing on the promises of a faithful God provides safety and hope for the current global refugees who are facing an uncertain future.

Irwyn Ince encourages the follower of Christ to believe that God empowers his people to live missionally in a broken world with the full assurance of hope. This entails living within the paradox of the suffering, gloried, and royal Savior. Ince lays out the intent of Hebrews clearly by expanding the description of the audience's plight in Hebrews 10:35–36. He says that the pastor's congregation was undergoing persecution and suffering, chaos and upheaval. They were losing hope and drifting away from Christ. They wanted to quit and abandon their faith and confidence. Wanting his flock to endure, the writer of Hebrews begins his letter with the supremacy of Christ as the sure hope of the eternal future in an upside-down world. "Christian hope bears witness to the world that Jesus is real and worthy of worship," as he sits at the right hand of the Father.

In part 3: Sigurd Grindheim maintains that Hebrews is God's way of divine communication. He asserts that the church is an effective witness through suffering and humility rather than from a position of power. Grindheim develops the theology of Hebrews by the superiority of the new covenant in Christ Jesus. To proclaim the kingly rule of God, the church's only proper form of communication is through the Lord Jesus in his humble witness by suffering and identifying with the poor and despised. God's missional communication is the suffering Son, Jesus.

After a thorough background survey of the epistle, Jessica N. Janvier says that the early antebellum African American community used Hebrews to understand the "grand schematic of Christianity." Additionally, Hebrews allowed them to understand their Black Christian lives in God and mission because of the ethnic and religious persecution they were experiencing. The epistle was used in the Black church's missional thinking to confront racial oppression in hope and prayer, believing that "it was the answer to the ills they saw around them." Lastly, Sarah Lunsford expands the missiological importance of making disciples from Hebrews 5:11–6:3, which provides discernment into the process of spiritual maturity and methods of discipleship. She sees that the teaching of Hebrews is central to discipleship.

Looking through the Lens of Exploring "Mission"

In part 1: Matthew Aaron Bennett defines the "gospel" message, but comes short of defining "mission." In part 3: Abeneazer G. Urga claims that Hebrews is a neglected missional writing and is concerned about the perseverance of the saints and evangelism. The recipients of the letter are exhorted to hold on to their salvation, the reconciling mission of God through Christ. The cloud of witnesses at the beginning of Hebrews 12 encourages believers to proclaim this great salvation.

Urga sees evangelism, or proclamation, as a missionary method in Hebrews to reach others for Christ and his kingdom. Unfortunately, the chapter is without any clear definition of evangelism or mission. The essay does not explain how Urga, or the writer of Hebrews, determines the difference between the two ideas. The chapter does highlight the context of suffering and persecution of the congregation and the exhortation of the epistle to persevere in hope knowing that they have an eternal home although having an alien status on earth. The salvation of God requires verbal proclamation, people to hear the message, and a faith response by the listeners. For Urga, it seems that the proclamation of the gospel of Christ is evangelism, and the entire process, which includes listening and responding, is mission.

Summary of Observations

When I analyzed *Reading Hebrews Missiologically* through the three hermeneutical lenses, I found the results to be mixed. In regard to an understanding of Hebrews within the biblical metanarrative, part 1 had three contributions, while part 2 only had one and part 3 had none. That is, out of the eleven chapters, only four made any reference to Hebrews having a function in the broader scriptural landscape of the *missio Dei*.

Regarding the awareness of the importance of the overall structure and purpose of Hebrews: the first part of the book had one donation, the second part had two, and the third part had three. In other word, 55 percent of the chapters broached this matter. Again, the contributors of the book were reluctant to interpret the Scripture as a whole—in this case a letter of the Bible.

To close this episode, there was no deliberation in any of the chapters about the meaning of the term *mission*, even though the freeway running through the volume was to read the Epistle to the Hebrews through a mission lens. Even if the editors included in their book's introduction an explanation of the word, it still wouldn't suffice if each author didn't separately address the issue. Each writer has his or her own perspective of the term because of the diversity of the authorship. No one definition at the beginning could possibly cover all scenarios of influence, since the concept is shaped by a continuum of theological traditions (Pentecostal to mainline), personal pilgrimages (Norway to Ethiopia), cross-cultural experiences (North Africa to Southeast Asia), and intellectual effects (University of Pretoria to Yale Divinity School).

Bosch Shines a Light on "Mission"

In "Evangelism: Theological Currents and Cross-currents Today," the South African missiologist David J. Bosch speaks of four ways in which theologians distinguish evangelism and mission from each other as referring to different realities.[6] Bosch regards mission as the wider concept and evangelism as

---

6 Bosch, "Evangelism," 98–103.

the narrower, but has problems with defining mission as "mission equals evangelism plus social action" because it leads to the question of which one is more important. This suggests that you can have evangelism without social action or the social component without evangelism.

In broad terms, David Bosch accepts the wider definition of mission as being the total task that God has set the church for the salvation of the world. Mission is the church carrying God's message of salvation across all sorts of barriers: geographical, social, political, ethnic, cultural, religious, and ideological. Mission involves the redemption of the universe and the glorification of God.[7]

The imprint of Bosch's research is the mindfulness that various theological practices across Catholic, Protestant, and Orthodox institutions have distinctive implications for the words *mission* and *evangelism*. This intuition is coupled with the realization that words change their connotation over time, fashioned around the cultural context. These alternatives extend all through historic eras and comprise a continuum of practices among similar Christian faiths, as well as organizations within the same traditions. A contemporary example is the designation "evangelical" that in northern America is no longer primarily associated with the proclamation of the centrality of Christ and his substitutionary work of salvation on the cross. The expression has taken on another life molded by the current socio-political trends of an affluent Western society.

Summing up, we cannot take for granted that when someone uses the word *mission* in a conference presentation or a peer-reviewed essay that they agree with how we think about the notion. Definitions of pivotal terms need to be at the forefront of our discussions. We may not completely agree with the author's or speaker's idea, but at least we know where they stand, and we can compare their hypothesis with our own reasoning. Hopefully this should alleviate any confusion or ambiguity in our scholarly endeavors and create a greater tolerance and appreciation of differences in academic opinion.

Conclusion

Reading Hebrews Missiologically is a significant contribution to the arena of biblical theology of mission, since it is rare to find a missiological

---

[7] Bosch discusses eight aspects of evangelism, suggesting that the expression may be defined as that dimension and activity of the church's mission which seeks to offer every person, everywhere, a valid opportunity to be directly challenged by the gospel of explicit faith in Jesus Christ with a view to embracing the Lord as Savior, becoming a living member of his community, and being enlisted in his service of reconciliation, peace, and justice on earth ("Evangelism," 100–102).

interpretation of any book of the Bible. The diversity of authors from varying cultures, ethnicities, educational backgrounds, and cross-cultural experiences allows a fresh missiological perspective of the letter to the Hebrews.

God's dealings with Israel were a meager shadow of the perfect reality in the man Jesus: absolutely God and absolutely human. He came to earth to establish his kingdom, and all that God had initiated in the old covenant to bring the Lord's blessing to his people is now no longer relevant. There is a continuity of theological understanding, however, as we move from the Old Testament to the letter sent to a group of Jewish believers in Christ. Then again, there is a discontinuity as the Perfect One has initiated a new human identity that is not linked to gender, culture, or ethnicity. The church of the new kingdom is now living on earth as if we are citizens of heaven, dispensing his moral and ethical teaching in word and deed via the Spirit of the Father. Jesus's loving and gracious presence is in our midst to empower his people to live the kingdom life he promised.

The mission of God in Hebrews is about staying true to Jesus Messiah, together with displaying the Lord's moral and ethical life, which is our calling. Being his representatives wherever he has planted us fulfills his will, as we dispense truth in grace, patience, and long-suffering, no matter what is going on around us that tells us that God does not care. Jesus is our model—on the cross, suffering with hope and holding fast to the Person of his Father, as he expressed enduring faith through his death prayers[8]—the pattern we should emulate, with the Spirit's assistance. There is no greater missional vocation than staying faithful to our Lord Jesus and fulfilling his purposes, whatever and wherever they might be in the mission of God.

The theology of mission in Hebrews affirms that there is no missional witness without enduring perseverance. Jesus says in Luke 8:15, "But the seed on good soil stands for those with a noble and good heart, who hear the word, retain it, and by persevering produce a crop." In Hebrews there is no *missio Dei* without enduring faith in the midst of trauma. Mission in Hebrews is the continuance of witness without exception to any struggling hardship and unstable circumstance. There is no mission without suffering

---

[8] The "death prayers" of Jesus from the Psalms refer to his heavenly Father even amid the hatred of the Jewish leaders, Roman military, and demonic hordes, all the while carrying the sin of the world. "About three in the afternoon Jesus cried out in a loud voice, '*Eli, Eli, lema sabachthani?*' (which means 'My God, my God, why have you forsaken me?')" (Matt 27:46 NIV; see Ps 22:1). "Jesus said, 'Father, forgive them, for they do not know what they are doing'" (Luke 23:34; cf. Ps 22:18 NIV). "Jesus called out with a loud voice, 'Father, into your hands I commit my spirit.' When he had said this, he breathed his last" (Luke 23:46 NIV; see Ps 31:5).

and persecution. And the Lord Jesus is still proclaiming, "Go! I am sending you out like lambs among wolves" (Luke 10:3 NIV).

Bibliography

Bosch, David J. "Evangelism: Theological Currents and Cross-currents Today." *International Bulletin of Missionary Research* 11, no. 3 (1987): 98–103.

About the Contributors

MATTHEW BENNETT (PhD, Southeastern Baptist Theological Seminary), along with his wife and three children, spent seven years living and ministering in North Africa and the Middle East. He currently serves as Assistant Professor of Missions and Theology at Cedarville University, and has written three books: *Narratives in Conflict: Atonement in Hebrews and the Qur'an*; *40 Questions about Islam*; and *The Qur'an and the Christian*.

JESSICA N. JANVIER (PhD candidate, Columbia International University), originally from South Carolina, graduated with an MDiv from Nyack College's Alliance Theological Seminary in 2017. Her degree focus was on Bible and Theology, with a concentration on the Hebrew Bible. Jessica went on to pursue a ThM in Church History from Princeton Theological Seminary. Her research and thesis project centered on the shaping of the antebellum Black church and Afro-Christology. From there, her studies have taken her to Columbia International University, where she is currently pursuing a PhD in Intercultural Studies, focusing her dissertation around the history of the antebellum Black evangelical experience. Lastly, Jessica is a proud graduate of Howard University—her foundational undergraduate institution and the place where she first became a disciple of Christ.

ROBERT L. GALLAGHER (PhD, Fuller Theological Seminary) is Professor of Intercultural Studies Emeritus at Wheaton College Graduate School in Chicago, where he has taught since 1998. He has served as the chair of the Intercultural Studies department (2011–18), president of the American Society of Missiology (2010–11), and an executive pastor in Australia (1979–90). His recent publications include co-authoring *Christ Among the Nations: Narratives of Transformation in Global Missions* (Orbis Books, 2021) and *Breaking through the Boundaries: God's Mission from the Outside In* (Orbis Books, 2019), together with co-editing *Sixteenth-Century Mission: Explorations in Protestant and Roman Catholic Theology and Practice* (Lexham Press, 2021) and *Contemporary Mission Theology: Engaging the Nations* (Orbis Books, 2017).

About the Contributors

SIGURD GRINDHEIM (PhD, Trinity Evangelical Divinity School) is Professor of Religion at Western Norway University of Applied Sciences, and he has also taught at the Ethiopian Graduate School of Theology, Trinity Evangelical Divinity School, and other institutions in Ethiopia, the US, and Norway. His publications include the forthcoming *The Letter to the Hebrews* commentary in the Pillar New Testament Commentary series, *The Crux of Election*, and *God's Equal*, as well as three other books and several scholarly articles on topics related to the New Testament, biblical theology, and missiology. He and his wife, Kidist Bahru Gemeda, have a three-year-old son, whose name is Per.

IRWYN L. INCE JR. (DMin, Covenant Theological Seminary) is the Coordinator of Mission to North America and a Visiting Lecturer in Practical Theology at Reformed Theological Seminary. He is the author of *The Beautiful Community: Unity, Diversity and the Church at Its Best*, and has contributed to the books *Heal Us Emmanuel: A Call for Racial Reconciliation, Representation, and Unity in the Church*, and *All Are Welcome: Toward a Multi-Everything Church*.

SARAH LUNSFORD (PhD, Columbia International University) has taught Theology and Global Studies at Liberty University since 2010. Her graduate degrees (MA Intercultural Studies, MDiv International Church Planting, and ThM) were earned at Southeastern Baptist Theological Seminary. She served as a marketplace missionary in Southeast Asia and then as a career missionary with the International Mission Board in East Asia for several years. She lives in the Atlanta area with her four children—Abigail, Elysa, Zachary, and Emilia—where they are active members at Johnson Ferry Baptist Church.

MICHAEL NAYLOR (PhD, University of Edinburgh) is Associate Professor of Bible at Columbia International University in Columbia, South Carolina. He is the New Testament book-review editor for the *Journal of the Evangelical Theological Society* and is the author of *Complexity and Creativity: John's Presentation of Jesus in the Book of Revelation*.

LINDA P. SAUNDERS (PhD, Columbia International University) is an adjunct professor of Intercultural Communication and Cultural Anthropology at Liberty University. Her published works include "The Future for the Evangelical Missionary Movement Must Include an Accurate Portrayal of Her Past" in *Advancing Models of Missions: Evaluating the Past and Looking to the Future* (EMS #29) and "The African-American Church's Absence from Global Missions: Providing Answers," in the *Evangelical Missiological Society Occasional Bulletin*.

EDWARD L. SMITHER (PhD, University of Wales; PhD, University of Pretoria) is Professor of Intercultural Studies and History of Global Christianity, as well as Dean of the College of Intercultural Studies, at Columbia International University. He is the author of *Mission as Hospitality: Imitating the Hospitable God in Mission* and *Christian Mission: A Concise Global History*.

JESSICA A. UDALL (PhD, Columbia International University) is the author of *Loving the Stranger: Welcoming Immigrants in the Name of Jesus* and has contributed to *Diaspora Missiology: Reflections on Reaching the Scattered Peoples of the World* (EMS #23) and *Crossing Barriers for the Great Commission: An Ethiopian Perspective*. She has also written for Evangelical Immigration Table, Zwemer Center for Muslim Studies, and A Life Overseas. She runs *Loving the Stranger Blog* (lovingthestrangerblog.com), which offers encouragement and provides resources for building intercultural harmony one friendship at a time.

ABENEAZER G. URGA (PhD, Columbia International University) lectures in Biblical Studies at the Evangelical Theological College in Addis Ababa and is an adjunct professor at Columbia International University and Ethiopian Graduate School of Theology. He is a member of Equip International and SIL International/Ethiopia. He has authored several books and articles. His forthcoming book is *Intercession of Jesus in Hebrews* (Mohr Siebeck).

ALLEN YEH (DPhil, University of Oxford) is Associate Professor of Intercultural Studies and Missiology at Biola University. His areas of geographical expertise are Latin America and China. He earned a BA from Yale, MDiv from Gordon-Conwell, and MTh from Edinburgh. Yeh has visited over sixty countries, on every continent, to study, do missions work, and experience the culture. He is also the author of *Polycentric Missiology: 21st Century Mission from Everyone to Everywhere* (IVP, 2016), and co-editor of *Majority World Theologies: Theologizing from Africa, Asia, Latin America, and the Ends of the Earth* (William Carey Publishing, 2018). He serves on the boards of the Foundation for Theological Education in Southeast Asia (FTESEA) and the Evangelical Missiological Society (EMS). Allen is an avid marathon runner and violin player. He is joyfully married to his wife Arianna (also a professor at Biola), and they have a delightful son, Asher (b. 2019).

Scripture Index

Genesis
1:26 25
2:17 10, 26
3:8 71
3:15 23–24, 29, 33
3:21 34
4:11–12 139
10:33–34 140
12:1–3 24, 72
12:2–3 90
12:3 42
12:7 33
13:18 73
14:18 32
15:5 90
17:7–8 27
18:4–8 74
18:8 74
18:16 74
22:16 90
22:16–17 42
22:17–18 41
23:1–4 130
47:9 130

Exodus
10:21 138
10:22 138
19:16 138
20:22–23:19 26
21:28–32 10
22:21 74
24:12 26
28–29 105

Leviticus
1:3–5 105
4:1–12 105
4:22–30 105
6:9 26
6:14 26
6:25 26
7:1 26
7:7 26
7:11 26
7:37 26
10:1–7 13, 17
11:46 26
12:7 26
16:16 12
16:20–22 31
17:11 12
19:33–34 74

Numbers
5:29–30 26
6:13 26
6:21 26
10:29 26
19:2 26

Deuteronomy
4:11–12 138
5:29 138
9:19 138
10:18–19 75
12:25 138
17:11 26
17:18 26
32:43 57

Joshua
2:1–22 79
2:12–13 79
6:25 80

Judges
6:11–13 80
7:1–8 37

2 Samuel
7:14 56, 107

2 Kings
6:8–23 112
6:16–17 112

1 Chronicles
17:13 56

Job
5:20 28
38:7 56

Psalms
2:7 56, 107
8:4 64
8:4–6 64
40 62
40:6–8 63
45:6–7 111
45:6–8 107
51:5 26
89:27 56
95:7–11 125
96:3 72
97:7 57
102 57
102:3–5 109
102:16–20 28
102:25–27 107–109
104:4 57
110 60, 61
110:1 58, 64, 106–107, 110–111, 124
110:2 111
110:4 33, 106–107, 136
110:14 111

Isaiah
3:5 24
6:8–10 104
19:23 49
42:7 28
42:18–19 104
53:2 43
59:16 24, 32
61:1 28
63:5 24–25

Jeremiah
31:31–34 29

Matthew
1:1–16 29
1:1–17 41
11:19 75
11:28 109
15:24 38
22:41–46 60
24:14 42
25:35 74
25:35–36 80–81
28:18–20 98

Mark
12:35–37 60

Luke
1:46–55 37
1:52–53 47
2:52 43
4:18 28
7:34 75
7:36–50 76
10:3 193
20:41–44 60

John
1:1 24
1:14 24
1:46 43
3:30 51
5:36 25
9:4 25
10:25 25
10:28 108
14:3 130
14:9 105
14:10 25
16:13 175
17:4–5 107

Acts
1:1 146
1:8 39
2:42–47 82
14:19–20 89
16:6–10 89

Romans
5:2–6 172, 175
8:3 27
8:34 32
11:13 40
12:2 176
12:8 173
12:13 81
12:15 178

1 Corinthians
1:8 175
2:6 179
3:1–2 171
7:26 145
7:27 145
7:28 145
7:32–34 145
7:38 145
13:7–8 93
13:12–13 93
14:20 179
15:1–5 3, 14
15:24–26 111

2 Corinthians
1:21–22 175
4:17–18 89
5:1 98
5:6 89
5:18–19 24, 27
11:33 89

Galatians
1:6–8 176
4:4–5 104

Ephesians
1:14 175
4:13 179
4:14 171

Philippians
1:6 175
3:5–6 40
3:15 179

Colossians
1:9–10 175
1:27 95

1 Thessalonians
1:3 90
5:21 172

1 Timothy
1:19 172
3:2 82
3:6 173
3:9 172

2 Timothy
1:14 172

Titus
1:8 82

Hebrews
1:1 66, 127
1:1–2 103, 135
1:1–4 6, 120, 123–124
1:1–14 122
1:2 56, 65, 112, 119, 124
1:3 6, 23–25, 28, 106–107, 110, 124, 140
1:3b 61
1:4 108, 112, 136
1:5 136
1:5–13 58
1:5a 56
1:5b 56

1:6b 57	5:5 106	8:2 61
1:8 56, 124	5:6 32, 136	8:6 61
1:10 110, 124	5:7 141	8:6–8 27
1:10–12 108–109	5:8 62	8:8–13 29
1:13 64, 106–107, 111, 124, 136	5:9 26	8:13 61, 137
	5:10 32, 61, 136	9:6–10 7, 62
1:14 30, 111–112	5:12 173	9:6–14 140
2:1 104	6:11 24, 101, 113	9:7 32
2:1–2 7	6:11–12 173	9:8 137
2:1–4 x, 64, 117, 119, 122–123, 125, 130	6:12 98	9:9 137
	6:12–16 30	9:11 42
2:1–14 118	6:13 29	9:11–12 105
2:2 10, 123, 136	6:13–14 42	9:11–14 29, 61
2:3 124, 126	6:13–20 89, 92, 175	9:12 33, 62
2:4 125	6:14 102	9:12–14 27, 32
2:5–9 64	6:17–18 30	9:12–15 28
2:8 108	6:18 90–91, 93–94, 96	9:13 140
2:9 7, 10	6:18–19 172	9:13–14 14, 28
2:10 18, 26, 62–63, 66	6:18–20 173	9:14 33, 137, 140
2:14 63	6:19 91, 101	9:18–20 140
2:14–15 172	6:20 32, 94, 136	9:18–22 32
2:14–18 28, 111	7:1–3 32	9:18–25 27
2:15 161	7:1–28 106	9:22 28, 34, 105
2:16 23–24, 29–30, 63	7:3 61, 105, 136	9:24–28 7
2:17 63	7:4–10 136	9:25 32
2:18 63	7:11 26, 32	9:25–26 62
3:1–6 136	7:11–14 61	9:26 14, 62
3:6 24, 172–174, 177	7:12 61	10:1 27, 106
3:7–11 175	7:15–17 32	10:1–2 11
3:7–19 125–126	7:16 61, 136	10:1–3a 137
3:12 126	7:17 41, 136	10:1–4 28, 62
3:12–19 126, 175	7:18–19 173	10:3 140
3:14 172	7:19 24, 26–27, 33, 91	10:4 27, 32, 105, 137
4:1 126	7:20–22 32–33, 61	10:5 63
4:1–3 x, 117, 125, 130	7:20–24 32	10:5–7 63
4:1–11 175	7:22 32	10:10 61
4:2 126–127	7:22–27 29	10:11 62, 106, 140
4:2–3 92	7:23–25 61, 105	10:11–14 61
4:6 92	7:24 14, 33	10:12 61, 106
4:7 55	7:25 31, 91–92	10:12–14 11
4:8 51	7:26 66	10:13 111
4:14 64	7:26–27 32	10:14 14, 61, 106, 137, 140
4:15 62, 141	7:27 61–62, 140	
4:16 64, 137, 140, 142	7:27–28 62, 105	10:15–17 175
5:1 31, 63	8:1–2 61	10:15–18 175
5:4–6 61	8:1–6 62, 105	10:16–18 29

10:18   7
10:19   27, 32
10:19–22   8, 14
10:21–25   173
10:22   137, 140
10:23   91, 98, 173
10:25   81, 140
10:29   32
10:32–34   118
10:32–35   77, 172
10:33   113
10:34   78
10:35–36   101
10:36–39   172
10:39   174
11:1   91
11:1–40   140
11:3   163
11:8–9   42
11:8–11   78
11:9   49
11:10   98
11:13   42, 79, 118
11:13–15   99
11:13–16   x, 117, 128, 129–130, 172
11:14   119, 130
11:15–16   130
11:16   163
11:22   79
11:25   162
11:25–26   141–142
11:27–29   79
11:31   80
11:32   55, 129
11:39   129
12:1   94
12:2   175
12:2–3   142
12:3   140, 172
12:4–13   173
12:14–17   187
12:18–21   137
12:18–24   8
12:22–24   139
12:24   140

12:28   97
13:1   93, 160
13:1–3   93
13:2   71–72, 78, 80–82
13:2–3   80–81
13:3   78
13:5–6   94
13:8   93, 110
13:11–12   140
13:12   49
13:12–13   141–142, 146
13:12–14   ix, 9, 94
13:13   37, 46
13:14   92, 142
13:20–21   175

James

2:19   171
2:25   80
3:1   173

1 Peter

3:15   95

1 John

2:1   32

Revelation

19:7   83
21:4   111

Visit us at missionbooks.org

Mission in the Way of Daniel
Empowering Believers to Live into God's Plan

Edward L. Smither | Paperback & ePub

Mission in the Way of Daniel probes mission theology and practice in the Old Testament, exploring the well-known story of Daniel through the lenses of mission history and mission practice. Providing relevant application for contemporary issues, the themes in *Mission in the Way of Daniel* advance the ongoing conversation about how to do mission.

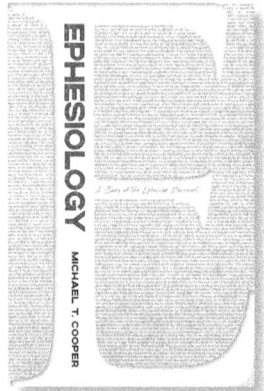

Ephesiology
A Study of the Ephesian Movement

Michael T. Cooper | Paperback & ePub

This book is a journey from the launch of the church in Ephesus as it became a movement grounded in God's mission and led by those who multiplied generations of disciples. Cooper focuses on Paul and John as missiological theologians who connected Jesus's teaching with the cultural context and narrative of the people in Ephesus. *Ephesiology* offers a comprehensive view of the redemptive movement of the Holy Spirit in this city.

Learning to Lead at the Feet of Jesus
Encounters with Grace and Truth

Todd Poulter | Paperback & ePub

Despite our best intentions, many of us struggle to consistently reflect Jesus in our leadership. The Gospels suggest a new posture. Building on Jesus's intimacy with the Father, *Learning to Lead at the Feet of Jesus* highlights the rich relational setting in which Jesus exercised leadership and developed his followers into leaders. In the context of his intentional "with-ness," Jesus generously shared his life and authority with the Twelve.

www.ingramcontent.com/pod-product-compliance
Lightning Source LLC
Chambersburg PA
CBHW071237070526
44583CB00017B/2228